CONTENT MANAGEMENT
Bridging the Gap Between Theory and Practice

Edited by

George Pullman and Baotong Gu
Georgia State University

Baywood's Technical Communications Series
Series Editor: Charles H. Sides

 Routledge
Taylor & Francis Group

LONDON AND NEW YORK

First published 2009 by Baywood Publishing Company, Inc.

2 Park Square, Milton Park, Abingdon, Oxon OX14 4RN
711 Third Avenue, New York, NY 10017, USA

Routledge is an imprint of the Taylor & Francis Group, an informa business

First issued in paperback 2017

Library of Congress Catalog Number: 2008009355
ISBN 13 : 978-0-89503-378-9 (hbk)

Library of Congress Cataloging-in-Publication Data

Content management : bridging the gap between theory and practice / edited by George Pullman and Baotong Gu.
    p. cm. -- (Baywood's technical communications series)
  Includes bibliographical references and index.
  ISBN 978-0-89503-378-9 (cloth : alk. paper) 1. Database management. 2. Technical writing. 3. Web site development. I. Pullman, George, 1962- II. Gu, Baotong, 1963-

QA76.9.D3C67144 2008
005.74--dc22

                                     2008009355

ISBN 978-0-89503-378-9 (hbk)
ISBN 978-1-138-63724-5 (pbk)

Table of Contents

PART I
CMS Implementation

PART II
CMS and Technical Communication Pedagogy

PART III
CMS and the Profession of Technical Communication

Introduction:
Mapping Out the Key Parameters of
Content Management

Baotong Gu and George Pullman

Any organization that gathers, produces, and provides information needs to have some systematic way to manage the process; it needs to know

- where the information comes from (authorship),
- how reliable it is (authority),
- when it was last updated,
- how many variations there are,
- how many iterations it has undergone,
- where it appears,
- whether it is intended for public, group, or private consumption,
- when it will expire, and
- and what other pieces of information it is connected to.

In addition, information producers have to ensure consistency in document design and style in order to maintain a consistent identity, a need traditionally provided for by boilerplates and style guides. In the days prior to Web publishing, the system consisted of an organizational structure and culture that would route information through a series of people: the knowledge worker(s), the typist, the editor, the section manager, the typesetter, and finally the distribution manager—whoever was in charge of getting the publication to its intended audience. Whether information management is embodied in a single individual or in many people, some systematic method for controlling the generation and distribution of

1

information is necessary, or else an organization has no idea what it is saying or how it sounds (see Boiko, 2005; Jeffery-Poulter, 2003).

The advent of Web publishing has increased the need for information management, because the complexity and expense of physical publication—document design, typesetting, and physical distribution—which tended to restrict who could say what within an organization and to whom on the outside, have been reduced and simplified. Given access to a Web server, anyone with even a minimal technological understanding can broadcast information to the world. Because information changes rapidly and going through the proper channels often slows down the process of distribution, people inevitably begin to use the technology to accelerate the process. Thus the volume of information being distributed has greatly increased while the control over information is becoming increasingly decentralized. When an organization's information isn't controlled by a central authority, the results can be duplication, inconsistency, invalidity, liability, and confusion. On the other hand, when an organization's information is controlled by a central authority, the results, from the knowledge workers' perspective, can be bureaucracy, delay, and a stifling of creativity. For technical communicators, this tension is felt most acutely when the expression "information management" replaces "communications" in discussions touching on how an organization addresses its people (internally) and its public (externally).

CONTENT MANAGEMENT SYSTEMS AND CONTENT MANAGEMENT SOFTWARE

A Content Management System (CMS), understood as a series of regulated steps taken by an organization to ensure control and integrity of information as it goes from creation to dissemination, is a system that can be tracked and even to some extent automated by software. This software has garnered such attention in the last five years that today when people hear the acronym CMS they assume it refers to a piece of software that tracks, organizes, and distributes information. The typical CMS consists of two parts: a database containing data and metadata and a Web template that controls the "look and feel" of information. From an organizational standpoint, the advantage of having all information presented via a single template or even a suite of related templates is consistency of brand and control over navigation. The advantages of using a database to store information, as opposed to files in a filing cabinet or proprietary software files on a stand-alone PC or even RTF files on a server, is that the separation of form and content can be strictly controlled, which enables information sharing and rapid republication in new formats and different contexts. Database storage of information also simplifies the process of tracking changes to a piece of information, knowing who contributed to its production, knowing how old it is, when it should expire, and how it relates to the other pieces of information in the system.

Perhaps a concrete example will illustrate the points involved here. Imagine a hierarchical organization, like a university, that has myriad semi-independent units functioning semi-autonomously. There are institutional rules for graduation; then there are departmental rules for graduation; and then there may be individual faculty beliefs about the departmental and university requirements for graduation. Given an uncontrolled information environment, a student might enter the information system from any one of several points and assemble an understanding of the requirements that might be different from another student's, who is following the same degree path but came into the information system using a different navigation scheme. One student might have the university rules in mind but no knowledge of the department's specifications, while the other might know the departments' rules but not know how the university regulations supplement them. Add to this the distinct possibility that a faculty member has his or her own ideas about what a student should do before graduating, which may or may not have any direct connection to what is required to achieve graduation, and you have an inefficient information system. So, if the first student looks for the answer to the question of what he needs to graduate by going to the university Web site, he might get one answer; while another student who seeks to answer the same question from a departmental Web site might get another answer; while a third who goes to a faculty Web page might get yet another answer. If there are multiple answers to the same question, confusion is inevitable.

By controlling who can answer what questions on a Web site, content management systems can control the information an organization presents to the world. While content management systems were developed in the days prior to Web-based publication, today a typical CMS consists of a Web browser front end that is accessed by any given knowledge worker through a login screen. Given a user ID and a password, the system decides what that user has authority to edit, contribute to, write, distribute, and publish. The system will alert a user when some piece of information is ready for one or more of these functions, track changes to a piece of information, keep multiple users from editing the same piece of information at the same time, or from including information in contexts where it doesn't belong. The CMS also controls the Web site's navigation, thus controlling access and context for understanding any given piece of information while providing a consistent user experience. The advantage, again from the bureaucratic perspective, is some control over how information from the organization is received and therefore a modicum of control over how it can be interpreted. At very least a CMS can reduce some instances of mixed messages. At the same time it can cull the system of documents that are no longer relevant, supersede antiquated versions, limit access, and maintain consistency of message. Although, to be strictly accurate, no CMS can do this for legacy documents, which still form the overwhelming majority of documents in most businesses and which need to be entered into the system if they are going to benefit. In effect, a CMS provides the electronic equivalent of a company spokesperson, a single authority in control of the company message, able to stay on message, and invalidate any unauthorized messages. All statements by people other than the spokesperson can thus be considered leaks and disavowed.

HOW WILL CMS AFFECT ORGANIZATIONAL STRUCTURES?

Because it promises such an increased level of control, a CMS is especially attractive to large organizations and even small organizations that generate a great deal of content. One of the consequences of implementing a CMS is that whoever is in charge of it is in charge of the design and distribution of the organizations' message, and thus some shifts in organizational structure may be inevitable.

What shifts may eventually occur in a given organization ultimately depends on what perspective people in that organization take regarding the three critical aspects within any content management context: system, people, and information. A systems-based approach, where content management is seen as systems managing people, will inevitably reflect a technologically deterministic slant and put the system ahead of people. Under such an approach, the features and capabilities of the particular CMS adopted become the focal point of, and often dictate, the organization's content management practice at the cost of the needs of its end users—the technical writers. Unfortunately, if the CMS has major flaws and limitations or is inappropriate for the organization's needs, it will place serious constraints on what the people in the organization will be capable of in managing their information. One of the primary complaints expressed by people who have been told they have to use a CMS is that it is unresponsive to their workflows.

A more technologically critical approach sees content management as people managing content/information. The focal point here is the organizational context, which encompasses its information needs and the needs of the people managing such information. The information needs determine what processes to implement and what system (CMS) to adopt. Such implementation and adoption decisions often come after careful, critical, and deliberate assessment of the capabilities of the CMS and how adequately the software system will be able to meet the organization's information needs and the needs of the people. The end result of such an approach is often more simplified content and a more streamlined process in addition to the reconceptualized approach.

Understanding a CMS and how it impacts an organization, particularly its documentation practice, is easier said than done. As Martin White (2002) has argued, "A CMS is probably the most complex rollout an organization will manage" (2002, p. 22). A project of such complexity dictates a project team of diverse makeup, often consisting of a project manager, IT personnel, authors, editors, and many more, depending on the particular organizational needs and context. Due to such a diverse makeup, content management teams are often confronted with two major issues: (1) some members may not have "an intimate understanding of the business requirements and problems," as Ray, Ray, and Hall (2001) found in their content management project at Tenix (p. 10); (2) "Very few people are willing to change the way they work in order to make somebody else's life easier," a lesson Mark Baker (2002) learned in his own experience of implementing a CMS. The problem could originate from any sector of the content management team. In a survey of people involved in CMS implementation projects, for example, Victor Lombardi (2004) found that training authors and editors was the second-biggest problem apart from hardware and software issues. In their investigation of the Web-content management project at Gonzaga University, Wayne Powel and Chris Gill (2003) found, not so surprisingly, that "the web manager became a bottleneck in the site's development and was criticized not only for being slow to meet the needs of offices demanding a Web presence but also for not keeping the site current" (p. 44).

A more serious problem in CMS implementation lies in organizations' tendency to neglect end users and their needs. Just as the most important people in a documentation project are product customers who will eventually be using the documentation, the most important people in a CMS implementation project are the content creators—technical writers and editors. As James Robertson (2002) has argued, "Without content creators, there would be no need for a CMS. Yet surprisingly, this user group is often the worst served by a new content management system."

Such an unfortunate state has two implications. One is that the managers put in charge of content management projects are often not content creators themselves and thus are inclined to take a systems-based approach toward content management, overemphasizing system parameters and capabilities and neglecting end users—the technical writers and editors. Another implication is that content management practice is redefining the roles of technical writers and editors. Unfortunately, this redefining does not always result in positive prospects for writers and editors, for reasons we mentioned earlier, and may present serious challenges. For example, a systems-based approach to content management may very well result in a devaluing of technical writers and editors and reduce their roles to those of assembly workers, where they are concerned only with producing discrete information chunks.

CMS AND TECHNICAL COMMUNICATION

For technical communicators and the people who train them, these shifts in organizational structure may be seismic. Whereas for the last 20 years or so professors of technical communication have been incorporating document design, desktop publishing, multimedia, graphics, photography, animation, movies, and Web design into our classrooms as preparation for people who will be entering various industries to become the people who present content to the world, these functions may well be performed by the CMS and the IT people who administer it. In such an organizational setting, the technical writers will be limited to writing rich text structured information chunks. They will not design documents or create layouts. They will have no control over how text is displayed or how the images or the data that should accompany the text will appear. They will have no control over the context in which their information appears or the uses to which it may be put. In fact, they will have no authority over their information at all. There will in a sense be no author, but rather an authorization process. The knowledge worker in sector seven, section G, cubicle four will have no distinct voice save that of one in a choir. The humanities-based technical communication degree will therefore be either all the more relevant or completely irrelevant, depending on your point of view. But one point is un-debatable: anyone who plans to directly participate in the communications processes of a contemporary organization needs to understand how CMSs work and how they alter the composition and flow of information within a given organization if they hope to do more than produce information chunks.

THE SEPARATION OF FORM AND CONTENT

A significant issue concerning content management systems, and also a major charge brought by critics of automated information management, is the strict separation of form and content. Traditional technical communication courses teach writers to produce documentation that seamlessly integrates form and content. We have taught, or have been taught, that content needs form to be effective and that a writer must consider form and content as simultaneously interrelated in order to design documents with maximum impact. Consider, for example, the following: 4043678940. Is this a sequence of numbers? Is it an area code followed by a phone number? Does its access result in a phone being dialed or a person's profile being printed to a screen? Or does it result in the next 10 digits in the sequence being accessed? For a human being, these questions are answered by visual design cues, data formatted to produce information: (404) 367-8940. Without the formatting, the 10 digits present a dilemma to the user. With the formatting, the dilemma is instantly resolved. Technical communication has concerned itself with the design of information in just this way, integrating form and content to create meaning.

The integration of form and content in this way, however, presents a problem for a database. The parentheses, the spaces, and the hyphen are not integers and thus cannot be stored in a field whose data-type is specified as integer. If we wanted to add these numbers up, we couldn't put them into the database as anything but integers. On the other hand, if we put them in as "varchar," we could keep our formatting. But if our company later decides to print all phone numbers using a different formation, or wants to connect its data warehouse to its voice over IP system and have the computer make the phone calls, we would have to write a script to access all phone numbers and reformat them. Given the current example, this is not a monumental task. But given a large corporation's infrastructure, getting it done might be absurdly time-consuming, since one would have to involve so many people.

Content management software operates like an interface between the world of data and the world of information. By accessing the data and formatting it according to the stylistic conventions chosen by the designers, it can interpret the data string 4043678940 as a phone number and thus present it as such, (404) 367-8940. In this way, the computer uses form to render data meaningful. The information design decision, that phone numbers should be printed according to a particular widely understood convention, is the purview of whoever designs the content management software and thus, if technical communicators are going to play a part in the CMS process, they need to understand both text and data, and they need to know how to interact with both in such a way that they get called upon to participate when such communications decisions are being made. A technical writer who cannot perceive the value of storing the expression "4043678940" as an integer in a database and insists on the "human" understanding that it is a phone number and therefore meaningless without the conventional formatting phone numbers typically receive (in North America) is positioning himself in opposition to a trend in communications practices that could vastly improve his employability.

CMS software may actually afford technical writers an excellent opportunity for participating in communications at the highest possible levels. In most organizations, the implementation of CMS software has been far from smooth. The systems are expensive, hard to customize, complex to use, and require the kind of careful forethought and planning about enterprisewide communication strategies and workflow practices that cannot be handled by a single group within an organization. A great many people and departments need to be involved in the implementation process if a CMS is going to be successful: designers, programmers, content providers, usability experts, workflow analysts, marketers, brand managers, system engineers, and lawyers; the list can easily exhaust the directory. So many people need to be involved because a CMS is ultimately not about software; it's about communications. Technical communicators, of all people, should understand this, and understanding it, they should be able to position themselves very handily in the implementation process, as long, of course, as they do not come across as wordsmiths.

NEW DEMANDS ON TECHNICAL COMMUNICATORS

The complex nature of content management and content management systems are effecting significant changes in the field of technical communication. To cope with the developing trend of content management approaches, our field has to adapt in several aspects:

- A shift of focus from tools to implementation: Technical communication has traditionally been concerned, at least in part, with making effective use of writing/design tools (mainly software)—understanding the capabilities and limitations of a particular software within a specific documentation-design context. This focus on tools, while helpful to technical communicators within the context of specific documentation tasks, falls short in serving the needs of an organization's overall information management. It must give way to a new focus, one that emphasizes implementation, where the technical communicators, as well as everybody else involved in content management, more critically assess writing/design tools not so much in relation to particular documentation tasks as in relation to overall information needs of the organization. More critical than the question of how a particular tool is going to affect a particular documentation task is the question of how the implementation of tools will affect everyone involved, from the users of the tools, that is, the technical communicators, to the users of information products, that is, the clients. Simply put, technical communicators will need more critical and global perspectives in examining writing/design tools.
- A higher demand for managerial capabilities: The changing and expanding role of technical communicators in content management, as discussed earlier, entails a higher demand for managerial capabilities. Although project management has been part of technical communication curricula, such managerial capacity has been more limited to individual documentation projects. Never have managerial capabilities become such an important asset and been so highlighted as in content management, which demands more global perspectives on the part of the technical communicators in their evaluation of the information needs of their organization, of the tools of information management, and of the implementation of such tools.
- A greater need for collaborative relationships: Since the makeup of a content management team is often diverse and multifaceted, technical communicators are required to collaborate with various groups: managers, programmers, IT specialists, graphic designers, and even subject-matter experts. Working with these groups is no longer an option but rather a requirement. The ability to maneuver among these groups can be key to implementing a most effective content management system.
- A shift from creation of content to its delivery: Technical communication has traditionally emphasized the importance of invention. With the advent of content management and with the datatizing of information at the invention stage, the delivery of this information transformed into a usable and meaningful context at the output stage becomes a more critical aspect in the content management process. The decontextualization at the input stage and the recontextualization at the output stage makes delivery even more important.

- A new set of skills: Finally, with all these new factors affecting technical communication as a result of content management, technical communicators' skills are being redefined. The shift of technical communicators' role from the creator of content to the manager of information, as discussed earlier, entails a new set of skills encompassing such areas as management, programming, graphic design, usability, and information technology in addition to the rhetorical skills of document design.

This list of changes (and the list is obviously not exhaustive) promises a change of revolutionary nature in our conceptualization of technical communication practice: what it is and what it entails. It is no exaggeration to say that content management is forcing us to step outside our familiar boundaries and tread some new yet important territory.

MULTIPLICITY OF VOICES IN
THIS COLLECTION

Although content management is not a totally new phenomenon in the field of technical communication, research into this area has been relatively limited in both depth and scope. In editing this collection, we have realized that our field's perspectives on many key issues concerning content management have been far from unified, and that the multiplicity of voices is what makes research into a new area all the more meaningful. In assembling this collection, although we as editors find ourselves not necessarily sharing all the authors' views, we have deliberately allowed multiple voices covering an array of different issues. Nevertheless, we hope that this multiplicity of voices has clearly come through in this collection, and that our thematic organization has made sense in grouping these different voices.

CMS Implementation

Authors in this section move into the more technical sphere of implementation, often relying on their own experiences, while also exploring various parameters that shape or are shaped by CMS implementation. Rudy McDaniel's chapter, for example, outlines the general requirements necessary for Web content management system (WCMS) construction and details a case study in which a specialized WCMS was created using narrative units of information. His case study reveals the ways in which specialized data collections can be represented, stored, and manipulated using common and freely available Internet scripting technologies and XML. Connecting WCMS-related practices to learning opportunities in the humanities classroom, McDaniel outlines a multitiered approach with some sample tasks and activities and provides student samples of CMS-related deliverables produced in his Digital Media course.

In contrast, Carol Johnson and Susan Fowler provide a cautionary voice against rushing to CMS implementation. Using three case studies of location-based, distributed, and expert (tacit) CMS, where CMS implementation is met with varying results, the authors explore what makes a content management system succeed or fail. Based on their analysis, they argue that technical communication practitioners need to learn how to analyze information environments and create systems that respond to the existing knowledge flow.

Finally, Julie Staggers, Meredith Zoetewey, and Michael Pennell examine three content management systems within different university settings. Their focus, however, is on how they, as new members of the junior faculty, struggle to negotiate new identities, new cultures, and new technologies—course management software in particular—in their first academic jobs. Their context-rich narratives depict the complicated overlapping of three problematic elements inherent in new and compulsory CMS: technology, pedagogy, and enculturation. Looking at CMS as more than a tool that can make or break a class, more than another technology choice, they conceptualize it as a potential stumbling block to professional development, especially for new technical communication faculty. The localized yet transferable strategies of coping and resistance they offer might prove helpful to many in similar contexts.

CMS and Technical Communication Pedagogy

A big purpose of our research on content management is to examine ways to integrate the topic of content management into our curriculum and to redesign our technical communication pedagogy to accommodate the changes at the workplace. This is exactly what the authors in this section strive to accomplish. Arguing that instructors should teach students how to analyze the technological situation and then select the most appropriate technical solution just as they teach students rhetorical repertoire, Becky Jo McShane contends that XML is a logical place for technical communicators to locate themselves as experts. She advises that technical communication instructors teach XML as the tool (a particular language) using single sourcing as the theory (a set of principles informing the implementation of a technology), modular writing as the methodology (a practice or way of doing something), and content management as the technology (a generalized set of skills or knowledge).

Exploring the use of open-source CMS, in particular Xoops and Drupal, as course management systems in delivering online graduate courses in professional and technical communication, Michelle Eble applies the classical rhetorical canons of arrangement, style, memory, and delivery in the context of content management. She argues that when we consider CMS, and the online courses/communities they help create, as rhetorical, then arrangement and style become design, memory becomes databases, and delivery becomes distribution.

Lisa Meloncon's chapter goes beyond practical pedagogical issues and constructs a framework using Edward Relph's method of "seeing, thinking, and describing" in combination with his "outsideness and insideness" to explore the use of content management systems as they relate to technical communication pedagogy. She argues that by accessing the CMS through these three lenses, teachers and students will be better able to situate themselves inside or outside the CMS landscape.

CMS and the Profession of Technical Communication

In this section, authors explore various key issues in content management. Robin Evans discusses the relationship between CMS and technical communication and argues that CMS is not a threat to the careers of technical writers but rather an enhancement. Jeffery Bacha, also noting this shift to content management at the workplace, warns of the danger of returning to positivistic, plain-style, and arhetorical technical communication practices. To counter such a threat, Bacha argues, writers will have to increase their ability to produce multiuse technical artifacts and overcome the traditional craftsman approach to document production.

Kirk St. Amant is concerned with the international aspect of content management. He points out that the export of information, or content, to nations with different legal systems creates new and different kinds of problems that must be addressed in the growing information economy. In reviewing practices related to international outsourcing and the content-related problems such practices can cause, St. Amant presents some content management strategies for addressing these problems and examines how such situations can provide opportunity for technical communicators to move into positions of management.

Nicole Amare's chapter focuses on the role of the technical editor as "new author" and explores the issues of authorship and authority within the content management context. Despite some negative consequences that come with this change in authorship, such as the feelings of loss of creativity and invalid restrictions on their writing style, Amare argues that this changing role of technical authorship through tools such as CMS is elevating the technical editor's role in document production, and she sees this as a positive shift.

Lyn Gattis examines the principles of coherence and cohesion and their relevance to the purported nonsequential, nonreferential writing modules in the content management context and seeks to identify means by which information can be easily repurposed and reused but cohesion can still be achieved at a certain level. Also examined by Gattis are issues of cross-cultural communication and the relevancy of contrastive rhetoric research to content management. Her chapter seeks to identify a satisfactory middle ground for repurposing text that is rhetorically and culturally appropriate for readers.

FAR FROM BEING CONCLUSIVE

Content management as a new practice and approach has yet to perfect many of its aspects. Content management systems leave even more to be desired. Even more complicated is CMS implementation (well, at least effective CMS implementation) that adequately serves the information needs of the organization and its users. Furthermore, as we have shown above, each major aspect of content management holds both promises and challenges, in some cases more challenges than promises. Yet as the title of one of the articles in this collection has implied, content management is becoming an inevitable reality, and the technical communication profession will eventually have to "roll with the tide." Research on content management and CMS has been less than abundant, although quality research already does exist. With this collection, we hope to give voice to different perspectives, deepen our understanding of content management, and open doors to new lines of research.

REFERENCES

Baker, M. (2002, November 17). *Structured content: What's in it for writers?* http://www.cmswatch.com/Features/OpinionWatch/FeaturedOpinions/?feature_id=79

Boiko, B. (2005). *Content Management Bible* (2nd ed.). Indianapolis, IN: Wiley Publishing.

Jeffery-Poulter, S. (2003). Creating and producing digital content across multiple platforms. *Journal of Medical Practice, 3*(3), 155-164.

Lombardi, V. (2004, February 9). *Managing the complexity of content management.* http://www.boxes and arrows.com/archives/managing_the_complexity_of_content_management

Powel, W., & Gill, C. (2003). Web content management systems in higher education. *Educause Quarterly, 26*(2), 43-50.

Ray, D., Ray, E., & Hall, W. (2001). Maintenance procedures for a class of warships: Structured authoring and content management. *Technical Communication, 48*(2), 235-247.

Robertson, J. (2002, March 5). *Losing Sight of the Content in a Content Management System.* http://www.steptwo.com.au/papers/kmc_content

White, M. (2002, November/December). *Content management: From vendor selection to successful rollout.* http://www.infotoday.com/online/nov02/white.htm

PART I

CMS Implementation

CHAPTER ONE

Experiences with Building a Narrative Web Content Management System: Best Practices for Developing Specialized Content Management Systems (and Lessons Learned for the Classroom)

Rudy McDaniel

In this chapter, I begin by examining the process of creating a specialized online content management system (CMS) and conclude by applying the techniques and lessons learned from this experience to classroom pedagogy. Specifically, I consider the development of a Web-based CMS that was created using stories as the raw material for propagating organizational knowledge (a more detailed description of this process is found in McDaniel, 2004). While the theoretical basis for such an effort is an interesting study in its own regard (see Denning, 2001; Post, 2002; Smart, 1999 for studies of storytelling at work in organizations such as the Bank of Canada, the World Bank, and NASA; or Kim (2005) for a discussion of narrative as it applies to the field of technical communication), the issues involved with the construction of such an interface deserve their own unique discussion. In addition, this humanities-friendly data model presents an opportunity for studying the implications of using content-compatible CMS design methodologies in a classroom with advanced writing, communications, or digital media students.

The chapter is organized into three sections. In the first section, I examine the fundamental components of a CMS and present several theoretical considerations for building a specialized CMS. For example, construction of a *narrative* CMS relies on research from organizational and business communication (Denning, 2001, 2004), from cognitive psychology (Bruner, 1991), and from computer science (Minsky, 1985; Schank, 1990). The process of building a narrative CMS is detailed in terms of a standard software development lifecycle, which begins with an abstract requirements and specification phase and gradually moves toward a more concrete implementation. This process can be adapted to other specialized CMS designs simply by transforming the content base, the encapsulating unit for this content, and the types of design decisions that will eventually be built into an interface. Many of the complex technological processes may require interdisciplinary collaboration from other fields such as information technology, engineering, computer science, or digital media.

I claim that this type of practice-oriented and interdisciplinary synthesis is precisely the type of activity that knowledge management researchers (Hughes, 2002; Wick, 2000) argue is necessary in order to empower technical communicators and situate them in more desirable positions within their organizations. In addition, I assert that writers and digital media specialists are well suited to be operators, administrators, or developers of such systems—that a knowledge and background supplemented with humanities expertise may improve the sterile and positivist pathways and applications of modern content management techniques. This is especially true given the tendency of IT firms to overemphasize technology, to misinterpret (or to wholly ignore) the needs of their audience, and to underemphasize the humanistic components of information applications (see Davenport & Prusak, 1997).

Next, I will detail the practical aspects of constructing CMS technologies and describe some of the decisions that were made during development of my own CMS. In the case of a narrative-based CMS, a system such as the one I discuss can be built using a modicum of student talent, open-source software, and a metadata classification system such as XML. As I discuss the process involved in building my own CMS, I will write about lessons learned from this experience with regard to user privacy; the selection, storage, and classification of relevant information; the use of open-source versus proprietary software; and the decision-making process behind building a genre-specific content management system.

The final portion of the chapter will focus on ideas for teaching by using CMS. My argument is that a thorough understanding of topics such as CMS, XML, and the practices for building such technological systems is essential for the students graduating with technical writing or new media degrees. Incorporating these topics through classroom exercises, readings, and discussions equips students to be better prepared with both the fundamental skills necessary for survival in the industry with the critical thinking skills necessary to truly innovate in the field.

As Zimmerman (2001) writes, it will not be long before autonomous computer agents write their own software documentation. We already have mechanisms in place for computer programming languages such as Java (JavaDoc) and PHP (PHPDoc), but such documentation is rather mechanical at this point and of use mostly only to other programmers and developers. The day in which computer algorithms begin to write useful instructions for end users is still some time away, but it is likely to be inevitable. When that day comes, the ability to translate core technical skills into other types of innovative ideas and projects will be essential for newly trained technical communicators and new media practitioners entering the workforce. CMS technologies provide a nice starting point for examining these sorts of issues. Their reliance on core Internet technologies, their ability to generate multiuse content for a variety of audiences and contexts, and their compatibility with metadata classification languages are all characteristics that position these complex systems as natively and inherently useful teaching tools for those courses in which the study of complex information is integral.

PART I: LIBRARY
(COMPONENTS OF A SPECIALIZED WCMS)

The process of designing, implementing, and managing CMS systems in online environments has been described as Web content management (WCM) (Yu, 2005). We can therefore describe the technologies supporting this task as Web content management systems (WCMS). In its most general form, a WCMS is nothing more than a database-driven Web site. Though some claim such a comparison is a bit oversimplified for CMS in general (see Goans, Leach, & Vogel, 2005), it is certain that the architectural basis for any online CMS generally involves a robust database paired with an interface capable of communicating with this data source. Such a scenario is also common for systems that *do not* rely on the Internet; complex configurations of content are generally only possible through the use of database technologies capable of sorting and shifting information in response to user commands. In a non-networked environment, such commands are simply generated by an interface from workstation application software rather than from a Web browser.

After these basic database and interface technologies have been configured, a WCMS can be customized for a variety of pedagogical and industrial applications, from monitoring and adapting student learning outcomes in fields such as mathematics and writing (Deacon, Jaftha, & Horwitz, 2004) to modularizing content in complex writing scenarios (Farkas, 2005; Goans et al., 2005; Surjanto, Ritter, & Loeser, 2000). A basic premise leading to the success of early WCM systems is the idea that a finite number of efficiently constructed information units, or nodes, can be coupled with database support to dynamically generate a large number of content configurations and documents. This emergent complexity is based on relatively simple changes to the requests made to the database server. The small number of template pages is then much easier to manage and maintain than vast collections of documents with individualized headings, inconsistent content, and stylistic disparities.

A specialized WCMS can be very useful for solving many of the issues encountered in large-scale Web development projects, especially when content is added in a distributed fashion. As Goans et al. (2005) note, such environments often rely upon multiple authors, each with their own technological backgrounds and ideas about how given content should be represented on the Web. While such stylistic and structural differences are interesting to observe, particularly in terms of emergent properties that may form when multiple authors consider a single topic from different angles, they also lead to serious problems when individual pages are collated and represented under a common organizational framework. A primary problem here is inconsistency, which contributes to an overall "lack of organizational voice and credibility" (Goans et al., 2005, p. 30). The architecture of a WCMS, which imposes a higher-level order and structure upon the data through the use of form fields and data verification tools, often alleviates many of these inconsistency issues. Furthermore, these architectures improve maintenance and administration of the content collection by trimming the number of editable files to a manageable number.

When a CMS system is housed on the Internet—thereby becoming a WCMS—additional server software is needed to manage communications between client and host computers. Using an interface, a Web server, and a database management system, an online content management system provides a dynamic and interactive alternative to information access and retrieval as opposed to traditional and static HTML delivery systems. The core of a general Web-based content management system is configured as shown in Figure 1. In any given transaction, a request for information is first relayed from the interface to the Web server, which sends any database queries on to the database server. Appropriate subsets of information are then returned to the interface, which displays records accordingly and filters information down to what is hopefully an absorbable and manageable level of granularity for the end user. Additional searches or sorts requested by the user will then be executed immediately, either with no additional requests to the two servers (client-side processing) or with additional round-trip visits to one or more servers (server-side processing).

The transformation of the relevancy of digital information as it moves in either direction through this system is worth noting. Using Davenport and Prusak's (1997) distinction between data, information, and knowledge, we see the process

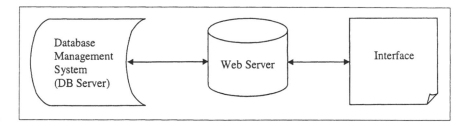

Figure 1. General CMS architecture.

of moving from raw data to usable knowledge as a filtering process, with the most useful, relevant, and appropriate sources representing information that will eventually be internalized and encoded as knowledge. This stored knowledge can then be transformed and adapted as new situations emerge that may require access to the same sorts of cognitively encoded memories and observations in a slightly different context. In Figure 1, assuming that data entry also occurs from within the interface, data primarily flows from the right to the left, starting in the interface and making its way into the database server. Information, though, will flow from the opposite direction, beginning its journey in the database server and eventually filtering through the Web server to arrive in the interface. Assuming that the WCMS is doing its job correctly and that the user has formed appropriate search parameters, the filtering process will be successful in separating data, or world observations, from information, or contextually relevant and useful world observations (Davenport & Prusak, 1997).

Given these three general requirements, it is quite possible for an entire WCMS to be developed and deployed on a single computer. In a testing environment, for example, it is not uncommon for developers to run Web server software, database server software, and programming or interface design software concurrently on a desktop or laptop computer. While a technical discussion of this installation and configuration is beyond the scope of this chapter, the point here is that the tools for constructing and creating a specialized WCMS are readily available and configurable for a wide variety of needs. In addition, many of these robust tools are available for free. Both commercial and open-source tools (see Deacon et al., 2004 or Goans et al., 2005, for a discussion of some of these applications) are available to support configurations of both specialized and general content management systems.

Developing a specialized WCMS, then, primarily involves manipulation of the data situated at either end of this general WCMS architecture. In other words, specialization occurs at both the database level, with the insertion of specialized sets of data appropriate for a given domain, and at the interface level, with the user-centered design of a product that meets the needs of those searching for information within that domain. The Web server, which coordinates the flow of specialized information in both directions, is largely unaffected by specialization. Examples of one such specialization technique—for both database and interface designs—will be discussed in Part II of this chapter.

Given this general architecture, the development of a specialized online CMS is largely concerned with soliciting the appropriate sources of specialized content. We can refer to this database collection as the *library* of the CMS. For example, a CMS concerned with automotive repair needs to gather and store data related to vehicle models and part numbers, service locations, service histories, technician personnel, and other types of data associated with vehicles and their parts. A CMS used by environmentalists for environmental awareness campaigns would instead populate their library with industrial propagation information, environment incidents, and public relations contact information, among other things. The key, of course, is to gather enough data so that a wide variety of problems can be addressed with the correct sources of information from the library. While information overload or lack of focalization can pose troublesome issues, these problems can generally be dealt with through the creation of a user-centered interface. Duplicitous or overlapping information can also be handled through database optimization techniques.

A primary concern with the library/database is describing its contents in a manner such that users without an expert knowledge of taxonomy will be able to find an appropriate number of usable sources. For example, a user of the automotive CMS looking for a specific recall part for the Ford Motor Company will want to peruse only vehicles from the particular year during the period of time in which this particular part was manufactured and installed. If the CMS were to classify each vehicle record as only "foreign" or "domestic," the results returned from a query would likely be too broad, and the user would be faced with a situation in which information overload was a significant possibility.

On the other hand, if the CMS library classified each record at too precise a level, perhaps by using the actual Vehicle Identification Number (VIN) of each Ford vehicle, the user would be subjected to the cumbersome task of navigating through each and every affected vehicle on an individual basis. For a specific task, then, such as mailing out letters to the owners of these vehicles, the operation would be far too time consuming to be used in a realistic scenario. The task would be much better suited to a batch mode type of operation in which letters were automatically generated based on a range of specific vehicle models and a filtering of relevant dates.

Fortunately, when constructing a CMS library, it is relatively easy to perform these types of sorts due to the inherent structure of databases in general. Specialized collections of content are generally grouped together in tables, in which each table will usually have a unique identifier that separates one row in the table from another. In a relational database, where various database tables and entities can have precise and defined relationships with other tables and entities, each column within a table serves as a potentially searchable entity within the database. For instance, a table in the database containing vehicle models, owners, and VINs can be searched by any of those three characteristics, thus enabling a variety of different search techniques depending on the particular data being sought. In addition, a second table might contain VIN-specific information, such as the year in which the vehicle was manufactured, its base configuration, and the manufacturing plant where it was produced. Fortunately for the user, complicated queries to these distributed, relational databases can be hard coded into the interface so that a given user will need to know only which button to click rather than the specific syntax and particularities involved with linking and selecting appropriate data and tables from the CMS library.

To summarize, building a specialized online CMS involves gathering the appropriate collection of specialized data (building the library) and then implementing access to this customized collection through a special interface. Queries, or commands designed to solicit specific subsets of information from the library, are designed to be attached to specific objects (buttons, scrollbars, links) that exist within the interface. In the next portion of this chapter, I describe a specific instance of this process through my experience in designing and building a narrative-based WCMS.

PART II: LAB
(CONSTRUCTION GUIDELINES)

Given the general requirements outlined in Part I of this chapter, we can now apply these design specifications to the construction of a specialized WCMS. The WCMS discussed in this section was developed as an accompanying software product for my dissertation (see McDaniel, 2004), and its purpose was to demonstrate how socio-organizational approaches to knowledge management might be embedded in positivist technologies, which generally focus more on the codification and transmission of data rather than on the influence of the environments and communities from which this data emerged. Wick (2000) provides a useful overview of several approaches to knowledge management (KM), which range from fully document-centered KM to technological and socio-organizational approaches. The most desirable approach is found in the practices of the "knowledge organization," which "emphasizes knowledge as the core source of competitive advantage" and "approaches knowledge management as a mission-critical issue affecting all areas of organization" (p. 520). The goal of this particular WCMS was to help encourage organizational growth toward a level of KM maturity by providing a means for collecting, storing, and disseminating tacit knowledge in the form of occupational narratives.

This WCMS operates by using a specialized database composed of narrative "objects," or textual stories represented in computational structures. In this context, the terms "narrative" and "story" are used interchangeably for simplicity's sake, though this practice deviates from the discussion of terms by some literary theorists who may choose to differentiate between the process of telling a story and the story itself, or to impose multiple and layered definitions on narrative (see Bal, 1997; Genette, 1980). Both terms in this chapter are used in the operational sense; they refer to the expression of a causal event sequence recounting some experiences of a primary character (protagonist) working within some environment to overcome some obstacle or obstacles (antagonists) in pursuit of some goal or goals. While this general definition is flexible enough to accommodate specialized forms of narrative (epic poetry, lyrical or musical storytelling, oral storytelling or story circles, etc.) the implementation of a CMS generally requires stories to be expressed in a format that can easily be encoded into a text-based (e.g., hypertext) medium. It is important to note that such encoding does not exclude multimodal storytelling, as images and audio information can also be accommodated by hypertext markup.

A narrative CMS is useful for many different types of applications, particularly in knowledge management scenarios in which specialized types of knowledge require discursive movements from subject matter experts to those audiences unfamiliar with its intricacies. Such applications are especially well suited to first-person-perspective experiential stories, in which a writer explains his or her experiences in dealing with some type of problem by telling a story about his or her situation. This technique is well known from Orr's (1996) observations of expert Xerox technicians and their tendency to swap stories about challenging technical problems during coffee breaks. Post (2002) writes of NASA's investigations into using the same type of narrative exchange in a written form, by having expert project managers compose narratives based on their knowledge and experience. These stories were then compiled into an internal newsletter and circulated to appropriate employees. Even highly technical concepts were able to be successfully shared through the careful use of storytelling and the creative use of figurative language and metaphor.

Stories are also useful for KM due to their native similarity to our own mental processes. Bruner (1991) writes of narrative's abilities to facilitate and engage on a cognitive level, citing such properties as normativeness (the ability to mirror reality), canonicity and breach (being able to surprise), and narrative diachronicity (following chronological patterns familiar to the reader from their experiences in the physical world). Others in the cognitive sciences have found that the scriptlike structure of narrative is especially compatible with the ways in which the brain processes information and scans for patterns (Fiore, Johnston, & McDaniel, 2007). Kim (2005) notes that narrative has some additional self-organizing characteristics, which can be helpful when deciding how to represent these structures in a CMS library. These characteristics include

- A reliance on causality and logical sequencing between various events and agent (character) actions, which, when taken collectively, represent the plot of a narrative,
- An anchoring to contextual information that influences both how the story is written and how the story is perceived by an audience,
- An environment regulated by boundaries such as time and place, and
- A definite beginning and ending, which provide impetus and closure for the narrative.

From these features, it is possible to develop several different methods for classifying and organizing this specialized CMS library. Stories can be classified according to environment, such as the time, place, or location of either the recounted events or of the narration itself—the environment of the story or the environment of its telling. They can be catalogued and sorted according to their obvious plot characteristics or their subtextual elements such as political or moral undercurrents. They may be classified by genre; for example, folklore stories might be separated into stories based around riddles, legends, or superstitious tales. Narrative characteristics provide a rich and varied source of potential organizing methodologies and are well suited for certain types of classification exercises within a CMS.

In the specialized WCMS I created, I chose to classify narrative using five primary features: the central character present within the narrative, the forces (human or otherwise) this character was matched up with and struggled to overcome, the environment in terms of both time and place, and the central theme or concern present in the story. To account for a variety of central themes, or plots, I also included a thematic dictionary system, which included topical listings of keywords. These keywords could then be searched for within narratives and, if a programmed threshold was exceeded, trigger an automatic classification of the story into one of the predefined topics. The final application was named EDNA-E, the Event-Driven Narrative Analysis Engine, and is described in more detail in McDaniel, 2004. Here I provide only a high-level overview of the process in order to relate how closely related the design process lies to fundamental CMS processes and procedures. The WCMS application is available online at: http://www.textsandtech.org/~rudy/edna-e/index.php.

Applying the traditional software lifecycle model (Hamlet & Maybee, 2001) yields five phases of development for a software product: requirements analysis, specification, design, coding, and testing. Developing a robust CMS, then, begins with a clear outline of requirements from a user-centered perspective. What exactly will users need to accomplish with this system? How will administrators enter data, and how will visitors or regular users then access it? Next, during specification, user requirements are implemented according to current process-oriented and technological capabilities. For instance, decisions must be made as to how the interface will function on a technological level and how the database and server will communicate with one another based on existing protocols and software configurations. During design and coding, the system is gradually transformed first into a formalized model, in the design phase; and then into a working prototype, during the coding phase. Testing then occurs to refine the system, and the cycle is repeated as necessary in an iterative fashion. Such development is often known as iterative software development or rapid application development (RAD).

As the content for this particular WCMS would be made up of employee generated stories, there were several considerations that needed to be addressed; namely the issues of scope, security, and quality. Scope concerned the process of soliciting appropriate stories that would be relevant to a given organizational problem, since this narrative WCMS was designed to be used for knowledge management. In other words, if a manager or subject matter expert were interested in reading stories pertaining to experiences with outsourcing or global-ization, then employees who were instead writing stories about technological issues would not be contributing valuable data. Scope, security, and quality were therefore driving factors throughout the development of the product and led to the creation of features such as

1. A *permissions system* to ensure that stories could be accessed by only those users with appropriate permissions or organizational status. This was used to tighten security in the WCMS.
2. An *event generation system* used to produce a database of organizational events open for soliciting stories at any given moment. In other words, only approved organizational events could be responded to by a contributing author. Sample events would include tasks related to major organizational change such as the adoption of new technologies, relocation to a new geographical environment, or perhaps the launch or release of a new product or documentation set. This was used to provide focus and control scope in the WCMS.
3. A *scripting and story administrator panel*, which was used to both define parameters upon the process of contributing new stories as well as to evaluate, edit, or delete stories already submitted. This allowed a "story administrator" to enforce some measure of quality control upon the WCMS.

With the narrative system described here, I began development with a require-ments analysis phase, during which I assessed and attempted to anticipate user needs. The database structure, or library, for this WCMS is composed of nine individual database tables (see Figure 2). The tables collect and store information related to both the content itself and the users and administrators who interact with and manage the system. A total of nine tables were designed in order to collect various types of data necessary for successfully soliciting and distributing narrative materials. These nine tables contained several important subsets of data that were critical for the operation of the WCMS:

- A *stories* table was used to encapsulate user-contributed stories and contained additional keyword metadata useful for searching.
- A *comments* table enabled user-contributed comments for particular stories based on reader interactions with stories.
- Both contributors and readers were assigned to the *users* and *groups* tables, allowing for complex permissions to be assigned according to different schema (organizational departments can be broken into different groups, for example).
- The *scripts* table was used to store data that communicated to a potential story author how their story should be created. Scripts were controllable in

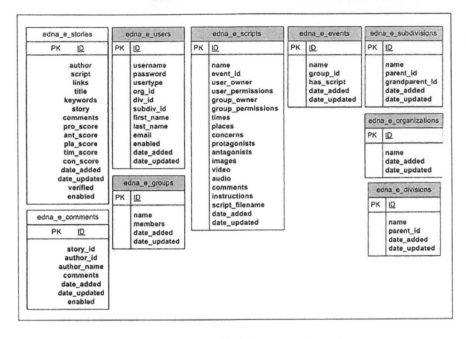

Figure 2. Narrative CMS library configuration.

terms of protagonist (what perspective should the story be told from?), antagonist (what is the opposing force this central character is dealing with?), environment (when and where did the story take place?) and central theme (what is the primary plot of this story and how does it relate to the organization?).

- The *events* table functioned as a library for organizational events and was queried during the story contribution process in order to find an appropriate topic and script.
- The *subdivisions*, *organizations*, and *divisions* tables were primarily used to support the permissions system in enforcing security for access to particular narrative objects. These default tables can be used to automatically generate groups and users based on their membership with default groups in the organization (such as the departments or divisions in which they worked).

Narrative scripts were created based on Schank's (1990) work with narrative and cognitive structures as well as Minksy's (1985) ideas about terminals, which are generic memory structures that he theorizes are filled in with specific details as we encounter variations of these objects in the real world. His idea of a story terminal, then, is a generic framework for a story with placeholders for protagonist, antagonist, place, time, and concern; this directly informed the construction of the scripting mechanism during the design and coding phases of WCMS development.

Finally, after the database had been implemented and populated, a secondary level of encoding was imposed upon the data using the eXtensible Markup Language (XML). XML, which is useful for documentation specialists in a variety of applications (Applen, 2002; Johnsen, 2001), provided a metadata framework to classify stories and dictionary items in a semantic fashion. A simple Web-based XML editor for configuring script files and editing thematic dictionaries was also included for convenience. Screenshots from the final application, which reveal selected components of both the content library management system and the administrative management interface, are shown in Figures 3 thru 10.

So far we have explored specialized Web content management systems from both theoretical and technical perspectives. What is particularly interesting about such systems, though, is that they also have uses as pedagogical tools.

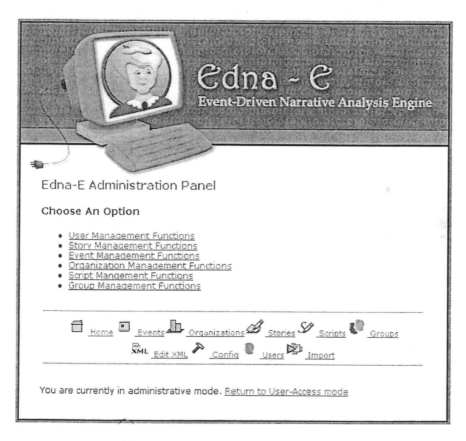

Figure 3. Administrative control panel.

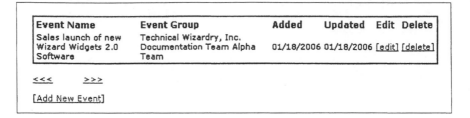

Event Name	Event Group	Added	Updated	Edit	Delete
Sales launch of new Wizard Widgets 2.0 Software	Technical Wizardry, Inc. Documentation Team Alpha Team	01/18/2006	01/18/2006	[edit]	[delete]

<<<　　　>>>

[Add New Event]

Figure 4. Event management panel.

Add A Subdivision

Name [   ] [Add]

Parent Division [Documentation Team ▼]

☑ Add Group for this Subdivision

Existing Organizations

Organization Name	Date Added	Date Updated	Delete
Technical Wizardry, Inc.	01/18/2006	01/18/2006	DELETE
---Documentation Team	01/18/2006	01/18/2006	DELETE
------Beta Team	01/18/2006	01/18/2006	DELETE
------Alpha Team	01/18/2006	01/18/2006	DELETE

Figure 5. Organizational management panel.

In Part III, I discuss several ways in which designing and evaluating specialized CMS applications can be incorporated into targeted learning objectives for the classroom.

PART III: LEARNING ENVIRONMENT (CONNECTIONS TO THE CLASSROOM)

Content management systems have interesting properties that make them suitable for certain types of learning, particularly in those courses dealing with information complexity, software documentation, usability, or project management. For one thing, they are technologically sophisticated and include many of the same types of technologies that graduating students will encounter in industry. For another, they provide an example of metadata classification systems at work, and they operationalize a concept that is oftentimes difficult for students to grasp without seeing it in action. Lastly, the ability of CMS implementations to

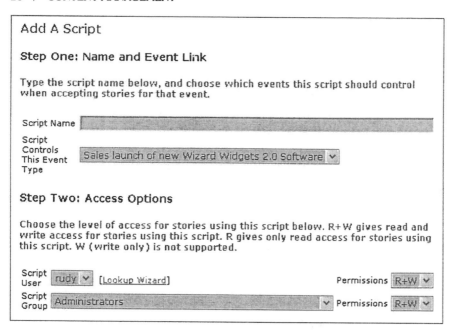

Add A Script

Step One: Name and Event Link

Type the script name below, and choose which events this script should control when accepting stories for that event.

Script Name

Script Controls This Event Type
Sales launch of new Wizard Widgets 2.0 Software

Step Two: Access Options

Choose the level of access for stories using this script below. R+W gives read and write access for stories using this script. R gives only read access for stories using this script. W (write only) is not supported.

Script User
rudy [Lookup Wizard]
Permissions R+W

Script Group
Administrators
Permissions R+W

Figure 6. Scripting panel.

cater to a wide variety of audiences and to meet varied informational needs using a single centralized data source seems representative of the trends in which practicing technical communicators and multimedia writers find themselves immersed in within industrial practice: trends like single sourcing and modular documentation designs.

The most challenging aspect of considering a CMS as a classroom tool is devising a framework for managing the complex technologies that make this type of system possible. It is relatively easy to see the benefits of having students design and construct specialized systems of their own: they learn about user-centered design, data flow, process management, audience analysis, and computational data structures, to name just a few topics, all in an operationalized context. Such tasks can be completed either individually or in group scenarios. It is very difficult, however, to provide students with a general framework for building such a system without investing large amounts of time and effort into the process of building a customized delivery system that needs only minor adjustments by each individual student or group of students. Even open-source portal software, freely available on the Internet, is often cumbersome to install, configure, and manage.

A more feasible goal, then, is to divide the construction of a hypothetical content management system into several smaller assignments, or perhaps into a

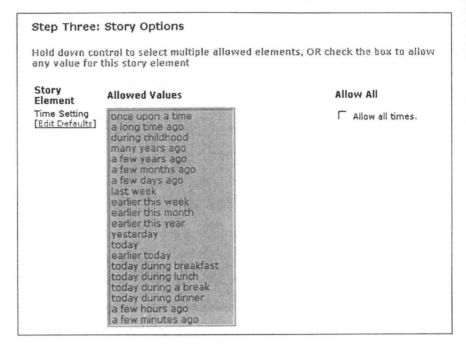

Figure 7. Scripting panel (time setting).

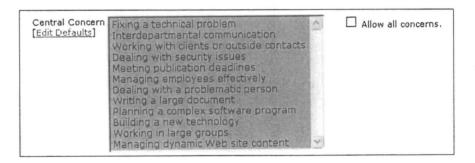

Figure 8. Scripting panel (central concern).

final group project for a semester-length computer software documentation course. Such division mirrors the decomposition model found in the software engineering process, wherein five or more phases occur during the completion of a large, team-produced software deliverable. During each phase, deliverables, or artifacts, are produced that reflect the progress of the CMS at that particular point in development. This division of process can be particularly useful for teaching

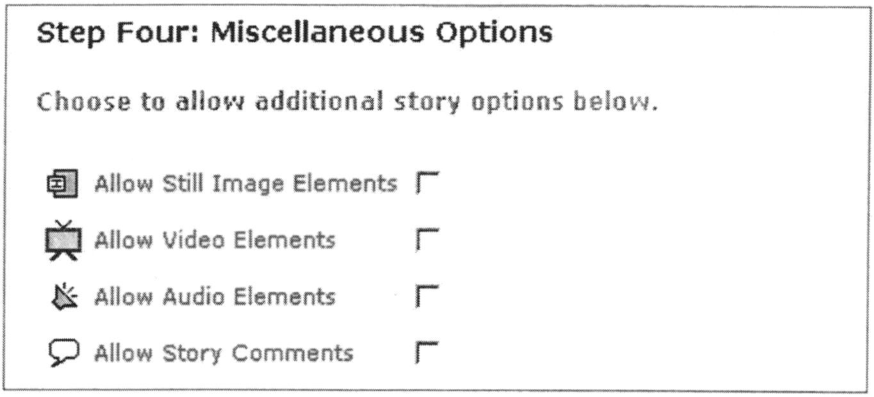

Step Four: Miscellaneous Options

Choose to allow additional story options below.

🖻 Allow Still Image Elements ▯

📺 Allow Video Elements ▯

🔇 Allow Audio Elements ▯

💬 Allow Story Comments ▯

Figure 9. Scripting panel.

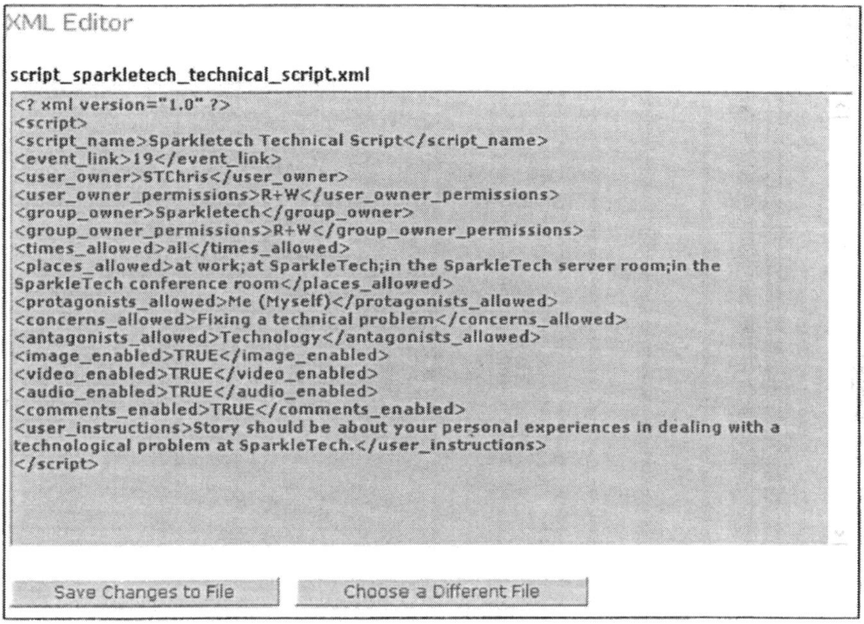

XML Editor

script_sparkletech_technical_script.xml

```
<? xml version="1.0" ?>
<script>
<script_name>Sparkletech Technical Script</script_name>
<event_link>19</event_link>
<user_owner>STChris</user_owner>
<user_owner_permissions>R+W</user_owner_permissions>
<group_owner>Sparkletech</group_owner>
<group_owner_permissions>R+W</group_owner_permissions>
<times_allowed>all</times_allowed>
<places_allowed>at work;at SparkleTech;in the SparkleTech server room;in the
SparkleTech conference room</places_allowed>
<protagonists_allowed>Me (Myself)</protagonists_allowed>
<concerns_allowed>Fixing a technical problem</concerns_allowed>
<antagonists_allowed>Technology</antagonists_allowed>
<image_enabled>TRUE</image_enabled>
<video_enabled>TRUE</video_enabled>
<audio_enabled>TRUE</audio_enabled>
<comments_enabled>TRUE</comments_enabled>
<user_instructions>Story should be about your personal experiences in dealing with a
technological problem at SparkleTech.</user_instructions>
</script>
```

| Save Changes to File | Choose a Different File |

Figure 10. XML editor with sample script loaded.

fledgling writers about the documentation or design process. Since each phase of development is concerned with different primary audiences, writing tasks will vary greatly from one phase to another due to the different informational needs of these audiences.

Table 1 shows one of several possible decompositions of a CMS development process in terms of potential writing tasks. These types of tasks are suitable for use in an upper-level computer documentation or writing for media course. In this table, development phases are indicated along with their primary milestones and some sample writing tasks. In addition, sample audiences are provided for each row and can be used to specify or customize the particular types of writing assignments requested for each phase.

An obvious benefit of this particular exercise is that it includes multimedia authors and technical communication students in the beginning of a complex design process rather than simply handing off a previously completed design to students and asking them to produce its documentation. This facilitates a process in which all team members are involved in all phases of development, and it minimizes confusion about how the product works or how it was designed during latter phases of production. This in turn leads to a truly reader-centered dynamic, in which writers can anticipate how a user or content contributor might feel when encountering the CMS for the first time. Such reader-centered expertise is critical for the development of both software and documentation that are more user-friendly as compared with items produced in a scenario in which documentation and design are fully independent.

An even more ambitious exercise would be to pair a software documentation course with a computer science, digital media, or engineering course in which the

Table 1. CMS-Related Assignments Useful for
Software Documentation Courses

Phase	Documentation milestones	Document artifacts	Audience(s)
Requirements	Achieve shared understanding between development team and client	Requirements analysis report	Client/Customer Design Team
Specification	Make technology choices based on capabilities and experience as well as on audience characteristics	Audience analysis, competition analysis	Design Team Project Manager
Design	Create blueprints for software model	Modeling documents and feature lists	Design Team Project Manager
Coding	Develop a working prototype from the abstract design	Prototype of software documentation	Design Team Project Manager
Testing	Refine prototype based on usability and quality assurance testing	Release version of software documentation	Design Team End User

software is fully programmed and implemented. This could be done either for a short period of time (perhaps for a final project) or in a full semester cooperative model, in which instructors collaborate throughout the development process. In either scenario, each course would exchange deliverables periodically—documents created by students from the writing course would go to the programmers for implementation and analysis, and beta software coded by the software engineering students would be delivered to the writing students for documentation.

While there is much potential for using a CMS in this type of software documentation course, these types of courses constitute only a small subset of what is generally available in technical writing and digital media departments. In more general types of courses, and in introductory technical communication courses, incorporating a WCMS into an existing course curriculum is more difficult, but not impossible. By separating the content of such courses into a set of modules, and by further imposing a hierarchical ranking of topics upon each module, it is possible to devise a simple pedagogical matrix that can be used for generating course ideas related to a given topic.

An example of this framework is shown in Table 2. In this structure, categories have been defined that list important skills and learning objectives one might find in an introductory technical communication or writing for media course. Sample categories for this table are defined for theoretical, technological, and professional development types of learning materials. Tiers are numbered according to increasing task complexity and represent various entry points for integrating traditional assignments with CMS development tasks. Each tier includes a sample (and arbitrary) task, topic, or activity related to a broader category of technical communication and could easily be expanded in either direction depending on the needs and objectives of a particular course. These tasks can then be wrapped around the design or *evaluation* of a CMS or WCMS application.

It is worth mentioning that Table 2 is not intended to represent discrete skillsets or categories; writing can be considered a type of technological skill, for instance, and knowledge of the eXtensible markup language (XML) could also be considered as representing a type of writing skill. XML might also be used to demonstrate an application of the theoretical topics related to the granularity or fragmentation of data in a CMS. "Theoretical topics" might be better described as "advisory frameworks," and so on. The idea is not to provide a rigid rubric for relating classroom activities to the design and production of content management systems, but rather to suggest some ways in which humanities expertise might be applied to the design of such systems by breaking down skills into certain topics related to the field that are especially pertinent. Many of these topics also generalize well to the broader discipline of software design. Additional categories could also be generated rather easily depending on the nature of the course (e.g., a category not mentioned here is business management skills,

Table 2. Skills Involved in CMS Design

Category	Topical task areas for generating classroom activities
Theoretical topics	Tier 0: Reader-centered design Tier 1: Audience analysis Tier 2: Granularity and fragmentation Tier 3: Knowledge models (logocentrism, constructivism) Tier 4: Digital rhetoric
Writing and rhetorical skills	Tier 0: Content generation Tier 1: Standardization of content and editing techniques Tier 2: Evaluating source credibility in WCMS Tier 3: Modular writing techniques Tier 4: Writing for extreme programming (XP)
Technological skills	Tier 0: Brainstorming and modeling tools in Word Tier 1: Working with collaborative writing software Tier 2: Database schema and design Tier 3: Producing eXtensible markup language (XML) Tier 4: Translation of unified modeling language (UML)
Professional development skills	Tier 0: One minute oral reports on brainstorming ideas Tier 1: Hybrid teams and team writing Tier 2: Analysis of job search tools as WCMS

which would include digital asset management, or the economic implications of reusable and accessible digital content, as a potential topic area).

An example of a Tier 4 theoretical topic that has some connections to CMS design is the branch of inquiry that has come to be known as "digital rhetoric." Zappen (2005), discussing Manovich's (2001) work, writes of the flexibility of new media methodologies when combined and arranged using online databases. He writes that new media "can appear in different versions (variability) so that a media database, for example, can produce an almost infinite variety of end-user objects, which can be customized for different users, manipulated through hyperlinks, periodically updated, and scaled upon demand" (p. 321). As this is precisely the type of scenario made possible by a WCMS, what better way is there to familiarize students with the potential power of new media configurations? A classroom discussion of digital rhetoric as it applies to WCMS technologies is likely to be interesting and productive, especially if students are asked to bring in several examples of WCMS technologies that they use on a daily or weekly basis. Discussions can then range from the properties of WCMS to the rhetorical characteristics that enable them to shape the same source of content for different audiences.

A Tier 4 technological skill would be translating unified modeling language, or UML (see Stevens & Pooley, 2006), documents from conceptual diagrams, such as use cases, activity diagrams, and sequence diagrams, into textual descriptions and features lists. These lists are important as they are the software design equivalent to the executive summary in the business world, enabling administrators to quickly absorb the most important parts of the design without wading through pages of documentation. In addition, translation allows technical concepts to be understood by other design team members not familiar with UML syntax. These individuals would include project managers and those individuals responsible for meetings with clients. Such descriptions might even reach end users or those responsible for adding content to the system, if the particular design features are stable enough to make it into the final release of the CMS. This skill is particularly valuable for all types of software documentation, and there is likely to be a significant increase in quality and disambiguation if technical writers and multimedia authors become attached to these types of design phase procedures.

An interesting exercise is to pair the most complicated theoretical exercises with the least complicated technological exercises during early development phases, then gradually adjust the intensities of each to maintain a stable level of difficulty throughout. For example, during the requirements phase, students can be asked to apply their knowledge of constructivist theories in order to produce a blueprint for a CMS design that will account for the needs of a wide variety of different discourse communities and subject matter experts. In this phase, a very low level of technological understanding is necessary, and ideas can be communicated using simple brainstorming software such as *Inspiration* or *Brainstorm* or even typed into a Word document or Excel spreadsheet for comparisons. As the designs move from the abstract realm to more specific ideas, the level of technological complexity will increase, but the theoretical material has been previously applied and can be tapered off or used in a postproduction context in order to produce evaluative usability feedback. By balancing the degree of technological difficulty with the degree of theoretical complexity for any given activity, the tool remains useful, but it is also easier to access and apply by students and to manage by instructors.

The activities shown in Table 2 do not take into account other ways in which CMS or WCMS technologies might be used in the classroom. For example, an instructor teaching in a multimedia classroom might find it meaningful to bring up examples of genre-specific CMS tools in order to demonstrate particular concepts such as information complexity, usability (or the lack thereof) of engineering systems, or concrete examples of single-sourcing methodologies that are used in industry or in open source applications. This would provide an example to *show* the types of systems being discussed. Evaluating existing CMS technologies therefore generates the opportunity for additional classroom connections in terms of classroom participation (discussion and evaluation), writing assignments (rhetorical criticism or evaluative essays), and even field work (usability studies or interviews with CMS personnel).

In my own teaching, I have used CMS examples in several different courses with varying degrees of success. As I am appointed both in an English department and in a digital media department, I generally teach at least one technical communication course each semester along with one or more digital media design courses. In English, I teach both introductory and graduate level technical communication courses, and in digital media, I teach courses in Internet software design, media for e-commerce (which focuses more on the application of technologies rather than on electronic business models), and interactive media.

At our university, digital media students, who come from humanities backgrounds and rarely have any type of background in engineering or computer science, have proven quite adept at designing and implementing their own CMS solutions. These students generally enjoy working with both artistic and Web-related content and appreciate the flexibility offered by CMS architectures in allowing them to create their own dynamic Web sites based on their own academic and professional interests. For example, in a course entitled "Media for E-Commerce II," offered in the spring semester of 2006, students designed CMS-like applications that we called "information fluency kiosks." In this particular course students were exposed to design tools such as Visual Studio .NET and PHP, and although most of these students did not emerge from programming backgrounds, they were able to develop skills sufficient to create basic CMS applications of their own. They could choose their own content for their information fluency kiosks as long as their designs met three objectives: they were required to be educational in some fashion, they were required to be interactive and to allow users to add content, and they were required to use database-driven technology.

These student-developed CMS kiosks were designed to draw from work done in the library sciences (primarily searching and database taxonomy) and digital media (interactivity and graphic design for interfaces) and used specialized content collections for pedagogical purposes. One student designed a CMS for students of beginning Spanish; the system would present data from the library in the form of virtual flash cards in which definitions and conjugation information could be layered and selectively shown based on whether or not a user was interfacing with the system in a "studying" or "quizzing" mode. Several others designed database-driven CMS wikis; rather than attempting epistemological ubiquity, though, they instead focused on specialized subsets of information specific to groups of students (film terminology or collections of tips and tricks for specific software applications, for example).

Using open-source programming and database languages such as PHP (http://www.php.net) and MySQL (http://dev.mysql.com/), students were able to produce and document these CMS applications over a period of four weeks

(Figures 11–14). While these applications are likely not full fledged WCMS applications due to their lack of advanced indexing and search features, they do demonstrate the basic characteristics of such systems in terms of database-driven design, interactivity, usability, and interface design.

In my English courses, I have had better luck dividing CMS design procedures down into smaller assignments as opposed to asking students to participate in building an entire system (although I still contend that this can be done and with valuable results). In a graduate-level professional writing course, one of my modules focuses on the use of XML in technical communication, and students are given the opportunity to examine modules of information (taken from a CMS and encoded in XML) in terms of their rhetorical efficacy. In another module, students are given the choice to either design a Web site system adhering to the principles of user-centered design or to evaluate an existing site through a rhetorical lens. Many students choosing the latter option have honed in on large commercial Web sites and examined the ways in which source credibility can be even further diminished by content management systems (see Warnick's 2004 discussion of online ethos and the complications involved with source assessment in "authorless" environments).

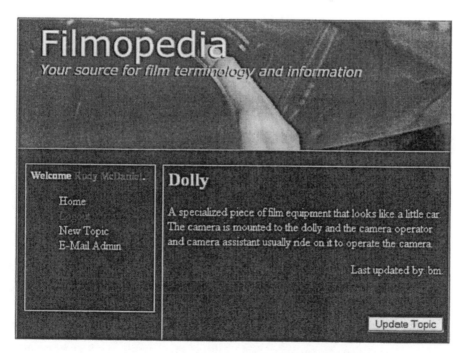

Figure 11. Student produced film terminology
wiki CMS.

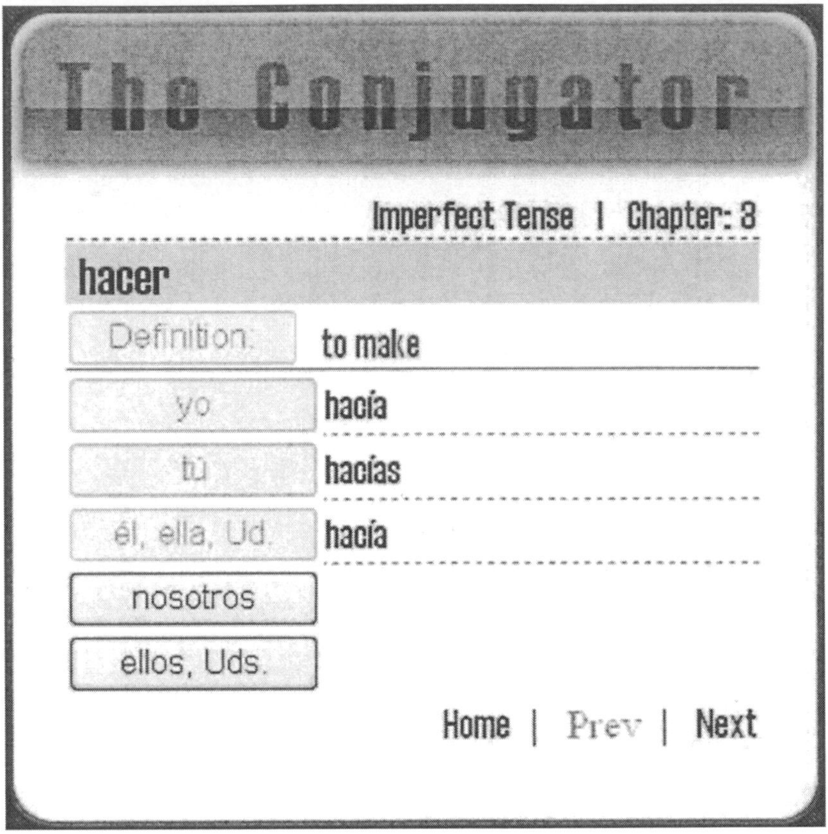

Figure 12. Student produced Spanish language study tool CMS.

CONCLUSION: IMPLICATIONS FOR WRITING IN NETWORKED ENVIRONMENTS

An understanding of specialized CMS processes and architectures is essential for technical communicators and multimedia authors hoping to position themselves as knowledge managers—or simply as effective and technologically literate documentation specialists—within their organizations. Luckily, such expertise is not difficult to obtain. As Hughes (2002) notes, those technical communicators who routinely practice user-centered writing are already working within a knowledge domain rather than an information-centric domain; he writes, "By reinterpreting technical information in user contexts, they are creating new knowledge by presenting that information in actionable terms and relating it to

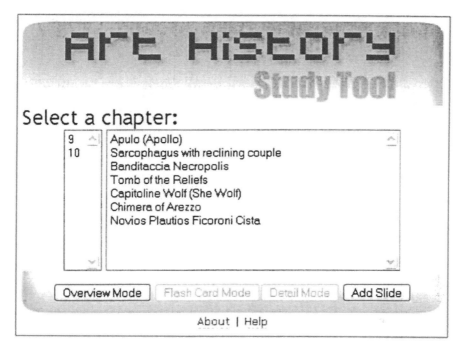

Figure 13. Student produced art history study tool CMS
(chapter view).

specific applications" (p. 276). By guiding the types of automated reinterpretation being done by CMS tools, technical communicators contribute valuable usability expertise to this process.

Likewise, the experience gained from working with CMS and WCMS technologies is highly desirable for those students studying in digital media and new media programs. By engaging with CMS frameworks in both directions—forward when designing and in reverse when evaluating—students are given the opportunity to interact with digital assets in a dynamic fashion while learning about critical concepts such as genre analysis, information granularity, modular design, and digital asset management. As digital media itself is such a new and emerging field—digital media programs across the country are being formed from programs as diverse as English, engineering, and art—CMS technology is rich enough to be studied from *all* of these perspectives, yet straightforward enough so as not to be overly intimidating and inaccessible.

Instructors also benefit from knowledge of CMS technology by better positioning themselves for interdisciplinary collaboration; such collaborations have the potential to yield measurable and tangible results. With a computer science and technical communication course partnership, for example, computer science

Figure 14. Student produced art history study tool CMS
(image view).

students are likely to appreciate the assistance with documentation and planning, while technical communication students will appreciate the chance to be involved in a project that is similar to what they will find in industry when they graduate. Faculty from both departments will appreciate the skills brought to the table by other disciplines. Administrators from cooperating departments may also see value in the collaboration; computer science Chairs often bemoan the poor writing skills of their students while technical communication and digital media administrators can have a difficult time replicating real-world technological problems in the classroom.

In addition to industrial utility, a knowledge of CMS applications can also be handy for use in the writing or communications classroom. By providing students with access to those principles guiding the development of industrial collections of data and corporate assets, these students are likely to recognize the value and necessity of fundamental communication tasks as they are applied to a more fully realized development cycle. Incorporating CMS-related activities into a technical communication, digital media, or information technology course is likely to generate at least two levels of benefit: at the short-term level, students will be exposed to complex technologies and gain some familiarities with the inner workings and applications of such technologies. At a more sustained (and arguably more valuable) level, students will also engage with these technologies on a critical level in order to reexamine and question the ways in which information technology networks operate in broader discursive contexts.

As we slowly but inevitably move toward the next-generation Internet technologies such as Web 2.0 and the Semantic Web, information overload will continue to be a very real problem, perhaps *the* problem professional communicators and managers of complex and specialized information are most unprepared to deal with. Technologies such as intelligent agents (Quesenbery, 2002; Soller & Busetta, 2003) may eventually mature to the point of viability as they take up residence in the pathways between interfaces and content databases and help users to construct accurate and focused searches through vast libraries of information. Regardless of new technologies, though, it is likely that students and faculty exposed to CMS tools and technologies in *any* context will be better prepared to deal with the continued growth and complexity of not only the Internet, but of distributed information systems in general.

ACKNOWLEDGMENTS

The author would like to thank several students in the Spring 2006 Media for E-Commerce II course at the University of Central Florida for agreeing to share their information fluency kiosks. In particular, Bryan Miller designed the kiosk shown in Figure 11, Paul Cox's work is shown in Figure 12, and the screen captures in Figures 13 and 14 are the work of student Gabriel Mariani. He also wishes to thank Carole McDaniel for her graphic design work on EDNA-E and her assistance in preparing Figures 1–10.

REFERENCES

Applen, J. D. (2002). Technical communication, knowledge management, and XML. *Technical Communication, 49*(3), 301-313.

Bal, M. (1997). *Narratology: Introduction to the theory of narrative* (2nd ed.). Toronto: University of Toronto Press.

Bruner, J. (1991). The narrative construction of reality. *Critical Inquiry, 18*, 1-21.

Davenport, T. H., & Prusak, L. (1997). *Information ecology: Mastering the information and knowledge environment.* New York: Oxford University Press.

Deacon, A., Jaftha, J., & Horwitz, D. (2004). Customising Microsoft Office to develop a tutorial learning environment. *British Journal of Educational Technology, 35*(2), 223-234.

Denning, S. (2001). *The springboard*. Woburn, MA: Butterworth-Heinemann.

Denning, S. (2004). *Squirrel Inc: A fable of leadership through storytelling*. San Francisco, CA: John Wiley & Sons.

Farkas, D. K. (2005). Explicit structure in print and on-screen documents. *Technical Communication Quarterly, 14*(1), 9-30.

Fiore, S. M., Johnston, J., & McDaniel, R. (2007). Narratology and distributed training: Using the narrative form for debriefing simulation-based exercises. In S. M. Fiore & E. Salas (Eds.), *Where is the learning in distance learning? Towards a science of distributed learning and training* (pp. 119-145). Washington, DC: American Psychological Association.

Genette, G. (1980). *Narrative discourse* (J. E. Lewin, Trans.). Ithaca, NY: Cornell University Press.

Goans, D., Leach, G., & Vogel, T. M. (2005). Beyond HTML: Developing and re-imagining library Web guides in a content management system. *Library Hi Tech, 24*(1), 29-53.

Hamlet, D., & Maybee, J. (2001). *The engineering of software: Technical foundations for the individual*. Boston, MA: Addison Wesley.

Hughes, M. (2002). Moving from information transfer to knowledge creation: A new value proposition for technical communicators. *Technical Communication, 49*(3), 275-285.

Johnsen, L. (2001). Document re(presentation): Object-orientation, visual language, and XML. *Technical Communication, 48*(1), 59-66.

Kim, L. (2005). Tracing visual narratives: User-testing methodology for developing a multimedia museum show. *Technical Communication, 52*(2), 121-137.

Manovich, L. (2001). *The language of new media*. Cambridge, MA: MIT Press.

McDaniel, T. R. (2004). *A software-based knowledge management system using narrative texts*. Orlando, FL: University of Central Florida.

Minsky, M. (1985). *The society of mind*. New York: Simon & Schuster.

Orr, J. E. (1996). *Talking about machines: An ethnography of a modern job*. Ithaca, NY: ILR Press.

Post, T. (2002). The impact of storytelling on NASA and Edutech. *KM Review, 5*(1), 26-29.

Quesenbery, W. (2002). Who is in control? The logic underlying the intelligent technologies used in performance support. *Technical Communication, 49*(4), 449-457.

Schank, R. C. (1990). *Tell me a story: Narrative and intelligence*. Evanston, IL: Northwestern University Press.

Smart, G. (1999). Storytelling in a central bank: The role of narrative in the creation and use of specialized economic knowledge. *Journal of Business and Technical Communication, 13*(3), 249-273.

Soller, A., & Busetta, P. (2003). An intelligent agent architecture for facilitating knowledge sharing communication. *Proceedings of International Conference on Autonomous Agents and Multi-Agent Systems* (94-100).

Stevens, P., & Pooley, R. (2006). *Using UML: Software engineering with objects and components* (2nd ed.). New York: Addison-Wesley.

Surjanto, B., Ritter, N., & Loeser, H. (2000). *XML content management based on object-relational database technology*. Paper presented at the First International Conference on Web Information Systems Engineering.

Warnick, B. (2004). Online ethos: Source credibility in an "authorless" environment. *American Behavioral Scientist, 48*(2), 256-265.

Wick, C. (2000). Knowledge management and leadership opportunities for technical communicators. *Technical Communication, 47*(4), 515-529.

Yu, H. (2005). *Content and workflow management for library Websites: Case studies.* Hershey, PA: Idea Group.

Zappen, J. P. (2005). Digital rhetoric: Toward an integrated theory. *Technical Communication Quarterly, 14*(3), 319-325.

Zimmerman, M. (2001). Technical communication in an altered technology landscape: What might be. *Technical Communication, 48*(2), 200-205.

CHAPTER TWO

Analyze Before You Act: CMS and Knowledge Transfer

Carol Siri Johnson and Susan Fowler

Content management, which includes document management, Web content management, digital asset management, and records management, is increasingly important in the digital age. CMSWatch, a vendor of content management analysis, publishes the CMS Report, a tool for CMS specialists to sort through the many products for a specific corporate environment. As of April 2006, the report compared 32 vendors of content management software systems and cost $895 for a single-user standard edition. Technical communication practitioners who face the expense and complexity of implementing a content management system need to be aware that before investing in software database systems, it is important to analyze the information environment and the flow of knowledge throughout the organization. Otherwise new document databases can slow existing communication, create extra work, and impede existing methods of knowledge transfer. This is especially true in organizations that create new knowledge, since clear and rapid communication between employees is critical to their success. In some cases, an outside vendor database is not necessary and, in fact, may impede the development of new knowledge.

Content management is complex: the content can include databases of customer records and inquiries, advertising copy, accounting data, technical specifications, chunks of XML and metadata, internal procedures, employee records, vendor correspondence, and more. The amount and types of content in any organization are specific to that organization, and thus no single solution is possible. In this chapter, we warn against relying on the implementation of software systems that do not take into account the complexity and specificity of each organization. Without a solid theoretical understanding of the knowledge flow within an organization, out-of-the-box systems can interrupt the flow of information. Our premise is that the most essential element to any information organization is an unimpeded lateral flow of knowledge between people; content management systems should be built to support that flow.

Technical communicators are uniquely positioned to move into the relatively new field of content management. We occupy the space at the interstices in many organizations, having access to information from many departments, groups, and subject-matter experts. Technical communicators are more likely to have an overall view of the knowledge flow within an organization than subject matter experts who concentrate on a specific portion of a project or process (or on a single project or process). As researchers, we are trained to locate information and make it available to others. The field of content management offers us an opportunity not only to create documents but to structure the systems within which they work. However, to be able to analyze systems that support tacit knowledge exchange, we need to be aware of the flow of knowledge within organizations. The final answer is not always to create a formal content management system.

DEFINITIONS OF KNOWLEDGE AND CONTENT MANAGEMENT

There are different forms of content management and little consensus on its definition. In *Managing Enterprise Content: A Unified Content Strategy* (2003), Ann Rockley focuses on "enterprise" content management "that spans many different areas within an organization, [is] created by multiple authors, and [is] distributed in many different media" (p. ixx). Enterprise content management connects databases from disparate sections of the organization, reducing the effect of silos (departments working in isolation) and creating a single source for all information regarding a specific topic. This approach takes knowledge and breaks it into chunks so that it can be reused in a variety of formats. For large corporations with legal issues, this enterprise content management is an absolute necessity. Addey, Ellis, Suh, & Thiemecke (2002) describe content management differently in *Content Management Systems:* they approach it as a practice specific to Web sites and Web content. They write, "It is probably best to think of content management as a broad concept that covers all aspects of publishing content with digital tools" (p. 12). Wikipedia (2006) notes that there are many different types of CMS such as wikis themselves, digital asset management systems, publication management systems, Web site databases, and more. Overall, the meaning of the term "content management" is still evolving. As the Darwin Web Team (2004) puts it, "The definition of content management remains a running target—one that isn't likely to slow down anytime soon."

Content management is truly something new. It has become necessary due to our increasing use of computers, the consequent explosion of data, and our need to sort and control the data. In *Control through Communication: the Rise of System in American Management,* JoAnne Yates (1989) describes a parallel cultural shift in the 19th century, when we moved from a premodern to an industrial economy. Her basic thesis is that, with the advent of the industrial age, workers and organizations had to "rise above the individual memory and to establish an organizational memory" (p. 6). The tools that she describes are early forms of content management: the typewriter, flat filing, letter presses, press books, and letter boxes. In the 19th century, the technological solutions were evolving, and they are still evolving now. Yates relates the 19th-century communication revolution to the present one when she wrote, it was "an office revolution since unequaled until the advent of the desktop computer" (p. 63). Now, however, the task is more complex, because the amount of data we can store is infinite; part of content management is to discover what is worth storing.

In this chapter we define content management as the method whereby an organization stores and distributes data and information. But to fully understand the distinctions between data, and information and their relation to knowledge, we need to look at knowledge management. In *Working Knowledge: How Organizations Manage What They Know,* Thomas Davenport and Laurence Prusak (2000) define data as undigested facts, information as organized data, and knowledge as "a fluid mix of framed experience, values, contextual information, and expert insight" that allows people to act (pp. 2-5). Knowledge management, which preceded content management as a corporate and professional issue, refers to the flow of knowledge within an organization. Since content management focuses on data and information, it is a subset of knowledge management. Data and information should be organized so that they are accessible to appropriate stakeholders; for instance, workers should have access to databases where their resources are stored. This is more difficult than it sounds.

Thus, although our definition of content management is simple—the method whereby an organization stores and distributes data and information—finding the theoretical bases for content management systems is complex. Content management systems should be built to facilitate knowledge transfer and generation. Therefore, in order to do so, designers of content management systems must first understand the knowledge flow within an organization. The volume of data and information is astounding: there are computer programs, backup systems, databases, networks, boxes of papers, filing cabinets, records stored at remote locations, tracking logs, libraries of modules, x-rays, statistical results, receipts, client records, graphics, e-mails, streaming video, and systems documentation, to name a few. Moreover, the content that we use to support knowledge generation is constantly changing. The technical communicator-turned-content manager visualizes the components and develops ways to connect them. This means making decisions about what is important to connect, what can be left in a silo, how knowledge moves from one person to another, what is important to keep, and what can be discarded. Every content management system will be different.

THEORETICAL BACKGROUND

Increasingly, knowledge is our major product. In *The Myth of the Paperless Office*, Sellen and Harper (2003) wrote, "One of the great changes of the past few decades has been the shift away from manufactured goods toward knowledge-based products and services. Workers are less likely to be using their hands and more likely to be using their minds to monitor, manage, and control the flow of information" (p. 51). Information flow is central to the production of knowledge. Thus, when considering a content management system, technical communication practitioners should start with an analysis of the existing knowledge environment.

One characteristic of knowledge environments is that in order to remain relevant, they are often temporary. Each project requires different inputs and produces different documents. Although existing documents are often used for templates, their lifespan is only as long as that set of knowledge elements is used. Sellen and Harper note that real-time content management systems are often scattered around the office in piles. The piles are meaningful, not just regarding their contents but in their locations and height.

> The information that [knowledge workers] keep is arranged around their offices in a temporary holding pattern of paper documents that serves as a way of keeping available the inputs and ideas they might have use for in their current projects. This clutter also provides important contextual cues to remind them of where they were in their space of ideas (p. 63).

The authors separate documents into three types of files: "hot files" (currently being used), "warm files" (finished or material for the next project), and "cold files" (unused, ready for storage) (Sellen & Harper, 2002, p. 164). Moreover, they note that filing systems are specific to each individual and to each project. When pre-arranged filing systems in content management software are instituted, they are usually incapable of providing the personalization, complexity, and visual clues that knowledge workers use. The authors conclude that digital repositories are most suited to cold (unused) documents (Sellen & Harper, 2002, p. 179).

One major feature underlying contemporary knowledge flow is that there is a great deal of uncertainty in workforce life. Research conducted at the AT&T Labs (Nardi, Whittaker, & Schwarz, 2000) discovered that the transfer of knowledge depends mainly on personal social networks. Due to "downsizing, outsourcing, merging, splitting, acquiring, partnering, and the constant redrawing of internal organizational charts," the structures of many corporations, including their content management systems, are unstable. Moreover, the responsibilities of each employee change frequently, as do their colleagues and reporting relationships. Thus, in our uncertain working environment, people have come to rely on the professional contacts they have made, rather than organizational databases. They interact within and outside their current jobs to get information. In this environment, tools such as "e-mail, voicemail, instant messaging, fax, pagers, and cellular telephones, as well as personal digital assistants" are key because they allow people to carry their knowledge with them (Nardi et. al., 2000).

There is uncertainty about the value of data and information as well: we don't know what data are worth storing. Brown and Duguid (2000), researchers from Xerox PARC, write, "a critical task ahead will be to stop volume from simply overwhelming value" (p. xiii). They remind us that despite the excitement of new software solutions, many technologies "create as many problems as they solve" (p. 3). They continue, "new technology often threatens not to help find a new equilibrium but rather to unsettle equilibria whenever they are found. The rapid innovation endemic to the technology can be destabilizing, even for large organizations with copious resources" (p. 75). At one company that we worked for, the implementation of a content management system required hours of training, cost over a million dollars, and then, because it was unnecessary for the production of work and hard to use, employees simply ignored it. In this case, the only disruption that occurred was the loss of money and time. In other cases, implementing a new system can disrupt production processes.

Computer systems cannot generate knowledge—knowledge is created by people. Computers can assist our knowledge-making activities and store the results. However, knowledge generation is a social endeavor. Working at the IBM Research Center, Erickson and Kellogg (2000) noted that inappropriate software can sever social ties: it can become "technologies that impose walls between people" (p. 80). Dodds, Watts, and Sabel (2003) wrote that problem solving requires "information-rich collaboration between individuals, teams, departments, and even different organizations" (p. 4). Much of this knowledge flows directly between people, in a human network, without the intercession of a computerized system or database. Vendor CMS systems are not responsive to specific situations, changing requirements or intrapersonal interactions. Thus, although they are well suited for storage, they are not well suited for human interaction. In many cases an intermediary, like a librarian, is required to negotiate the pathways to information.

Wenger, McDermott, and Snyder (2002) have suggested that "communities of practice" can create their own documentation and content management systems. A community of practice is a group of people that works together on a joint enterprise and shares knowledge as they do so. Communities of practice themselves are fluid, gaining and losing members as the project develops and changes. The shared knowledge that communities of practice use is a collection of resources that cannot easily be cataloged: "They range from concrete objects, such as a specialized tool or a manual, to less tangible displays of competence, such as an ability to interpret a slight change in the sound of a machine as indicating a specific problem" (Wenger et al., 2002, p. 39). The knowledge that they share is both tacit and explicit. Explicit knowledge is that which can be captured; but tacit knowledge happens of its own accord. Therefore, content managers need to be aware of communities of practice and provide space and time for them to exchange tacit knowledge. The strength of tacit knowledge is that it is powerful and fast, but explicit knowledge can span the boundaries of space and time. In fact, our ability to store explicit knowledge has made complex technology possible.

Human interaction is essential in any organization that relies heavily on knowledge making. In their article written for the Center on Organizational Innovation, Kelly and Stark (2002) discuss the power of "strong personal ties, lateral self-organization, and nonhierarchical relations" (p. 1523). After the September 11 attacks, they held a roundtable discussion with IT and communication executives from the World Trade Center. Many of the organizations had been able to begin operating soon after the attacks, and the participants in the roundtable credited the fast recovery to people, rather than technology. One executive explained,

> It was getting into the systems, [figuring out] the IDs of the systems because so many people had died and the people that knew how to get into those systems . . . were all gone. The way that they got into those systems? They sat around the group, they talked about where they went on vacation, what their kids' names were, what their wives' names were, what their dogs' names were, you know, every imaginable thing about their personal life . . . (p. 1524).

By accessing personal information acquired in social situations, the group was able to guess the passwords of the IT personnel and thus restart the systems. The greatest knowledge generation and transfer occurs between people. Thus, the first step to creating a useful content management system is to read the information environment—how people find what they need, how they communicate, and how they generate knowledge—and incorporate those realities into the CMS design.

THREE CASE STUDIES

In this section, we describe three case studies from the literature that demonstrate some characteristics of knowledge databases. From these case studies we can isolate the signals that colleagues and students can use to read the information environment, thereby discovering and creating knowledge databases on their own. The first case study occurred at the University of Jyväskylä in Finland; the second at the Xerox Palo Alto Research Center (PARC); and the last at the School of Computing, Mathematics, and Statistics at the University of Waikato, New Zealand. In all of these cases the analysis was undertaken by academic and professional researchers. Unfortunately, in the working world we have known, corporations undervalue research, and thus they rely on the advice of commercial vendors such as those listed in CMS Watch. Technical communicators, then, have the opportunity to identify a problem, theorize a solution, and present it to their management. As will be seen below, intelligent solutions can be much simpler than IT solutions.

Papermill Electronic Diary

The first case study is a report on the creation and use of an electronic "diary" from a Finnish papermill. The authors, researchers from the University of Jyväskylä in Finland, studied papermill and oil-rig work with the intention of using CSCW (computer supported cooperative work) software that they had at their disposal. Their first step was to analyze the working environment. In an ethnographic study using interviews, observation, and participation carried out over a period of 18 months, they collected findings on information systems and information use in papermills. Overall, they found that "the information systems in use are primarily designed for some other user-group than operating personnel" and that there was a "lack of access to organizational memory" (Auramäki et al., 1996, pp. 371, 375). Based on their observations, they developed an electronic diary to be shared among the workers that would facilitate knowledge exchange for the purposes of solving technological problems.

Paper manufacturing is one of Finland's most important industries. Papermills run 24 hours a day, with three shifts, to recoup the original investment in the very expensive equipment. Production lines can be as long as 500 feet, and the rolls of paper are up to 30 feet wide and 20 feet high. It takes time to walk around them, so other workers are often out of sight. The level of noise is high as well, so communication between workers on the same shift is nearly as difficult as between workers on different shifts. Downtime costs up to $20,000 an hour, so the mill workers try to keep the mill running at all times. Rather than stop the machine for small repairs, they adjust what they can and then wait for major breakdowns to do all the maintenance and repairs at once (Robinson, Kovalainen, & Auramäki, 2000, p. 65). This means that the mill workers have to keep track of problems and troubleshoot whatever they can (for example, holes or tears in the paper) during and sometimes across shifts.

At the beginning of the study, the papermill had a paper diary (a logbook) kept in the shift foreman's office. This diary was used for the "morning meetings," when the managers got together to check progress and resolve problems. However, as it was a paper diary and it was located in the manager's office, it was not very accessible to (or used by) the mill workers. The managers who did write in the paper diary didn't use any particular format except date and time, and the entries were used primarily as agendas for the morning meetings. The rest of the data was temperatures and other numbers collected from the machines at various points during each shift. It wasn't searchable except by flipping through the pages.

The authors set up what they thought would be an electronic version of the diary using Lotus Notes. Computer terminals were set up at distributed locations on the shop floor, and all mill workers had access to the terminals. The format was simple: the e-diary had an automatic date and time stamp, job roles, and an area for free-form notes.

To their surprise, the e-diary took off—the starting group of 35 mill workers and two managers quickly grew to 100 workers and 13 managers (Kovalainen, Robinson, & Auramäki, 1998, p. 49). The purpose of the original paper diary expanded into a communal problem-solving and communications tool that recorded the daily functioning of the mill and was searchable. Instead of cryptic notes for the morning meetings, entries became a running commentary on the state of the machines, problems, solutions, and general comments. It became a way for the mill workers to communicate with each other over time and across space to managers; to other workers on the same shift but out of sight or earshot; to workers on following shifts; and to mill workers coming onboard after their days off (mill workers are scheduled nine days on, five days off). The purpose and power of the diary expanded so that it became a tool for knowledge transfer. For example, here is a short cross-shift dialogue (Robinson et al., 2000, p. 67):

> *17.5.97 morning, shift foreman, finishing:* Sensor problem in PL72 . . . Night shift will make the next trim. Then we will see if the fault occurs again.
> *17.5.97 evening, shift foreman, finishing:* Making trim on PL72 went fine.

The e-diary was also used for dialogues between workers during shifts in order to overcome noise and distance between workers. The interactions followed the same general format (Robinson et al., 2000, p. 68):

> *10.11.96 evening, shift foreman, mass sector:* Some yellow rolls have been wrecked.
> *Mass operator, mass section:* The lock on the yellow ink drum has been removed (it will run until it's empty). . . .
> *Roll person:* It is rattling along here too.

In addition to recording "soft" information such as interesting events and experiences, the e-diary entries had more structure, with headings and roles. It was also searchable—workers could pick up all related entries and look for patterns.

What was even more interesting to the authors, however, was the unexpected nature of the communication. First, unlike e-mail systems, the messages were not directed to anyone in particular. The addressee was self-defined—it was whoever answered or took action based on an entry. Another surprise was "hanging entries," which were write-ups about particular problems or machinery peculiarities. What made them hanging was that they were left unresolved, at least within the e-diary. The authors found out later that some were resolved "by other means"—in conversations, by workers simply seeing that something has been done, in morning meetings, and in other ways. However, some of them remained unsolved and were repeated many times. The lack of resolution for these problems itself was significant—they marked areas that might require technical attention. Overall, the e-diary facilitated and recorded conversation that could take place across distance, noise, and time. This conversation enabled greater knowledge transfer than the paper diary in the manager's office, but it was also linked to the ongoing methods of human communication. The only software tool that was necessary for this new process was the relatively common Lotus Notes.

Xerox Technicians and Knowledge Transfer

According to Graham (1996), Xerox created its R&D division, the Palo Alto Research Center (PARC), in 1970 to define "the office of the future" (p. 374). Much interesting research has come out of this group. Since part of this effort was to understand work as a social process, the multidisciplinary research center included "a cadre of academically trained anthropologists who spend their time studying how people interact with machines, and with each other" (Buderi, 1998, p. 44). Brown and Duguid (2000) both worked at PARC. In their book *The Social Life of Information,* they discuss the following two examples of analyzing knowledge flow within an organization.

In a now famous case, the anthropologist Julian Orr studied the methods by which Xerox technicians solved problems with machines at customer sites. Since there was an existing document database, and the technicians were generally successful in solving the problems, his fellow researchers questioned the need to study the situation at all (Brown & Duguid, 2000, p. 100). However, Orr's groundbreaking study showed that it was not the document database that enabled the technicians to repair the machines; instead, it was the stories that they told each other over breakfast.

At that time, Xerox technicians were provided with "directive" documents that listed error messages and mapped symptoms to potential solutions. However, the machines were so idiosyncratic that the documentation could not take into account all of the different errors that could occur in different parts of the machine at different times, so the technicians never used the documentation. Brown and Duguid write that "Although the documentation claimed to provide a map, the reps continually confronted the question of how to travel when the marked trails disappeared and they found themselves surrounded by unmarked poison oak" (p. 100). The documentation simply could not take into account the number of variables in the process flow. As Auramäki and colleagues noted above (1996), "the central expertise in immediate process control is knowledge of process interdependencies, and the ability to evaluate probabilities of different cause combinations" (p. 312). The combinations were nearly limitless, and the technicians had to use their combined expertise to discuss possible causes and evaluate and test solutions.

By following the technicians in their daily routine, Orr observed that they discussed the complexities of machine interactions during their breakfast. In fact, they held conversations like this on a daily basis, and it was these conversations, not the documentation, that enabled them to get their work done. Orr discovered that narrative was a powerful tool in complex problem solving (Brown & Duguid, 2000, p. 106). As a consequence, Xerox provided the technicians with two-way radios so that they could consult each other whenever necessary. They also started a knowledge-capture system called "Eureka" that allowed the technicians to enter solutions that were then peer-reviewed. Both of these solutions have been successful.

At the same time, Xerox was trying to lower the number of site visits by technicians, which were expensive. If call-center phone technicians could help customers solve simple problems, they would save money. At first they tried a case-based expert system. Case-based systems provide call-center technicians with a series of prompts—questions to ask—to help define the problem and thus arrive at a solution. However, this process did not work, and the customer would usually ask for a technician to travel to the site anyway. Another researcher from PARC, Jack Whalen, analyzed the performance of different call center technicians and discovered that those who were most successful overheard the calls of other technicians and thus learned more about the common problems than they were able to learn by the scripted case-based system. The solution, in this case, was to restructure the call center so that there were fewer barriers between the call desk technicians (Brown & Duguid, 2000, p. 132). This is another example where a content management system did not answer the real needs of the organization. Graham (1996) stresses "taking account of the subtleties of work practice when incorporating new information technologies into an existing work culture" (p. 373). Technological solutions are often not the best answer to optimize the flow of information.

Lab Technicians in a New Zealand University

Cunningham, Knowles, and Reeves (2001) present a case of analyzing a knowledge flow in a university IT support center. Their original goal was to create a digital library to provide a source of knowledge for the contractors who worked at the support center. Due to their analysis, however, they discovered that a digital library was not necessary. They collected data on six consultants who served 700 faculty, staff, and students at the University of Waikato, New Zealand. Their methods included "interviews of participants; 'shadowing' participants as they worked; observation of semi-social discussions in the School tearoom; and examination of various work artifacts (email, bookmarks, webpages, office bulletin boards, etc.)" (p. 191). Their ethnographic study of how university technical support personnel gather information can be related, on a broader scale, to the way we search for information in general.

Although some of the consultants' task-based work was well defined, much of it was unique problem solving. Most universities have technical support departments that are responsible for simple tasks such as configuring individual e-mail accounts, connecting printers, and providing basic answers to users. These departments are also responsible for more undefined tasks such as locating conflicts within and between programs, databases, and networks; setting up new facilities; and providing the administration with information about current and future needs in hardware and software. As the authors note, "For some of the tasks there is a level of repetition. . . . Some of the tasks, however, fall into the category of 'one-offs'," in which the research and resolution will not be used again (p. 191). At the beginning of this study, they were considering using Greenstone, software created by the New Zealand Digital Library Research Group (http://www.nzdl.org), which provides multiple entry points for searching document collections (p. 190).

However, after studying the activities of the technical support consultants, the researchers concluded that the standard search functions provided in database software such as Greenstone were not useful for the types of searches that the IT consultants used. The following are some of the reasons that they felt a digital library would not be helpful:

- Formally published documents usually aren't useful
- Many documents are ephemeral
- Documents may not be trustworthy
- A primary information source is other people
- Information might not look like a document (pp. 192-196)

Moreover, existing digital library systems make the assumption that people find information by creating a search string. However, many people find information by browsing remembered locations and using personalized information resources. Some of the IT consultants, for example, saved files on their desktops. Others used color as well as location to keep track of information. One consultant used colored stickies at his workstation and another used colored nodes in a mind map file (p. 195). If documents are necessary, they are often produced by the consultants themselves.

Search faculties in digital databases are too far removed from immediate tacit human knowledge flows to be useful in a just-in-time situation. They are less likely to be used than less formal documentation that is written on scrap paper, pinned to the walls, or transferred between people. In *The Myth of the Paperless Office,* the authors note that people leave papers "around their offices in a temporary holding pattern" (Sellen & Harper, 2002, p. 63). That holding pattern leaves visual and tactile clues as to where useful information can be found. Digital libraries require remembering a verbal search string, or a search route, that was successful in the past. Since the documents themselves are in "cold storage," several steps removed from human activity, it requires time to find, access, and assess them before they can be brought into the live working environment. Although digital libraries may be useful in long-term, research-oriented professions, they are inconsequential for the immediate task of keeping up with changing technology.

Cunningham, Knowles, and Reeves (2001) conclude that, too often, "system developers concentrate on creating an information system, rather than on ensuring that the system created is useful and usable, or even investigating whether a system should be created at all!" (p. 198). Software developers are generally not trained in usability or human-computer interaction. The gap, then, must be filled by others, including technical communicators.

CONCLUSION

In an information economy, where knowledge is our product, it is necessary to carefully analyze the existing knowledge flow in an environment before implementing a content management system. Established knowledge (as well as data and information) can be contained in content management systems, but current working knowledge is far too fluid to be captured and placed in a database. If a business or corporation is required by law to have consistency in disseminating data and information, then a full content management system is necessary. However, if a business or corporation relies on the development of new knowledge or the rapid exchange of existing knowledge, it must rely on the seemingly disorganized and uncontainable flow of human interaction and communication. This may mean making changes to workplace environments rather than building new IT systems.

All of the case studies shown here emphasize that the most effective knowledge exchange can happen with relatively simple technology. Researchers at University of Jyväskylä discovered that a simple application of Lotus Notes, distributed through a complex paper-making factory, allowed people to locate and solve mechanical problems. At Xerox PARC, researchers discovered that scripted documentation was useless for solving complex problems, whereas verbally exchanging tacit knowledge was successful. At the University of Waikato, researchers discovered that a database of documentation was unnecessary because lab technicians assembled their own dynamic "libraries" as they solved problems. A formal content management system was not necessary in any of these situations.

Technical communicators, especially those trained in academic settings, are well placed to take on the challenge of proposing and implementing content management systems. As generalists, rather than specialists, we are often at the interstices of organizations, so that we can see the flow of knowledge (or lack thereof) between departments and silos. Inherently interdisciplinary and experienced in continually understanding new concepts, we are especially attuned to seeing entire organizations rather than parts. For us, as well as for the organizations that we serve, we should know that the best CMS solution is not always an IT solution, but an intelligent solution.

REFERENCES

Addey, D., Ellis, J., Suh, P., & Thiemecke, D. (2002). *Content management systems*. Birmingham: Glasshaus.

Auramäki, E., Robinson, M., Aaltonen, A., Kovalainen, M., Liinamaa, A., & Tuuna-Väiskä, T. (1996). Paperwork at 78kph [Electronic version]. *Proceedings of the 1996 ACM conference on computer supported cooperative work.* Boston, MA, pp. 370-379.

Brown, J. S., & Duguid, P. (2000). *The social life of information (2002).* Boston, MA: Harvard Business School Press.

Buderi, R. (1998). Field work in the tribal office. [Electronic version]. *Technology Review, 101*(3), 42-49.

CMS Watch. (n.d.). Retrieved April 6, 2006 from http://www.cmswatch.com/CMS/Report

Cunningham, S. J., Knowles, C., & Reeves, N. (2001, June). An ethnographic study of technical support workers: Why we didn't build a tech support digital library [Electronic version]. *Proceedings of the 1st ACM/IEEE-CS joint conference on digital libraries,* Roanoke, VA, pp. 189-198.

Darwin Web Team. (2004, December 28). *Content management.* Retrieved January 10, 2006 from http://guide.darwinmag.com/technology/web/content

Davenport, T. H., & Prusak, L. (1998). *Working knowledge: How organizations manage what they know (2000).* Boston, MA: Harvard Business School Press.

Dodds, P. S., Watts, D. J., & Sabel, C. F. (2003, April). *Information exchange and robustness of organizational networks.* Retrieved November 30, 2005 from Working Paper Series, Center on Organizational Innovation, Columbia University Web site: http://www.coi.columbia.edu/pdf/dodds_sabel_watts.pdf

Erickson, T., & Kellogg, W. A. (2000). Social translucence: An approach to designing systems that support social processes. *ACM Transactions on Computer-Human Interaction, 7*(1), 59-83.

Graham, M. (1996). Changes in information technology, changes in work [Electronic version]. *Technology in Society, 18*(3), 373-385.

Kelly, J., & Stark, D. (2002). Crisis, recovery, innovation: Responsive organization after September 11. *Environment and planning A.* Retrieved October 30, 2005 from Working Paper Series, Center on Organizational Innovation, Columbia University Web site: http://www.coi.columbia.edu/pdf/kelly_stark_cri.pdf

Kovalainen, M., Robinson, M., & Auramäki, E. (1998). Diaries at work. *Proceedings of the 1998 ACM conference on computer supported cooperative work* [Electronic version]. Seattle, WA, pp. 49-58.

Nardi, S., Whittaker, S., & Schwarz, S. (2000). It's not what you know, it's who you know: Work in the information age. *First Monday, 5*(5). Retrieved March 31, 2006 from http://firstmonday.org/issues/issue5_5/nardi/index.html

Robinson, M., Kovalainen, M., & Auramäki, E. (2000). Diary as dialogue in papermill process control [Electronic version]. *Communications of the ACM, 43*(1), 65-70.

Rockley, A., Kostur, P., & Manning, S. (2003). *Managing enterprise content: A unified content strategy.* Indianapolis: New Riders.

Sellen, A. J., & Harper, R. H. R. (2002). *The myth of the paperless office (2003).* Cambridge, MA: MIT Press.

Wenger, E., McDermott, R., & Snyder, W. (2002). *Cultivating communities of practice.* Boston, MA: Harvard Business School Press.

Wikipedia. (2006). *Content management system.* Retrieved September 19, 2006 from http://en.wikipedia.org/wiki/Content_management_system

Yates, J. (1989). *Control through communication: The rise of system in American management (1993).* Baltimore, MD: Johns Hopkins University Press.

CHAPTER THREE

Learning with Limits: New Faculty and Course Management Systems

Julie Staggers, Meredith W. Zoetewey, and Michael Pennell

JULIE'S STORY:
THE PATH OF LEAST RESISTANCE

"Are you sure *you didn't have anything to do with designing this Web site?" a skeptic demanded from the front row. He was one of her better students, and he was uncharacteristically irked.*

"Positive. I assure you, I have no horse in this race," Julie said. "Why? What's up?"

"When we do class evaluations, I need to talk some serious smack about this textbook thing. It's just a collection of links," he asserted. "You might as well do it in WebCT; that's what we all use. That's what we LIKE."

On her way back to her office, Julie passed the open door of a colleague who was spitting bad words through clenched teeth as he fought to import his beautiful Web pages into WebCT. For its business and technical writing service courses, her program uses a course management system developed by the publisher to accompany their in-house online textbook. For distance education versions of the service courses, her program was required to use the campus standard CMS, which is WebCT. When she told her student she had no horse in the course management system race, she meant it. She had come to academia fresh off a year in industry, developing Web-based training for pharmaceutical manufacturing using an impossibly clunky and cumbersome commercial content management product. After a year on a system that required 16 distinct key strokes to insert a graphic onto a Web page, she never wanted to see the words "content" and "management" in the same sentence again. From her perspective, her course management system was a slight variation on a tool that was decidedly lacking in utility and slowed her productivity to a crawl. WebCT vs. her program's in-house product? From her perspective, it was six of one, half a dozen of the other.

Despite her industry-fueled antipathy to CMS, however, Julie opted to use her program's online textbook and its associated course management system during her first year on the job. She had a dissertation to finish, and she was hoping that with the course mostly preplanned and with nifty features like an automated grade book and self-grading quizzes it would make her life easier. Beyond that, she felt obligated to test drive the system. Her program is locked into both the textbook and the CMS for the foreseeable future, and she will eventually be responsible for providing support to the instructors—mostly PTIs and grad assistants—required to use it.

After nearly two full semesters using the system, she found herself telling her student, "Talk as much smack as you like. I'm not in love with it either." She had mixed feelings about the in-house product and was fairly certain WebCT would be different but not markedly better or worse. Some of the features had made her life easier, but she wasn't sure the system had made her teaching any easier or better. She had taught straight off the syllabus and straight out of the textbook as never before. She'd used technology far less than normal and with less than her usual creativity. While she had taught essentially the same projects for the same courses she had been teaching for six years as a graduate student, most of her previous pedagogy and the materials that supported it went out the window. Importing them was simply too time consuming. With lots of new demands on her time and a course already in the can, she opted for the path of least resistance.

INTRODUCTION

When we were grad students, scarcely more than a year ago, the young crop of assistant professors in our graduate program took great delight in assuring us—frequently—that our lives would never again be so easy. Like demented senior summer campers hell-bent on torturing the young ones, they spun out tales of woe about the impossible hours and the unimaginable quantities of work and the pressure to please all parties at all times that were part and parcel of being a freshly minted member of the junior faculty.

Over the past year we've struggled to negotiate new identities, new cultures, new technologies in our first academic jobs. It seems sometimes as if we've become the senior summer campers ourselves, and we've picked up where our beloved—if demented—junior faculty left off, trading frequent stories about our new lives on new jobs. Perhaps predictably, the reality is both better and worse than we might have anticipated. The hours are long, our workloads vary from just-about-manageable to insurmountable, and we all feel like we're on socially and professionally shaky ground from time to time as we negotiate the intricacies of new departmental cultures and co-worker personalities. As we embarked on careers this year, we found that different as they may be (a mid-sized public R1 university in the Northeast, a tiny private engineering college in the Midwest, a fast-growing R2 university in the Southwest) our respective campuses share a common bogeyman: the course management system.

Our technology experience in graduate school was characterized by cutting edge hardware and software—an embarrassment of riches. Early morning IM sessions and late night, long distance phone calls during that first year on the job, however, revealed that our preparation was, in some ways, inadequate. We found ourselves unexpectedly and continually bumping up against course management systems (CMS). The stories we shared with each other showed a surprising number of similarities despite our superficially different circumstances. These stories allow us to look within and across our varied contexts to speculate about the common impacts of course management systems on new academics making their first jump onto new professional terrain.

During our transitional year, we have come to see the value of storytelling. As Brenton Faber has noted in *Community Action and Organizational Change,* "Stories broker change between social structures and individual agency. . . . [They] help us negotiate between those factors that restrict and limit our possibilities and our free ability to pursue our own choices" (2002, p. 25). Stories are interpretative acts; they provide security and continuity, they create resistance, opposition, and conflict. As such, they have the power to help us enculturate into and intervene in the disciplinary machinery in our new institutions.

In this chapter, we offer three stories from our first year on the job, our transition narratives, to tap into this power. We began with Julie's story. Now we turn to Meredith and Michael.

MEREDITH'S STORY: BETWEEN A ROCK AND A HARD PLACE

Though she hadn't taught a canned class since she was a first semester's master student, Meredith was actually looking forward to it. Using someone else's pedagogy for a technical writing service course would free up a few more precious weeks in August so she could unpack the dishes in her new house in her new town before the start of classes. She was about to begin her first job as an assistant professor at a private engineering college in the Midwest. The

*top-ranked school where she would begin teaching had an outstanding repu-
tation, earned in part because it put the newest technology available into the
hands of students and instructors alike. On one of the first campuses in the
country to require all incoming students to purchase laptops, Meredith's students
were instantly recognizable by the matching, overstuffed black backpacks they
used for hauling around their 8-pound, $3,800 laptops, PDAs, tablets, and MP3
players (only the last of which were not institution-issued).*

*Sitting in a conference room with three service course veterans, who were
generously giving up a summer day to orient her, she worked hard to keep up with
the acronym-studded, shorthand phrases the others easily traded back and forth.
ANGEL Learning Management Suite wasn't required, technically, but since it
was the mechanism the other service course instructors used to trade and archive
the files Meredith needed to teach the course, it certainly felt required. Meredith
chafed at the layer of complication the course management system presented. It
wasn't even that this particular course management system wasn't particularly
user-friendly. But as a graduate student, she created substantial class Web sites
using Macromedia Studio 8 and Adobe CreativeSuite 2. Her control of her class
Web sites was limited only by her ability to learn and apply software. She spent
several years teaching other instructors how to integrate proprietary and open
source software into their own pedagogies. To Meredith, relying on course
management systems meant that one didn't care to sincerely engage with the
technology. And, since her research and teaching straddled the boundaries of
technical communication and computers and composition, she had veered as far
away from CMS for as long as she could.*

*Now, on the day after she has unpacked her dishes in her new house in her new
town, with $1900 worth of Web development software she had negotiated into
her contract and 500 MB of easily expandable server space, she confronted a
hard truth: She could embrace the cumbersome course management system
and be seen as a team player, or she could fight for what she saw as a better
way and be seen (potentially) as a hiring mistake.*

WHY WE'RE CONFRONTING COURSE
MANAGEMENT SYSTEMS NOW

Course management systems (CMS), in both open source and commercial
forms, continue to spread across and envelop classrooms throughout a range of
higher education institutions. By the time commercial CMS giants Blackboard
and WebCT merged in early 2006, the two systems shared roughly 3,700
academic clients (Blackboard and WebCT http://www.blackboard.com/company/
press). Moodle, arguably the dominant open source academic CMS, claims some

18,000 user sites worldwide (Moodle Sites http://moodle.org/sites/index.php).[1] Marketing materials for commercial CMS vendors promise a host of benefits for institutions, instructors, and students alike. They assert that CMS will engage learners, allow universities to increase enrollments without investing in capital facilities expansion, and enhance assessment (The WebCT Vision http://www.WebCT.com/vision/). The press release announcing the 2006 merger of WebCT and Blackboard characterized WebCT as a powerful tool for facilitating "faculty empowerment, administrative efficiency, and student outcomes" (Blackboard and WebCT Announce Agreement to Merge, 2005, http://www.blackboard.com/company/press).

Robert B. Kvavik (2005), who conducted a 2004 study of technology use by 4,374 students at 13 institutions in five states, asserts that course management systems have great potential to significantly reduce the restrictions of time and space on learning for students and faculty. Course management systems, he suggests, promise to

> enhance learning quality by enabling instructors to convey information more effectively, helping instructors meet the needs of students with varied learning styles, as well as enriching the interactions students have with each other and with their instructors.

Proponents of CMS argue that these systems can be part of a technological infrastructure that promotes student-centered learning, but Kvavik's (2005) study found that faculty and students used course management systems mostly for communication of information and administrative activities; both groups used CMS much less in support of learning (p. 7.17). While it appears that students themselves are embracing the technology—in Kvavik's (2005) study 83% of students had used a course management system and 76% of them were positive about the experience[2]—the interactive features used least by faculty were the very features students indicated contributed most to their learning (p. 7.15).

Course management systems, and especially proprietary CMS, are not without critics. Observing that their study "contests the notion that culturally neutral content is even conceivable, let alone attainable in online settings," intercultural communication researchers Reeder, Macfayden, Roche, and Chase (2004) noted that learning platforms such as WebCT may pose special problems for

---

[1] Clients for Blackboard and WebCT were predominantly in higher education and K-12 environments, but also include corporate, government, and commercial academic institutions. Moodle users run an eclectic gamut from institutions of higher education to community-based online learning initiatives; their 18,000 sites include both Cal State-San Bernardino and the Addictive Aquatics Classroom.

[2] Only 6.6% of Kvavik's (2005) survey participants were negative or very negative about their experience with CMS.

intercultural learners because they are rooted, in a Western-style notion of efficiency (p. 100). The ubiquity of learning platforms like WebCT and Blackboard tends to obscure the value systems in which they are rooted because the technology becomes invisible as students gain familiarity with the CMS. At the University of Nevada at Las Vegas, Jeff Jablonski and Ed Nagelhout (in press) opted to have the publisher of their in-house textbook develop an alternative to the campus standard WebCT because

> We were cynical about WebCT's potential as a transparent communication medium . . . one of our pedagogical goals when using electronic writing technologies is to foster critique of the tool itself, to discuss with students how the technology opens up or constrains discourse. When a campus adopts a particular course management systems platform, its use becomes ubiquitous, comfortable, and invisible.

There is a burgeoning open source movement out there that is mounting a critique of proprietary course management systems based on its incompatibility with the epistemological, collaborative, and liberatory ideals of academia. As Colleen Reilly and Joseph Williams (2006) rightly assert, various forces push the adoption of CMS, especially institutional mandates.

> Due to time constraints, inadequate technical expertise, and institutional mandates, both proactive and implied, many instructors select commercial courseware—such as Blackboard and WebCT—when teaching their distance-learning courses (p. 69).

Particularly for new faculty, it is important to note that whether a campus has adopted proprietary or open source CMS, such adoption has taken place within a specific institutional infrastructure and culture. DeVoss, Cushman, & Grabill (2005) explain:

> We know many people, including ourselves, who have been prevented from working in certain ways as teachers and writers because it was infrastructurally impossible in a given context. Not intellectually impossible. Not even strictly technologically impossible. Something deeper (p. 17).

DeVoss and colleagues are getting at the way institutional arrangements—spatial dynamics, material conditions, technological mandates and constraints, political practices—disrupt or facilitate new media writing instruction. Although the authors illustrate infrastructure in light of a new media course, it applies equally well to any transition that involves technology. They highlight the critical role of place and context in our deployment of technologies. Place and context matter like never before because CMS is no longer solely the domain of distance education. Like technology in general, CMS has found its way into classes across campus. Within technical communication, this digital turn is especially pronounced. Increasingly, instructors find themselves relying on, or compelled to use, CMS in both online and face-to-face settings.

Thus far, when technical communication has discussed content management, attention has mostly been paid to single sourcing: its effects on teaching (Eble, 2003) and its implications for writers and writing (Albers, 2003; Carter, 2003; Kramer, 2003; Rockley, 2001, 2003; Sapienza, 2004; Williams, 2003). When we work our way around to course management systems, it's more often on listservs or in hallways than in our journals. Our published discussions about course management systems—few and far between—tend to ask, How can faculty aid its implementation (White & Myers, 2001)? How can course management systems enhance students' skills and instructors' performances (Hutchins, 2001)? These analyses are helpful in that they highlight the classroom implications and possibilities of course management systems.

While rhetoric and composition focus a fair amount of attention on the use of technology by new teachers (Dufflemeyer, 2003; Klem & Moran, 1992; Takayoshi & Huot, 2003), technical communication has devoted less attention to the issue (see Selber, 1994 for an early example of such articles). Even within rhetoric and composition, however, the transition of new faculty members to new technological settings has received little attention. In a field that trains its graduates to take a critical view of technology, especially in the teaching of writing, little scholarship has focused on the transition of new technical communication faculty to new institutional contexts. Our stories give us a way into issues of technology, pedagogy, and enculturation.

MICHAEL'S STORY:
THE MOTHER OF INVENTION

"Just use WebCT,"[3] plainly stated the grizzly bearded man as he appeared from behind a gray cubicle wall.

In the basement of the university library, Michael had just explained his issue to the undergraduate student maintaining the help desk at the university computing center. He seemed perplexed at the dilemma, and Michael, in turn, explained it a couple of times. He was a new faculty member at the university—an assistant professor in the writing program. He was trying to build his business communication course Web site, and he had quickly exceeded his personal Web space quota. Michael was looking for suggestions as to where to find more space. Surely, he assumed, there must be more than 500 kilobytes available for him to use.

---

[3] This exchange occurred before Blackboard purchased WebCT.

It was on the third explanation that the man emerged from behind the cubicle with the directive to just use WebCT. He asked Michael to explain the situation again, and he nodded throughout, again emphasizing, "WebCT is your only option." Hoping to avoid WebCT, Michael asked for alternatives to WebCT, which drew blank stares and a comment from the help desk student, "What do you have against WebCT?" After he tried to explain his desire to create the sites himself without the WebCT structure, the man added, "Your students will appreciate you using WebCT; they use it in a lot of classes and like it. They are used to it." When Michael asked about an e-mail list, the man told him that WebCT has a bulletin board; not the same, but for Michael's purposes, apparently sufficient.

Needless to say, the walk back to Michael's office was not pleasant as he plotted how to avoid WebCT. Michael had been creating Web sites for courses for the past four to five years at a previous institution and, while he figured there would be some bumps in the transition, this brick wall was unexpected. His colleagues offered sympathy, but few suggestions. Michael did avoid WebCT throughout the semester. Through uploading and deleting files in a very calculated and orchestrated manner during the semester, he was able to get the most mileage out of his 500Kb personal space. At one point during the semester, as Michael was walking through some documents on the Web calendar, he complained about his limited server space. After class, a student approached Michael and asked if he had considered using WebCT.

When Michael realized he would be teaching two sections of Writing in Electronic Environments in the spring semester, he made two early decisions. First, he would track down more university Web space. After some back and forth with the university webmaster, Michael was granted access to more server space (20 MB). This increase came with the advice that he keep only current files on the server. Second, Michael gave in to WebCT. He created a course site within WebCT, complete with a calendar and resource files. Michael forced himself to work through his prejudices of and frustration with WebCT—for one semester.

UNPACKING OUR NARRATIVES

Our stories are a first step toward examining the role of course management systems in mediating our transition from graduate student to assistant professor, a transition from having a surprising amount of control over which technologies to engage with in the classroom to having little. We found ourselves struggling with a pedagogical and technological disconnect at the same time we were struggling to enculturate into a new infrastructure and culture. Situating our narratives within DeVoss et al.'s (2005) work on infrastructure helps us illuminate and problematize the adoption of CMS. Essentially, each of these narratives depicts the complicated overlapping of three problematic elements inherent in new and compulsory CMS: technology, pedagogy, and enculturation. While it may prove tempting to read each narrative through one of these problem lenses, we find it more accurate and potentially useful to unpack the ways in which the strains intertwine in each story.

Technology

On the surface of these stories lies a technological disconnect. This disconnect is the most popular and easy way to characterize CMS issues. With new developments in campus technologies, including the rise in CMS, teachers in general are overcoming and embracing technologies in their pedagogies—whether it's teaching in computer classrooms, meeting occasionally in computer classrooms, using a CMS, or just referencing computers and expecting students to be familiar with computers. Granted, there are tremendous differences in the technology available and employed in various writing classrooms and campuses, but the number of writing teachers believing that computers have little to no influence on writing and writing pedagogies is dwindling.

In these three stories, each new professor encountered a different technological situation—in the form of a CMS—from their former institutions. We thought we were well prepared intellectually to enter workplaces with less access to the abundant technology of our graduate program. We thought we were prepared to do without. We were used to treating technology as a buffet. We weren't prepared for a three-course *prix fixe* set menu that required us to use technologies about which we were dubious and to use them in ways that were narrowly prescribed and proscribed. For all three of us, building course materials in the CMS took longer and yielded less effective materials than we could have produced on our own in Dreamweaver. Even though one of the benefits touted by CMS developers is a shallow learning curve, it is still a learning curve. The very features that make CMS an effective tool for novices, make it painfully cumbersome for experienced Web designers. We vented our spleens frequently at the lack of visual control of Web pages, our inability to link to targets, and myriad other nuisances.

Pedagogy

Ultimately the new classes and students were not our only pedagogical transition. The adoption of a CMS into our teaching affected all other aspects of our pedagogies. Clearly these three stories represent more than just a technological disconnect. Because we regularly teach with technology, it's impossible for us to consider technology separately from our pedagogies. A change in technology, especially in the form of CMS, is a change in pedagogy. Consider Michael's story. There is little pedagogical difference between a WebCT discussion board and an e-mail list to the Information Technology support on campus. They are similar group communication technologies that accomplish class discussion and announcements. Within Michael's particular approach to a class, however, they offer and enable different approaches to extracurricular communication. Pedagogically, there is a world of difference between the type of external-to-class communication and collaboration fostered by a BBS and a class listserv. The BBS demands that students go to the message source. It's less fluid, less instantaneous; to access information, students must log onto WebCT, go to the BBS, and find the information. In contrast, the class listserv sends the information directly to the students, wherever and whenever they check e-mail, which our students pretty much do constantly. Whether one opts for the listserv or the BBS, incorporating that technology in a way that capitalizes on the student-centered learning promised by CMS requires different pedagogical strategies. Push technologies, like e-mail or a class listserv, which move information from the online learning platform to the student, create a different (and to our way of thinking, more dynamic) learning community than a BBS. The listserv finds the student, whenever he or she checks e-mail. Pull technologies, like the BBS, require students to find the online space where the information resides.

Although WebCT contains push technologies such as e-mail, within the interface, students must still log onto the system and navigate to the class in order to receive a message. To the tech guys administering WebCT, it's a minor difference in setup. For Michael, it means rethinking his approach to collaborative writing, to teamwork, even to homework. Rethinking pedagogy, of course, isn't in and of itself a bad thing when it's born out of classroom experience or scholarly knowledge. But shifting pedagogical approaches because of campuswide technology initiatives that have more to do with contract negotiations and technology budget changes than with pedagogical initiatives is not rethinking. If Michael envisions a learning community that revolves around a continual, free-flowing conversation, he might really need a listserv. (Or he might need to figure out how to rig up a work-around in WebCT to simulate a listserv.) If he wants an exchange of information that has discrete perimeters, that is bounded—if not by the walls of his physical classroom—by the walls of his online classroom, a BBS is precisely what he needs. A combination of push and pull technologies and delivery methods should be available to students and teachers; matching the technology to your pedagogy and giving your students the kind of learning community you think they need is the real trick.

For different reasons, Meredith's and Julie's familiar pedagogies all but vanished during their first semesters using CMS in their new institutions. The CMS Meredith used brought with it an extremely detailed class plan and set of instructional materials that left her little choice about what to do in class or how to do it. The technology facilitated a top-down approach to pedagogy, which sought to ensure the greatest degree of uniformity possible between various sections of the course. While Julie had the freedom to teach with or without the designated CMS, the set syllabus, and even the approved textbook, she found herself overdependent on all three. Focused more on finishing her dissertation than on bending the CMS to her will, she simply gave up on using any of her own teaching materials and lesson plans because importing them or adapting them to the CMS was simply too labor intensive. Instead, she used the CMS to mount class assignments, taught out of the textbook far too often, and avoided using the computers in her computer classroom whenever possible, a significant departure from her normal routine. With her time at a premium and with good basic materials in the can, she defaulted to the materials available. Her class wasn't terrible, but she spent time wrestling with back-end administration issues instead of generating in-class activities tailored to her new students.

Enculturation

Campus cultures can be tricky to maneuver, especially for new members of the community. The transition from graduate student to assistant professor represents a difficult process of enculturation. Our enculturation into our respective campuses was complicated by our institutions' investment in CMS, in part because the CMS at each of our institutions is imbricated in an infrastructure. It took us quite some time—and countless e-mails, IMs, and early morning phone calls—to understand that we weren't just whining. Trading stories helped us identify the issues of local culture that the CMS sometimes highlighted and sometimes obscured.

Meredith spent her first year adapting to a campus culture that values conformity. The desire for a uniform and consistent approach extends well beyond the desire to ensure that one's assignment sheet for the memo project matches those of one's colleagues. Conformity is a core value of her institution. At Michael's campus, he has slowly learned the philosophy of doing a lot with a little. Implicitly and explicitly, members of the land grant university in a very small state with a budget crisis are encouraged to always make resources go further. While the campus may not have some of the resources of the Ivies nearby, it does have a community that can accomplish at the same level.

Julie is still finding her way in a program that is committed to bucking the establishment (WebCT) on one hand and replicating the system (with its own far-from-perfect CMS) on the other. Her program's use of CMS grows out of a particular philosophy about the critical use of technology in writing classrooms; she's still gauging how far she can or should go in requiring students and instructors to use a system many of them like less than WebCT. The flexible approach to CMS use at Julie's institution leads her to believe she has some latitude in suggesting changes, but she's not entirely confident of that.

As new instructors, though, none of us really know how much space we are allowed in terms of critiquing the infrastructures and cultures into which we are entering. We think that, as newcomers, we're well poised to offer unique insights into our experiences (Zuboff, 1998), but even articulating our stories for this chapter gave us pause. When we first presented this chapter as a conference talk, we ruffled some feathers. Upon returning from the conference, a senior colleague angrily confronted Meredith about the presentation. Didn't she like the new job? A "real" salary? Having conferences paid for? In this particular case, some explaining was required in order to reassure the colleague that a critique of a favored technology did not imply a critique of her or the program she worked so hard to build. Clearly there is more at stake than simply using some software to prepare a class students can access over the Web. A wholesale embrace, or critique, of classroom technologies opens up the possibility that we will be seen as innovators, slackers, team players, lone wolves, rebels with/without causes, or conformists.

LEARNING FROM OUR EXPERIENCE

We are focusing on the connection between CMS and enculturation because we see CMS as more than a tool that can make or break a class, more than another technology choice; we see it as a potential stumbling block to professional development, one that can be particularly difficult for new technical communication faculty to negotiate.

Besides illustrating the disparate yet related scenes within which CMS is implemented, our narratives push us to develop strategies for TC faculty, especially new faculty, who find themselves up against "labor practices and institutional business decisions" not of their own making (Reilly & Williams, 2006, p. 68).

We know faculty, in general, can make or break technological initiatives (White & Myers, 2001), but new faculty are in a particularly tenuous position as they find their footing. Cultivating agency in unfamiliar environments takes time and confidence, and new assistant professors are likely to come up short on both counts. How, we ask, can academics in our position say no to WebCT, for example, when our new institutions have already said yes?

We close this chapter by offering a few local, yet transferable, strategies of coping and resistance that we've developed in light of our stories.

- **Move beyond the tendency to see the course management system as a (ubiquitous) technological artifact into a more profitable view of the software packages as a methodology** (Ament, 2003). Kurt Ament positions single sourcing as a "methodology not a technology" (p. 1). When we treat CMS as a technology, it becomes a transparent delivery system. When we treat it as a methodology, it functions as a lens that colors the way we interact with our infrastructure—material, political, spatial, technological, and social arrangements. New faculty members must seek out and uncover their campus infrastructures. Investigating CMS as a methodology on our campuses forces us to interact with and discover the complicated campus networks, of which CMS may be only a part. As Michael's story illustrates, he uncovered the people responsible for maintaining, promoting, and changing the implementation of CMS in his pedagogy. We might also uncover the histories and potential futures of CMS use on our campuses or within our departments. Even for institutions as a whole, decisions regarding CMS are rarely technology choices only.

- **Embed other, more public applications within the CMS interface.** As David Fahey (2000) comments, "Courseware makes a faculty member put data into the categories that the software designer thinks make sense. In other words, there is not the flexibility of a website built by or for a particular course or professor" (p. 31). Most CMS systems offer some option for integrating external applications with its interface. For example, Michael linked a class blog, as well as student blogs, to his WebCT site. Meredith opted to frame public Web pages in the ANGEL interface rather than keeping closed files inside the system (Courseware lacks a distinct URL). These moves allow us to enhance the functionality of the system. They also promote the sharing of ideas among geographically dispersed instructors by keeping key course materials available over the Web instead of bottling them up inside the system. This strategy has the added benefit of thwarting the corporate university's drive to co-opt privately developed materials imported into CMS.

- **Capitalize on the power of stories for enculturation and intervention.** We think it's important—especially in an assistant professor's first year—to listen a lot and talk a little. Whether she has been thrown up against a CMS that she loves or a CMS that she hates, one of a new professor's most important coping mechanisms is to listen to the stories that the institution is telling about CMS. For Meredith, a way to enhance her enculturation is to ferret out the secret story about CMS at her school to understand why more experienced faculty are drawn to it. For Julie, the first step in reconfiguring CMS at her institution is to gather the stories of longtime and novice instructors alike. Our stories, though overlapping in some respects, suggest that there is no one story when it comes to new professors and CMS. Tapping into the range of stories helps highlight the places where people can be brought together as well as the fissures that offer the opporunity for intervention.

REFERENCES

Albers, M. J. (2003). Single sourcing and the technical communication career path. *Technical Communication, 50*(3), 335-343.

Ament, K. (2003). *Single sourcing: Building modular documentation.* Norwich, NY: William Andrew Publishing.

"Blackboard and WebCT Announce Agreement to Merge." (2005). Blackboard, Inc. Retrieved Sept. 10, 2006 from
http://www.blackboard.com/company/press/release.aspx?id=767025

Carter, L. (2003). The implications of single sourcing for writers and writing. *Technical Communication, 50*(3), 317-320.

DeVoss, D. N., Cushman, E., & Grabill, J. T. (2005). Infrastructure and composing: The when of new-media writing. *CCC, 57*(1), 14-44.

Dufflemeyer, B. B. (2003). Learning to learn: New TA preparation in computer pedagogy. *Computers and Composition, 20*(3), 295-311.

Eble, M. F. (2003). Content vs. product: The effects of single sourcing on the teaching of technical communication. *Technical Communication, 50*(3), 344-349.

Faber, B. (2002). *Community action and organizational change: Image, narrative, identity.* Carbondale, IL: Southern Illinois University Press.

Fahey, D. M. (2000). Blackboard course info: Supplementing in-class teaching with the Internet. *History Computer Review, 15*(1), 29-37.

Hutchins, M. (2001). Enhancing the business communication course through WebCT. *Business Communication Quarterly, 64*(3), 87-94.

Jablonski, J., & Nagelhout, E. (in press). Technology as a site of praxis: The role of assessment in professional writing program design. In J. Allen & M. Hundleby (Eds.), *Assessment in technical and professional communication.* Albany, NY: State University of New York Press.

Klem, E., & Moran, C. (1992). Teachers in a strange LANd: Learning to teach in a networked writing classroom. *Computers and Composition, 9*(3), 5-22.

Kramer, R. (2003). Single source in practice: IBM's SGML toolset and the writer as technologist, problem solver, and editor. *Technical Communication, 50*(3), 328-334.

Kvavik, R. (2005). Convenience, communication, and control: How students use technology. In D. Oblinger & J. Oblinger (Eds.), *Educating the net generation.* Educause http://www.educause.edu/content.asp?PAGE_ID=5989&bhcp=1

Reeder, K., Macfayden, L. P., Roche, J., & Chase, M. (2004). Negotiating cultures in cyberspace: Participation patterns and problematics. *Language Learning and Technology, 8*(2), 88-105.

Reilly, C. A., & Williams, J. J. (2006). The price of free software: Labor, ethics, and context in distance education. *Computers and Composition, 23*(1), 68-90.

Rockley, A. (2001). The impact of single sourcing and technology. *Technical Communication, 48*(2), 189-193.

Rockley, A. (2003). Single sourcing: It's about people, not just technology. *Technical Communication, 50*(3), 350-354.

Sapienza, F. (2004). Usability, Structured Content, and Single Sourcing with XML. *Technical Communication, 51*(3), 399-408.

Selber, S. A. (1994). Beyond skill building: Challenges for technical communication teachers in the computer age. *Technical Communication Quarterly, 3*(4), 365-392.

Takayoshi, P., & Huot, B. (2003). *Teaching writing with computers: An introduction.* New York: Houghton Mifflin.

White, J. T., & Myers, S. (2001). You can teach an old dog new tricks: The faculty's role in technology implementation. *Business Communication Quarterly, 64*(3), 95-101.

Williams, J. D. (2003). The implications of single sourcing for technical communicators. *Technical Communication, 50*(3), 321-327.

Zuboff, S. (1998). *In the age of the smart machine: The future of work and power.* New York: Basic Books.

PART II

CMS and Technical Communication Pedagogy

CHAPTER FOUR

Why We *Should* Teach XML:
An Argument for Technical Acuity

Becky Jo Gesteland McShane

In this chapter I claim that just as we teach students how to analyze the rhetorical situation and then choose the most appropriate stylistic solution (rhetorical tool), so too should we teach them how to analyze the technological situation and then select the most appropriate technical solution (technological tool). To do this, we must provide students with opportunities to discover technology's limitations, to interrogate tool availability within an organization, and to articulate alternative software selections. Rather than teach students how to become automatons, I believe we should teach students how to think critically about the tools available to them, how to evaluate their options, and how to discover new methods for document creation and delivery, thereby making them valuable players in the technological sphere.

Taking a cue from Albers, I want to sort out some terminology. In his introduction to *Technical Communication*'s special issue on "The Future of Technical Communication," Albers (2005) explains the importance of distinguishing between tools and technologies. For example, he says that a particular Web design tool such as Dreamweaver is a tool; a technology is all the Web design tools and how they're used. He cautions that writers and students can no longer ignore technology and that new graduates need a technological skillset (pp. 268-269). The problem, Albers contends, is that practitioners have been too focused on technology and academics too focused on rhetoric: "we need to move both sides closer to a middle ground" (p. 270). For my purposes I define *technology* as a generalized set of skills or knowledge (content management), *tools* as particular utensils or languages (XML), *methodology* as a practice or way of doing something (modular writing), and *theory* as a set of principles informing the implementation of a technology (single sourcing). I explain these terms in further detail throughout this chapter.

Many scholars have discussed the changes that content management, single sourcing, and Extensible Markup Language (XML) will require teachers of technical communication to make to their curriculum (Albers, 2003; Applen, 2002; Battalio, 2002; Clark & Andersen, 2005; Eble, 2003; Hart-Davidson, 2001; Rainey, Turner, & Dayton, 2005; Sapienza, 2002). Clark and Andersen (2005) articulate the problem this way: "managers are not coming to technical communicators for solutions to complex, rhetorical informational problems, the natural domain of technical communication" (p. 293). Therefore, they argue, we need to train technical communicators to critically analyze technology from an organizational perspective so that they can sell ideas to management (p. 295). I agree and believe that one way to address this need is to teach the technologies, rather than leaving them to industry, which often fails to analyze and critique them. As teachers of technical communication we should embrace technologies such as content management and tools such as XML, because they offer us—and our students—an opportunity to employ the full-range of our rhetorical skills.

Therefore, I argue that technical communicators should be able to write, edit, and manage XML documentation, including XML tags, document type definitions (DTDs), XML schemas, and Darwin Information Typing Architecture (DITA). In his presentation at the 2006 STC Conference, Michael Priestly of IBM said, "technology should not be an excuse for not doing the right thing . . . it should be an excuse for doing the right thing" (Priestly, 2006). And we, as teachers of technical communication, should be teaching relevant technologies, tools, methodologies, and theories to our students.

THE THEORY: SINGLE SOURCING

Hart-Davidson (2001) argues that "we need theory" and encourages practitioners and academics to make "the core expertise of technical communication explicit" (p. 147). My experience in the corporate realm of training serves as a cautionary example. In 2003 I attended RoboHelp's "Basic/Intermediate Training Version X4" so that I could teach a course on help applications. During the course I was frustrated by the lack of explanation for why we were structuring our help projects the way we were and the lack of discussion about why we might want to create a help project in the first place. To put it another way, I wanted some theory to support my practical application. The trainer would not, probably could not, analyze the particular tools or the general technology of help applications. This was something I had to do for myself; as a teacher I could do it for my students.

When I looked for an appropriate text, I was surprised by the scarcity of theoretical approaches. There are plenty of books about using XML to do single sourcing but few that discuss the rationale behind the method. Finally I found *Single Sourcing: Building Modular Documentation* (2002) in which Ament argues that the key to successful single sourcing is modular writing. So I decided to combine the methodology of single sourcing with the technology of a help applications tool and teach our senior-level issues class as "Single Sourcing Using RoboHelp."[1] I hoped, thereby, to demonstrate for students the importance of applying theory to practice. At a CPTSC conference I was advised not to do both single sourcing and RoboHelp in one course, because the purposes are different and the topics are too broad to cover in one semester. I agreed that ideally we could offer two separate courses—one on single sourcing with XML and one on help applications—but given the constraints of our program I decided to combine help applications technology with single sourcing methodology. Hence I developed my course around the notion of modular writing:

1. Evaluate content
2. Break content into the smallest possible modules
3. Label these modules
4. Configure them into meaningful hierarchies
5. Link these hierarchies to related hierarchies (Ament, 2002, p. 1)

Ament (2002) claims that "single sourcing is a methodology, not a technology" (p. 1). When he distinguishes between tools and technologies, Albers (2005) states that single sourcing is a technology (p. 267). However, Rob Hanna defines single sourcing as "any process used to systematically create information products from a single defined source of information" (as cited in Kahn, 2003). Clearly, the term has many different interpretations. It can be a methodology, a technology, and a process.

In order to clarify the term for myself and my students, I placed it alongside some other familiar terms: content management, XML, and modular writing. I decided that "content management" means different things depending on the situation. The software, language, or system used to manage content varies widely, but the skills and knowledge remain the same. They are a particular kind of technology: the technology of content management. As for "XML," it is one kind of language or system. It is a tool. The term "modular writing" is a way of writing, a process really. Thus I decided that methodology best described this term. I decided that Ament's use of "single sourcing" seemed more like a theoretical approach than a method. Single sourcing is a concept, a notion, a principle, a belief that there is or can be a single source. It is a theory.

---

[1] Weber State University offers a minor in Professional and Technical Writing. When I offered this course (2004), the minor consisted of four required courses in the English Department—"Professional & Technical Writing," "Technical Editing," "Issues in Professional & Technical Writing," and "Seminar & Practicum in Professional & Technical Writing"—and two interdisciplinary courses to be determined in consultation with an advisor.

Based on these definitions, I wrote the following description for my "Single Sourcing Using RoboHelp" course:

> In this course you will learn the methodology of single sourcing and the technology of a help applications tool (RoboHelp Office X4). Your objectives are to
> - Incorporate the principles of modular writing as you compile a help project,
> - Create writing standards and guidelines for your project,
> - Develop a document production strategy that foregrounds usability, and
> - Practice outputting your project to various formats (McShane, 2004).

Because most of my students are English majors and Professional and Technical Writing minors, they worry about an increasingly automated and mechanized approach to writing. Early in the semester of my "Single Sourcing" course, I asked them to define single sourcing and discuss why they might want to use this methodology and why it might be problematic. One student wrote that

> The more I read about it, the more I think of modular office furniture: similarly colored and themed pieces of furniture that can be moved around/ stacked and reconfigured to meet the needs of the office workers. This is single sourcing's strength AND weakness—you can come up with a variety of useful cubicles and combinations, but in the end, it can be homogeneous and redundant and mainly suited to "office space"—would you decorate your house with your cubicle elements (Ciccone, 2004)?

Another student commented, sarcastically, that

> Single sourcing is a wonderful gift from the information organization gods! Information is organized into small stand-alone modules for later assembly into larger documents for any and all uses. It saves our time, our money, and can increase our document quality by allowing each module author to focus on his or her area of expertise. We are saved from the monotony of real thinking through the gift of stringent writing guidelines that we all get to follow. From the efficient uniform templates of module organization to the glorious mechanization of document "assembly," I for one see a bright future for those choosing a career in technical assembly-line-writing (Braegger, 2004).

I forged ahead despite my students' misgivings. Dayton and Bernhardt (2004) discovered a similar concern among faculty when they conducted a survey of ATTW members. Faculty believed that one of their students' biggest challenges was "How to find a job that doesn't construe them as automatons, that recognizes them adequately as professionals, and that doesn't work them to death." The solution to this perceived problem lies with us—the way we teach writing and, especially, the way we teach technology.

What we need is a shift toward content management; we need to separate content from format and incorporate technology into our teaching. Eble (2003) argues that single sourcing "is a way of thinking, a reconceptualization of the relationship between audiences, purpose, and documents" (p. 345). She describes the effect of single sourcing on the teaching of technical communication. We must teach students how to separate content, data, and information from presentation, format, and design. Eble believes that we should teach single sourcing in the classroom through information modeling (determining the information to be created in a single source) and structured writing (tagging that information to create elements) (pp. 346-347). This was a struggle for my students, who've grown up applying formatting to their documents, watching the groovy things that Word can do. But they learned the concept of separating format from content.

As the course progressed students discovered that new methodologies and technologies did not necessarily mean they would become automatons. A typical comment at the course's conclusion was this one:

> This project has helped me to scrutinize the elements and implementation of modular writing. I enjoy organizing things—especially thoughts and ideas into realities (i.e.—this project). The idea of re-usable "chunked" information is a concept I've unintentionally employed at different points in my life without realizing what I was doing. Single Sourcing and RoboHelp helped me move the concepts of modular writing from abstract to tangible in my mind (Lavicka, 2004).

Although the combination of RoboHelp software with modular writing was less than ideal, I found the nature of writing help applications to be very similar to single sourcing a document set. And at the end of the course my students were ready and eager to learn XML. They discovered what so many technical writers discover every day: often, you cannot choose the software you use; software has its limitations; and putting theory into practice can be frustrating.

Single sourcing has already affected the career paths of technical communicators. Albers (2003) envisions careers moving away from the craftsman model and toward specific job responsibilities such as information analysts, information designers, information architects, and information technologists (p. 341). "Gone are the days of each writer crafting an entire chapter," he says (p. 342). My single sourcing course worked well as a topics course, but afterward I'd become convinced that all of our professional and technical writing students needed to learn single sourcing. In order to provide a rationale for including a required course on single sourcing in our curriculum, I changed the title to

"Content Management" and lobbied to have the course added to the minor.[2] The course description broadened considerably:

> This class teaches the theory and application of content management. Students will learn how to evaluate content, divide content into reusable elements, label these elements, and then re-configure them into usable structures. Using the principles of single sourcing, modular writing, and structured authoring, students will map content for reuse, evaluate available authoring tools, implement state-of-the-art technologies, and develop project strategies. Throughout the semester students will come to understand the history of information management and current trends such as information architecture and knowledge management (*Courses in Professional & Technical Writing*, 2006).

I then justified the course as follows:

> The concept of managing content—whatever technology is in favor—will never go away. Really, this is a concept we've been teaching for a long time, though perhaps the terminology is different now. Professional and technical writers create content, then they edit, track, format, and assemble that content before they deliver it to the customer. The entire process between creation and delivery is "content management." It's just that word processing programs have given individual authors the ability to jump from creation to delivery, sometimes without a lot of content verification along the way. Because our students will be expected to author, manage, and deliver content in a variety of outputs, they must learn the core concepts of content management (*Course Proposal Results*, 2006).

JoAnn Hackos (2002), who has been teaching content management strategies in the private sector for over 20 years, claims that "content management is no longer an option . . . it is a necessity" (p. 1). My current content management course teaches the theory and application of content management. In this course students learn how to evaluate content semantically, divide content into reusable elements, label these elements for DTD schemas—the simplest schema for beginners to employ—and then reconfigure them into usable structures (Ament, 2002). Using the principles of single sourcing, modular writing, and structured authoring, each team of students creates an information model, reuse map—identifying "where content is reused in [an] information set" (Rockley, 2002, p. 31)—and small-scale content management project. Along the way each student evaluates and practices using various tools, such as XML and other open-source software.

---

[2] In 2006 we added two new courses to our minor: "Document Design" and "Content Management." These replaced the interdisciplinary requirement.

THE TOOL: XML

One of the most common languages used in content management is Extensible Markup Language or XML. Castro (2001) explains that XML's usefulness comes from its extensibility: you design your own custom markup language—an XML application—and then use this language to mark up your documents (p. 13). She defines XML as "a grammatical system for constructing custom markup languages" (p. 21). XML was developed from Standard Generalized Markup Language (SGML) and originally was designed for large-scale electronic publications (W3C, 2006). XML became a standard in 1998. Bridges (2006) describes XML as "an electronic 'lingua franca.'" Microsoft's senior director of XML architecture and one of the co-creators of XML 1.0 with the W3C, Jean Paoli explains that "XML is about creating documents in which the content is delimited, or set apart, by tags that explain the meaning of that content" (*Q&A*, 2005).

In the third edition of *XML in a Nutshell*, Harold and Means (2004) describe XML as "a metamarkup language for text documents" (p. 3). The tags are not fixed; they are extensible. Further, they explain that it is "a structural and semantic markup language, not a presentation language" (p. 4). They emphasize that it's "not a programming language" (p. 5). It's "an incredibly simple, well-documented, straightforward data format" (p. 6). The appeal to technical communicators is that it's all text—"XML documents are text"—they're data, markup, and tags created in a text-based format. In other words XML is not math, not calculus, not engineering, Harold and Means tell us. "Java promised portable code; XML delivers portable code" (p. 7). With XML there's no need for any special editors. Technical communicators can use Notepad or any text editor, for that matter (see Houser, 2000, for a discussion of other editing tools),

So, for example, I can use Notepad to write

- XML tags, which label elements for reuse. In this case, the tag name is "title":
```
<title>Writing XML</title>
```
- Document type definitions (DTDs), which define rules for handling tags. In this case, the tag will contain only text:
```
<!ELEMENT title (#PCDATA)>
```
- Cascading style sheets (CSS), which apply formatting to HTML output (another option is XSLT). In this case, to the "title" tag:
```
title {display:block;font-weight:bold;font-
size:18pt;width:100%;text-align:center;}
```

These tags, schemas, and style sheets are shown in their complete context below.

Because technical communicators write the content, structure the content, and know how to reuse the content, they should be the creators of the single sourcing project. Indeed, Sapienza (2002) argues that because of its rhetorical focus, "technical communicators are uniquely poised to seize upon opportunities that integrate rhetorical craft with technical wizardry." Moreover, he speculates that they'll "probably have to integrate the two areas of knowledge" when one day "all organizational documents are saved in XML format" (p. 157). If technical communicators develop schemas and DTDs, then they acquire a great deal of power, "potentially shaping how the organization structures knowledge about products and processes" (p. 161). In other words, "the person developing a DTD will be asked to write a new linguistic context, and perhaps a new language, that an entire organization or several organizations must be willing to adopt and share" (p. 161). Again Sapienza emphasizes that "XML may become the data format for all technical documents in the future" (p. 165). XML requires technical communicators to think in terms of data management (p. 166). "Students are using data management and computer programming skills to solve a *rhetorical* problem, not a *computer* problem, and it is also for this reason that technical communicators may be the best ones to prepare such projects" (p. 167). The literary skills of technical communicators parallel the technical skills of XML developers, but he reiterates that "a technical communicator must also be technical" (p. 168).

Similarly, Applen (2002) claims that technical communicators "can expand their territory into the realm of knowledge management by learning how to model knowledge using XML" (p. 307). He explains that "technical communicators who serve as knowledge managers can work with others in their organizations to rewrite the XML code" (p. 311). Unfortunately Applen stops short of suggesting that technical communicators actually "write" XML—they should only "rewrite" it—and he seems to view it as a programming language or database system. Although I disagree with him on this point, I am encouraged that he advocates writers to become knowledge managers and use XML to get there.

XML will produce changes in technical communication programs, and Battalio (2002) offers concrete solutions. Our program has designed a variation on his adaptations: a required course on content management that includes a section on XML (Battalio calls his required course knowledge management). He concludes that "though language skills are ones with which technical communicators have been traditionally most comfortable, the ultimate XML model may in fact demote the position of writer/editor to that of data-entry operator filling in the blanks on preprogrammed interfaces created by front-end developers" (p. 241). After reading Battalio's article, taking the content management course, and working for many years as a technical writer, one of my nontraditional students, Leslie Harris (2005), argues that "perhaps a more accurate outlook for technical communicators involves change more than obsolescence" (p. 1). She believes that "technical communicators *will* ultimately work with XML—the level of interaction will be determined as the XML continues to evolve" (p. 2).

In my content management course I teach a section on XML. As they work through instructions for writing XML, I quiz students on their progress. All they need for these quizzes is a text editor. Each quiz tests a step in the process of readying an XML document for use.

1. Prepare an XML document by typing the tags and content into a text editor or other tool:

   ```
   <?xml version="1.0"?>
   <cont_mgmt>
   <quiz1>
   <title>Writing XML</title>
   <question>1. Write an XML declaration.</question>
   <question>2. Define "root element."</question>
   <question>3. What are child and parent elements?</question>
   <question>4. What is an attribute?</question>
   <question>5. What does<![CDATA[&lt;]]> represent?</question>
   </quiz1>
   </cont_mgmt>
   ```

2. Create a document type definition (DTD) and add it to the XML document:

   ```
   <!DOCTYPE cont_mgmt [
   <!ELEMENT cont_mgmt (quiz1)>
   <!ELEMENT quiz1 (title?, question+)>
   <!ELEMENT title (#PCDATA)>
   <!ELEMENT question (#PCDATA)>
   ]>
   ```

3. Include a stylesheet. If you want to output to HTML, for instance, you would need to include a cascading style sheet (CSS).

   a. Add the stylesheet type to the XML document:

   ```
   <?xml-stylesheet type="text/css" href="CSS.css"?>
   ```

   b. In a separate text file, write the CSS:

   ```
   cont_mgmt
   {display:block;font-family:Verdana,Arial,sans-serif;}
   title {display:block;font-weight:bold;font-
   size:18pt;width:100%;text-align:center;}
   question {display:block;padding:20px;}
   ```

4. Validate or parse the XML document to check it for well formedness and adherence to a DTD, using a tool such as W3C's Markup Validation Service (2006) (see Figure 1).

5. View the output, or XML information transmitted to an application. In this case, HTML viewed in a browser (Figure 2). The source is shown in Figure 3.

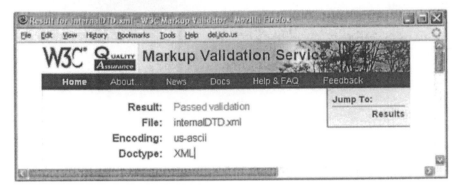

Figure 1. XML validation results.

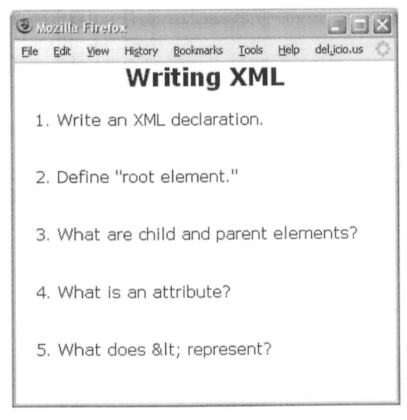

Figure 2. XML document.

The source looks like this:

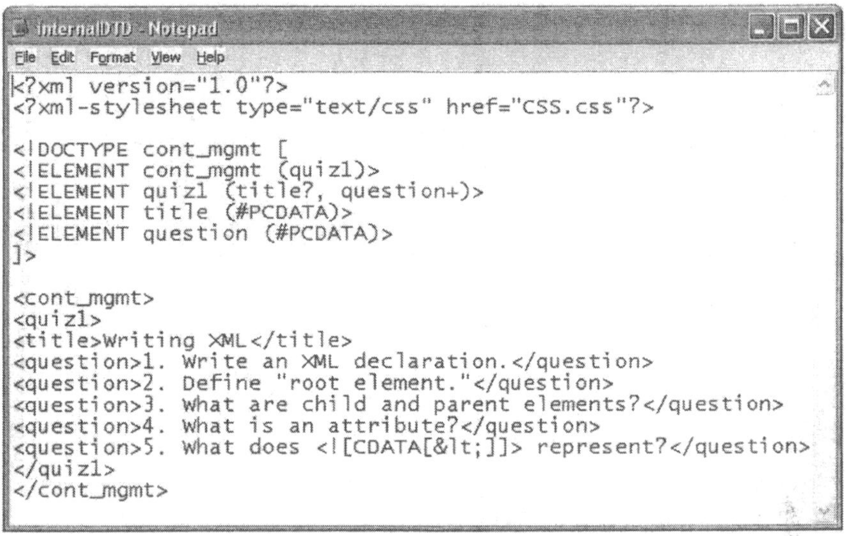

```
InternalDTD - Notepad
File  Edit  Format  View  Help
<?xml version="1.0"?>
<?xml-stylesheet type="text/css" href="CSS.css"?>

<!DOCTYPE cont_mgmt [
<!ELEMENT cont_mgmt (quiz1)>
<!ELEMENT quiz1 (title?, question+)>
<!ELEMENT title (#PCDATA)>
<!ELEMENT question (#PCDATA)>
]>

<cont_mgmt>
<quiz1>
<title>Writing XML</title>
<question>1. Write an XML declaration.</question>
<question>2. Define "root element."</question>
<question>3. What are child and parent elements?</question>
<question>4. What is an attribute?</question>
<question>5. What does <![CDATA[&lt;]]> represent?</question>
</quiz1>
</cont_mgmt>
```

Figure 3. XML source.

By the end of this section, students should understand the basic concepts of writing an XML document, writing a DTD, writing a CSS, validating an XML document, and outputting an XML document to an XML application, in this case HTML.

CONCLUSION

Most scholars agree that we should teach content management, single sourcing, XML, and other relatively new approaches to technical communication, but they caution that we must teach these concepts critically. I think we all agree. Because of XML's text appeal, I believe that this tool is a logical place for technical communicators to locate themselves as experts. But we must teach it with the theory (single sourcing), the methodology (modular writing), and the technology (content management) to support, apply, and guide it. Moreover, we must critique the practitioners' texts (Ament, 2002; Castro, 2001; Hackos, 2002; Harold & Means, 2004; Rockley, 2002) and perhaps write our own. Our students—future technical communicators—must understand the complexities of the technological landscape: outsourcing solutions, open-source tools, international consortiums, wikis, and so on. In addition, they need to know the basic ins and outs of traditional desktop software—not just word-processing but Web-based, graphic-design, and illustration tools. Of course they can choose to specialize; however, before they do we should give them a broad, inquiring sense of the options available to them, and we should give them a deep, critical knowledge of technology and a solid set of technical skills.

REFERENCES

Albers, M. (2005). The future of technical communication: Introduction to this special issue. *Technical Communication, 52,* 267-272.

Albers, M. (2003). Single sourcing and the technical communication career path. *Technical Communication, 50,* 335-343.

Ament, K. (2002). *Single sourcing: Building modular documentation.* Norwich, NY: William Andrew Publishing.

Applen, J. D. (2002). Technical communication, knowledge management, and XML. *Technical Communication, 49,* 301-313.

Battalio, J. (2002). Extensible markup language: How might it alter the software documentation process and the role of the technical communicator? *Journal of Technical Writing and Communication, 32,* 209-244.

Braegger, B. (2004, January 21). Re: About single sourcing. Retrieved February 15, 2004, from http://vista.weber.edu/webct/cobaltMainFrame.dowebct

Bridges, S. (2006, March). Getting to know your Xs. *IEEE Newsletter, 50*(3). Retrieved April 13, 2006, from http://www.ieeepcs.org/newsletter/pcsnews_mar2006_xml.php

Castro, E. (2001). *XML for the world wide web: Visual QuickStart Guide.* Berkeley, CA: Peachpit Press.

Ciccone, V. (2004, January 21). Re: About single sourcing. Retrieved February 15, 2004, from http://vista.weber.edu/webct/cobaltMainFrame.dowebct

Clark, D., & Andersen, R. (2005). Renegotiating with technology: Training towards more sustainable technical communication. *Technical Communication, 52,* 289-301.

Course Proposal Results. (2006). Retrieved May 15, 2006, from http://documents.weber.edu/catalog/submission_form_interface/results1/results_page_substantive.asp

Courses in Professional & Technical Writing. (2006). Retrieved May 15, 2006, from http://departments.weber.edu/ptw/courses.htm

Dayton, D., & Bernhardt, S. (2004). ATTW member survey 2003. *Technical Communication Quarterly, 13*(1), 35.

Eble, M. (2003). Content vs. product: The effects of single sourcing on the teaching of technical communication. *Technical Communication, 50,* 344-349.

Hackos, J. (2002). *Content management for dynamic web delivery.* New York: John Wiley & Sons, Inc.

Harold, E. R., & Means, W. S. (2004). *XML in a nutshell* (3rd ed.). Cambridge, MA: O'Reilly & Associates.

Harris, L. (2005, December 14). *English 4100 Final Examination,* 1-5.

Hart-Davidson, W. (2001). On writing, technical communication, and information technology: The core competencies of technical communication. *Technical Communication, 48,* 145-155.

Houser, A. (2000, November 16). *Creating XML documents with the tools you already have.* Retrieved May 14, 2006, from http://www.groupwellesley.com/talks/STCPGH11.2000/creating_xml.htm

Kahn, P. (2003, October). Single-sourcing deconstructed. *Toronto STC Chapter Newsletter.* Retrieved January 24, 2005, from http://www.stcsig.org/ss/articles102003/SingleSourcingDeconstructed.htm

Lavicka, J. (2004, May 5). *Final Exam: RoboHelp Project Evaluation.*

McShane, B. J. (2005, November). Quizzes. Retrieved May 15, 2006, from http://faculty.weber.edu/bmcshane/4110/quizzes.htm

McShane, B. J. (2004, February 6). *Syllabus for English 4100.* Retrieved May 15, 2006, from http://faculty.weber.edu/bmcshane/old/4100_SS/syllabus.htm

Priestly, M. (2006, May 8). *Intro to DITA: An open-standard, XML architecture for documents.* Presentation at STC's 53rd Annual Conference in Las Vegas, Nevada.

Q&A: Microsoft co-sponsors submission of Office open XML document formats to Ecma International for standardization. (2005, November, 21). Retrieved April 12, 2006, from http://www.microsoft.com/presspass/features/2005/nov05/11-21Ecma.mspx

Rainey, K., Turner, R. K., & Dayton, D. (2005). Do curricula correspond to managerial expectations? Core competencies for technical communicators. *Technical Communication, 52,* 323-352.

Rockley, A. (2002). *Managing enterprise content: A unified content strategy.* Berkeley, CA: New Riders Press.

Sapienza, F. (2002). Does being technical matter? XML, single source, and technical communication. *Journal of Technical Writing and Communication, 32,* 155-170.

W3C. (2006, February 5). *Extensible Markup Language (XML).* Retrieved April 13, 2006, from http://www.w3.org/XML/

W3C. (2006, November 14). *The W3C markup validation service.* Retrieved February 27, 2007, from http://validator.w3.org/

CHAPTER FIVE

Digital Delivery and Communication Technologies: Understanding Content Management Systems Through Rhetorical Theory

Michelle F. Eble

This chapter describes content/course management systems (CMS) as a type of information communication technology (ICT) (see Grabill, 2003; Grabill & Hicks, 2005 for a discussion on the convention of this term) and how they have been used in delivering online courses in a professional and technical communication graduate program. Early discussions about the online teaching of writing courses often focused on the practical use of technology and how online learning compared and contrasted with face-to-face teaching and learning (as examples, see Mehlenbacher, Miller, Covington, & Larsen, 2000; Miller, 2001). The proliferation of online teaching and learning within colleges, universities, and organizations during the last decade is well documented in the journals of our field (see Blakelock & Smith, 2006). Discussing the use of Internet communication technologies to deliver these online courses as well as the implications and applications of this digital delivery in learning contexts are also certainly beginning to take place. For example, *Online Education: Global Questions, Local Answers,* edited by Kelly Cargile Cook and Keith Grant-Davie (2005), focuses on important questions for scholar-teachers and presents best online education practices within technical writing programs. They write, "online education in the early 21st century is at a theory-building stage, a stage at which we need not only to take stock of what we are doing with the new technologies, and what we might do with them, but to also examine and discuss our rationales for those practices" (p. 2) (see also Hewitt & Ehmann, 2004). Within this context,

I have created several online courses informed by rhetorical theory and delivered using CMS.

CMS can be used to deliver courses or information online where interaction with and feedback from the audience/users are primary concerns. After a brief introduction to open source content management systems, I discuss the research and writing of scholars who write about secondary orality, electronic rhetoric/ discourse, and more recently, digital rhetoric. This research serves as a theoretical foundation for discussing CMS as a type of ICT that can be used for a number of purposes, but can best be understood through a rhetorical framework that uses the repurposed rhetorical canons as a heuristic to facilitate the interaction and communication in these online environments. In other words, CMS allow content to be delivered to students and enable students and teachers to engage and interact with the content and with each other through writing.

The second half of this chapter introduces two open source CMS—Drupal and Xoops—which I have used on several occasions in teaching courses online and face-to-face. While CMS, including the ones I have chosen to discuss in this chapter, can be used for a wide variety of purposes: to create and design Web sites, portals, virtual communities, blogs, and so on, this chapter focuses on the use of CMS as well as the other ICTs (forums, chat, instant messaging, etc.) embedded within them in courses delivered in online environments. While I have limited the discussion of these CMS to one context, (teaching and learning in online environments), I hope the rhetorical framework presented here can be used as an heuristic for those interested in using a CMS to deliver content for other purposes and audiences not necessarily addressed in this chapter.

Although computers and desktop publishing affected the way people would write/design texts (see Bernhardt, 1993; Hawisher & Selfe, 1999; Johnson, 1998) and hypertext changed the way audiences might read and interact with a text (see Bolter, 1993, 2001; Howard, 1997; Johnson-Eilola, 1997), CMS allow audiences to help create texts/ discourse, respond to the texts/discourse in other instances, and even interact with other audience members. They can also be used to create discourse communities where knowledge can be created and shared by its users. And last, I will discuss the use of CMS to create discourse communities and the implications for instructors and students when writing in these environments, where content creation is often times separated from design and layout decisions, and where the characteristics of oral discourse (exemplified most often in instant messaging or chat) are presented through written discourse in online environments.

WHAT ARE CONTENT MANAGEMENT SYSTEMS (CMS)?

Gu and Pullman (2005) define content management generally "as the process of creating, managing, and publishing information with a conscious, purpose driven approach, using some kind of specially designed system or software."

CMS enable administrators to set up Web sites, establish the interface (which includes the layout and design), write and label content, delineate the permissions, dictate who can access the content and create content, and manage and update the site through a control panel type interface. CMS are used in public and private companies and organizations for intranets, customer relationship management, document management, and Web sites. Blackboard, WebCT, Moodle, and Angel are CMS commonly used in higher education. While a variety of ICTs (networked computers, e-mail, instant messaging, chat, discussion board, shoutboxes, wikis, podcasts, blogs, Web sites) have been used in writing classes for years now, many of these writing technologies have become more mainstream in higher education with the help of these proprietary systems (see Gurak & Duin, 2004; Hawisher & Selfe, 1999; Porter, 2003; Selber, 1997). These proprietary web-based systems have become particularly popular with those instructors not accustomed to writing technologies because they find them easy to use, and they can deliver course content to their students outside the classroom.

However, many of us in computers and writing as well as professional and technical communication choose alternatives for using technology in our courses. Those who advocate open source software (see Faber & Johnson-Eilola, 2005; Lowe & Barton, 2006) have pointed out the numerous interfaces created by open source alternatives rather than supplementing or using proprietary CMS software adopted by our universities. Opensource.org (2006) writes that "the basic idea behind open source is very simple: When programmers can read, redistribute, and modify the source code for a piece of software, the software evolves. People improve it, people adapt it, people fix bugs." Although these open source solutions are not supported in traditional terms like Blackboard and Microsoft, all open source software systems have communities of developers and users that help support the system. We also use open source CMS for their flexibility and the customization they allow with regard to design and layout.

Those new to open source CMS should investigate opensourcecms.com. At this site, a user can demo over 50 CMS and see some of their features and characteristics. All open source CMS share common characteristics, and the differences tend to be with administration and their capabilities. Drupal and Xoops are no exception. I chose these two to discuss in this chapter because I have the most experience with them, not because I think they are the best. Both systems are updated regularly and offer effective and usable documentation. Both systems have a large community of developers and have been around for at least five years. The Drupal system can be used to foster an online community through blog technologies while the Xoops system acts as a portal to foster online interaction for a set of users. In this example, the difference between them is subtle.

Content and discourse as well as information and knowledge can be created, communicated, shared, revised, and presented using CMS. The communicative acts that occur in these online environments can happen through instant messages, podcasts, discussion boards, and chat boxes and, in these cases, the discourse seems oral while blog entries and other writing seems more like print. In light of the discourse—which often shares characteristics of orality and print—in these online environments, it seems important to use prior research on secondary orality, electronic discourse, and digital rhetoric, along with the classical rhetorical canons, to understand these communicative acts and online environments.

SECONDARY ORALITY, ELECTRONIC RHETORIC/DISCOURSE, DIGITAL RHETORIC

Walter Ong (1982) defines secondary orality as "present-day high-technology culture, in which a new orality is sustained by telephone, radio, television, and other electronic devices that depend for their existence and functioning on writing and print" (p. 11). Kathleen Welch (1990), who bases much of her work about electronic discourse on Ong, wrote more than 15 years ago that the "canons of classical rhetoric have been reconstituted and revivified by secondary orality" (n.p.). Early scholars in composition and rhetoric argued for the role of classical rhetoric in the teaching of writing and pointed to the rhetorical canons as a structure that could be used by students, but the emphasis was normally placed on invention, arrangement, and style.

This understanding of secondary orality through the rhetorical tradition, especially the canons of memory and delivery, serves as a powerful example for current investigations of digital rhetoric and its technologies. In John Frederick Reynolds' (1993) edited collection, *Rhetorical Memory and Delivery: Classical Concepts for Contemporary Composition and Communication,* scholars discuss "orality and literacy within a secondary orality that blends written and spoken and visual and aural language" and understood secondary orality and later electronic discourse through the "revival of the classical canons of memory and delivery" (Horner, 1993, p. ix). This early work also emphasized the use of rhetoric for both reception and production of texts/discourse. Welch's (1991) definition of rhetoric, "as a faculty and field of study," provides a useful heuristic for studying digital rhetorics (pp. 159-160). She writes,

> Rhetoric . . . provides not only the means of analysis for all these symbol systems but the means of producing new kinds of material as well. No other system for the production and reception of texts in all symbol systems possesses the completeness of rhetoric and its definitive connection to systems of education and to cultures (pp. 159-160).

As for the relationship between orality and print literacy in secondary orality, which is also pertinent today in writing technologies like e-mail, instant messaging, blogs, and CMS, Welch (1991) writes,

In primary orality, the dynamism of the word is powerful but transitory. In secondary orality, the dynamic of the spoken word is not only powerful, it is lasting. We have returned to a state of interdependence of oral and written discourse. With the technology of secondary orality, the spoken word and the written word are empowering each other in ways that previously were not possible. This situation makes classical rhetoric, which accounts for encoders, decoders, and cultures as well as texts, a newly powerful area (p. 161).

Much of this early work focused on the proliferation of film, TV, and radio. However, hypertext help change the way we discussed written discourse delivered in electronic environments. Bolter (1993) uses the term "electronic rhetoric" when he writes about the rhetorical canons and writing technologies in the early nineties.

Delivery once again becomes central, because the electronic text itself is defined in the act of delivery. Hypertext moves delivery back from the margin of the rhetorical canons toward the center, and in so doing it disrupts established relationships with invention, arrangement, style, and memory. Electronic technology disrupts both literary theory and composition theory. It disrupts literary theory by admitting a whole new body of materials (interactive texts) that need theoretical treatment. It disrupts composition theory by providing new faculties (for interactivity and multimedia presentation) that will need to be incorporated into the pedagogy (pp. 99-100).

Bolter was referring to the traditional notions of hypertext before the widespread use of the Web; however, his words prefigure what continues to be discussed in humanities departments in the 21st century. He also forecasts many of our current discussions related to the teaching of writing: "Achieving a new balance between verbal and visual presentation will be a principal task for writing pedagogy in the coming decades" (p. 111).

More recently, Welch (1999) introduced the term "electric rhetoric" and defined it as an "emergent consciousness or mentalité within discourse communities" and the "new merger of the written and the oral, both newly empowered and reconstructed by electricity and both dependent on print literacy. Electronic technologies have led to electronic consciousness, an awareness or mentalité that now changes literacy but in no way diminishes it" (p. 104). Her focus on this change in awareness is important to a discussion of delivering courses online since so many are opposed to it because they are unfamiliar with it. At the time, she was referring to video, TV, and film and acknowledged the influence computers and screens would continue to have on literacy, communication, articulation, and our consciousness.

Within the last couple of years we have begun to see scholarship on digital writing, digital spaces, and digital rhetoric. At least two characteristics of digital rhetoric are important to this chapter as writing in online environments emphasizes: 1) all of the rhetorical canons; and 2) audience interaction. The WIDE Research Collective (2005) defines digital writing as the "art and practice of preparing documents primarily by computer and often for online delivery. Digital writing often requires attention to the theories and practices of designing, planning, constructing, and maintaining dynamic and interactive texts—texts that may wind up fragmented and published within and across databases. Texts that may, and often do, include multiple media elements, such as images, video, and audio" (n.p.).

The following definition of digital writing by Grabill and Hicks (2005) describes both the role of the rhetorical canons as well as the emphasis on audience interaction in online environments:

> From a rhetorical viewpoint, writing concerns not only the words on the page (the product), but also concerns the means and mechanisms for production (that is, process, understood cognitively, socially, and technologically); mechanisms for distribution or delivery (for example, media); invention, exploration, research, methodology, and inquiry procedures; as well as questions of audience, persuasiveness, and impact (p. 304).

Using this definition, digital writing is not just writing "printed" on the screen or writing produced through the use of word processing software. Digital writing entails more than the electronic version of print documents as well.

The characteristic of digital rhetoric that likens it to secondary orality is its emphasis on audience interaction. CMS, used by applying digital rhetoric theories and practices, make for effective online environments where learning can occur. However, defining digital rhetoric has also been as complicated as defining rhetoric at times. Nevertheless, according to a group of students and faculty at MSU, digital rhetoric "shifts the productive *techne* of the rhetorical process (as typically instantiated in composition and other writing courses) from primarily invention-driven to a broader rhetorical approach that privileges arrangement as a focal activity and reclaims the importance of delivery and memory as key areas of rhetorical practice" (Digirhet.org, 2006, n.p.). They also introduce three goals for learning about digital rhetoric: the need for community, engagement, and application (Digirhet.org, 2006, n.p.). These are similar to the goals of any online course in our program: develop a discourse community; foster engagement with readings, other material, and classmates; and initiate and provide response and feedback on writing projects that are informed by the theories and discussions of the course.

The digital spaces that CMS help to create can facilitate the interaction between writers and audiences. One of the differences between literacy and secondary orality is audience consideration and interaction. "Oratory has always dealt partly with large audiences. Electronic discourse mostly speaks to large audiences" (Welch, 1999, p. 152). This notion of audience is important as one tries to build a community of learners. "Performance in the electronic symbol systems means that the fourth and fifth canons come to life again after centuries of atrophy and in turn help to reconstitute the familiar first three canons of invention, arrangement, and style" (Welch, 1999, p. 152). Electronic discourse shares characteristics of orality, literacy, and secondary orality and fosters audience interaction. That is, internet communication technologies like content management systems and blogs call for interaction with the audience in order for the articulations to continue. Blogs, alone or within CMS, incorporate oral characteristics, such as leaving feedback or commenting on an entry, print characteristics (blog entries are time stamped and are similar to journals or diaries) and secondary orality through the use of multimedia components and podcasts. A socially situated context helps foster learning, and within the interaction between the interface and the audience, learning occurs. Delivery in the rhetorical tradition was always about interaction and feedback with an audience (Porter, 2005). As a result of these interactions in an online course, knowledge can be created and shared, and learning occurs especially if we remember "the role language plays in the knowledge production process, which is characterized in every respect as social in nature" (Selber, 2004, p. 79).

Building on Digirhet.org's framework and its emphasis on community, critical engagement, and practical application as well as Stuart Selbers' (2004) definition of rhetorical literacy as "the thoughtful integration of functional and critical abilities in the design and evaluation of computer interfaces," the next section discusses the repurposing of the rhetorical canons to create interfaces that foster learning and interaction (p. 79).

REPURPOSING THE RHETORICAL CANONS

Rhetorical theory, especially the rhetorical canons of memory and delivery (arguably the two most neglected canons during the 20th century in writing pedagogy), provides writers/designers a theoretical framework in which to implement ICTs such as CMS. These digital environments and the discourse and communication that takes place within them are best planned and understood through the repurposing of the rhetorical canons of invention, arrangement, style, memory, and delivery. Not only does this repurposing help establish a theoretical foundation for CMS as rhetorical, digital environments, it also provides a pedagogical theory for the creation of online courses that are delivered through an informed, interrogated interface. These database-driven online environments or communities share both oral and print discourse characteristics. When we consider CMS, and the online courses/communities they help create, as rhetorical, then the canons become a useful heuristic for these environments. Invention involves content creation, audience consideration, purpose, and planning; arrangement and style can illuminate layout, design, and metadata decisions;

memory applies to the database backend, archiving capabilities, and syndication feeds; and delivery focuses on interface issues, distribution and medium.

The teaching and learning experiences (communicative acts) in online courses are best understood through a rhetorical framework where the CMS delivers the content of the course to students, and the communication technologies enable students and teachers to engage and interact with the content and with each other while also fulfilling class projects, getting feedback, and revising writing projects. The rhetorical framework I have used as a heuristic to implement a CMS includes repurposing the classical rhetorical canons for delivering electronic discourse to a specific audience for a particular purpose. In my own use of CMS, my students are my audience, and engagement, production, and learning are my purposes.

Any implementation of a CMS for an online course begins with the rhetorical canon of invention and includes overall planning. It involves a consideration of all of the elements of an online environment, which might include the content and interface design as well as the layout, content descriptors, interactivity, and distribution. The framework introduced below is not linear, and the repurposed canons are recursive and interrelate with each other. The delineation between each of the repurposed canons is more fluid than the five parts of oratory; nevertheless, they serve as a useful heuristic for implementing a CMS for an online course.

Classical Canons	Repurposed Canons	Heuristic
Invention	Content Creation	What content needs to be written and delivered to audience?
Arrangement	Layout	How will the content be structured or organized to meet audience needs? How will the interface be accessible and user-friendly? How will you adapt the CMS templates? How will students go through the content?
Style	Design	What should the interface look like? How will students interact with the content and each other? How will you customize the cascading style sheets (CSS)? How will they find things?

Memory	Database/Archives	How will content be stored? How will content be labeled? What taxonomy (tags) will you use to label content?
Delivery	Interface/Distribution	How should it all be distributed? What aspects should be public? What sections should be private? How will students interact with the online environment?

The layout and design elements of the CMS combined with the content and the database results in the interface. In online environments, "delivery refers to issues related to matters of appearance, material design, access, interoperability and interactivity, and the politics and economics of information distribution. It is of central concern to the writer who wishes to communicate with their online audience" (WIDE, 2005, n.p.).

Using CMS relies on the separation of content from design in the customization and writing of content. The arrangement/layout and the style/design of an online environment, which can be created separate from the creation of any content, are generated through a sophisticated combination of PHP and cascading style sheets as well as easily modifiable templates. Once content is invented (written and labeled according to its purpose or its content), which is normally done using a WYSIWYG editor similar to word processing software (and allows for image and audio insertion), the content is stored in a database (memory) and delivered or distributed as the infrastructure (layout and design) of the CMS dictates.

This rhetorical framework offers us a lens to understand CMS and how they work in delivering online courses while also complicating the notion of what it means to write/create/design. CMS are unique communication technologies in that the delivery of content, whether text, information, knowledge, audio, video, or images is done through the interface. The audience/users can then interact with the content and with each other to create more content, thus creating recursive rhetorical acts that build on this interaction. With CMS, the creation of content and design elements is separated, but that doesn't mean that content is created with no purpose or context. Creating and designing interfaces informed by digital rhetoric and the repurposed rhetorical canons can also help build discourse communities where knowledge sharing and knowledge creation can happen, which is especially important in an online course.

CREATING AN ONLINE DISCOURSE COMMUNITY:
DRUPAL AND XOOPS

Drupal is "a software package that allows an individual or a community of users to easily publish, manage and organize a wide variety of content on a Web site. . . . Drupal includes features to enable content management systems, blogs, collaborative authoring environments, forums, newsletters, picture galleries, file uploads and downloads" (http://drupal.org/about). Features of this content management system include user and permission management, personalization, templating or theming, discussion forums, syndication, aggregation, tagging taxonomy, and a wide variety of modules or plugins—such as chat, instant messaging, image galleries, polls, and easylinks, which allow users of the site to suggest links to other sites—that extend the capability of the core software.

Xoops stands for "eXtensible Object Oriented Portal System" and is a system "that allows administrators to easily create dynamic websites with great content and many outstanding features. It is an ideal tool for developing small to large dynamic community Websites, intra company portals, corporate portals, Weblogs and much more" (http://xoops.org/modules/wfchannel). Features of this CMS include user and permission management, personalization, theme-based skinnable layout and interface, and a repository of modules (similar to Drupal) for extending the usefulness of the site.

Administration for both of these CMS is Web-based, so you can access, administer, and manage the interface through any Web browser. The documentation and support for both CMS, including manuals, user discussion boards, and FAQ for both Web administrators and users, is extensive. The documentation for both sites suggests modules or plugins to install for common Web site types, like community or organizational-based Web sites, Weblogs, and collaborative online communities. Drupal even has a distribution especially for using Drupal in educational settings (http://drupaled.org). Most people in computers and writing may be familiar with Drupal because it is used to host Kairosnews (http://kairosnews.org) and Plone.

Open source CMS, unlike proprietary versions like Blackboard and WebCT, can be customized and adapted to meet instructor and user needs. Both Drupal and XOOPS have developers working to improve and update the software. Using an open source solution also helps to dispel the myth that the Blackboard or WebCT interface is what online courses look like. Putting lectures online and linking to content along with user interaction in the form of discussion boards or even chats doesn't necessarily ensure learning; and neither do open source CMS for that matter. However, the philosophy of open source software can serve as an epistemological model for students and can help foster a community where the creation and sharing of knowledge evolves through the interaction. For example, once an instructor has defined learning goals and projects for the course and provides the readings, resources, and project explanations, the job of the instructor is to facilitate student learning. The way he or she does this in an online professional writing course is through the interface of the online environment through the delivery of content, interaction with content or each other, and through communicative acts that help create new knowledge. As a result, students interact with the content and with each other and the teacher to create more content. This pedagogy emphasizes a community that is student centered, learning centered, student created and based on the social construction of knowledge. Proprietary CMS can also help do this to a certain point, but like any large-scale implementation, they can be limiting. CMS, like Blackboard, WebCT, and Angel, allow faculty who want to enhance their course with technology without having to know any programming languages.

Part of my frustration with proprietary CMS popular in higher education, like Blackboard and WebCT, are the metaphors they help instill into our culture and thus students and other faculty about online teaching and learning. The virtual schoolhouse and virtual chalkboard or blackboard are no longer useful metaphors for online teaching and learning because many see virtual as an alternative to "real," and why would you have an "unreal" schoolhouse and "unreal" chalkboard? Moreover, in this context, how could "real" learning occur? The metaphors also emphasize the object so that learning occurs in a schoolhouse, building, or classroom and from a chalkboard or professor standing in the front of the classroom. Almost by default, these metaphors put teaching and learning in online environments at a disadvantage. I prefer to emphasize the learning and interaction in online courses rather than the distribution method. In this way, learning can occur in a wide variety of ways and in various contexts.

I spend my time building an online environment where students can engage with course content and where knowledge can be created and shared. More and more students are familiar with learning and writing in these online environments, and most students are very familiar with online communities. My students belong to a wide range of communities where they learn from others and others learn from them. Just this last semester, I had students who were members of Massive Multiplayer Online Role-Playing Game (MMORPG) communities, stock & mutual fund groups, geocaching organizational Web sites, and various health condition/support group communities.

A customizable online environment where I decide which parts are public and which sections are private, where students can communicate with me and other classmates through various communication technologies—instant messaging, chat, forums, links, blogs, comments, file and image attachments—and where students receive responses and feedback on their writing and projects makes for an impressive learning community.

The delivery of courses in online environments depends upon a carefully designed and user-tested interface that the creator/designer/writer creates to deliver content, foster interaction and communication through digital writing. Content can be text, audio files, images, and video. Interaction includes blogs, forums, chatboxes, and instant messaging. Other capabilities of Drupal and Xoops include calendars, quote blocks, list of links and resources, polls, and member lists. Arrangement of the content and where the interaction will occur can be customized according to user needs and instructor wants. For example, forum/discussion board postings might be arranged according to weeks or topics or even by discussion leader, and they might be private to registered users only. All blog postings, which will appear on the home page in the order they are written, might be public, but you have to be registered to comment on them. Content labeled as news might be placed in an additional section on the site, and content labeled as resource may go to the resource page. The administrator determines how these content areas will work together during the creation/designing/writing the course phase. Once students register and log on to the site, they will have the ability to change some of their own settings like themes or blocks depending on the rules the administrator has defined for the user group.

In addition to implementing and customizing a CMS by using a rhetorical framework and by trial and error, I have also used Swales' definition of a discourse community as a pedagogical foundation for delivering courses online. Swales (1990) defines a discourse community as "socio-rhetorical networks that form in order to work towards sets of common goals" (p. 9).

One example of this type of discourse community consists of a group of graduate students and an instructor working toward a common set of goals through an online interface informed by rhetorical theory and pedagogical critique. Customizing a CMS, open source or proprietary, for a course online or to enhance a F2F course, depends on the course goals and outcomes and the community of learners. CMS can provide interfaces to foster a discourse community where knowledge is constructed and contingent upon the specific community where it is created (Bruffee, 1986). According to Bruffee,

> A social constructionist position . . . assumes the entities we normally call reality, knowledge, thought, facts, texts, selves, and so on as constructs generated by communities of like-minded peers. Social construction understands reality, knowledge . . . as community-generated and community-maintained linguistic entities . . . that define or "constitute" the communities that generate them (p. 774).

In other words, an online community can share and construct knowledge if the members of an online community interact and communicate with each other and agree upon, with the help of an instructor, the goals of the community. Thus, the social construction of knowledge is achieved through discourse. In the case of online courses, knowledge is shared and created through digital writing and an interface.

DELIVERY AND INTERFACES IN
ONLINE ENVIRONMENTS

My discussion of CMS in this chapter focuses on one use of them—for online course delivery in a graduate program in professional and technical communication. Using CMS to create/design/write interfaces conducive to learning and interaction is a complex process that involves issues of accessibility, design, usability, and technical know-how, as well as questions involving pedagogical issues. Given earlier research on secondary orality, electronic discourse, and more current research on digital rhetoric/writing and the repurposing of the rhetorical canons for digital delivery, CMS will continue to provide interesting digital environments/interfaces for research. This type of course delivery involves students' prior experience with other CMS within educational establishments or in their own interests outside of school. I taught a class just this summer where students were continually e-mailing to ask why a particular aspect of Blackboard wasn't included in the CMS we were using for our course. Another student e-mailed me to let me know about another discussion board option that had a better, more user-friendly interface than the course's Web site. I wasn't sure what to say. I don't use Blackboard for a number of reasons. I don't want students to think there is one kind of online course or interface or arrangement for an online course, because if they encounter a different user interface, then it must not be online learning or they are resistant to it. However, with the continual proliferation of CMS, students/users are bringing with them expectations for this specific interface—the online course interface. Grabill (2003) uses the term interfaces "to describe cultural, theoretical, institutional, and technological interactions" and "as actual computer interfaces that inscribe those interactions" (p. 469). How ICT interfaces are created/designed/written and how they communicate with students are questions that need to be asked as these technologies are adopted in more and more situations (see Selfe, Selfe, & Richard, 1994). Grabill (2003) writes, "Any attempt to design ICT interfaces that are class or race or ethnicity or gender interventions must deal with a set of infrastructural-level decisions that once made are perhaps irreversible, as well as equally complex decisions at the surface of the interface" (p. 466). Questions related to students'/users' experiences with these technologies are certainly worth exploring: What are students' experiences with these interfaces? What is their experience of writing and learning in this environment? What do they expect from an online course interface? How have they come to expect this type of interface?

My students' comments made me realize how important it is to use different interfaces in my online courses and at the same time value their critique of the interface. Selber (2004) writes, "rhetorical literacy concerns the design and evaluation of online environments" (p. 182). I think that the use of CMS in online teaching and learning helps foster students' rhetorical literacy of online environments. We need to focus on the writing/discourse created by the instructors and the students through the use of the CMS. Porter's (2003) view of writing technologies is not focused on the computer as tool or the genres produced through ICTs but instead defines "technology as use—as the human and machine working in concert (joined in the interface) and writing in a particular social, political, and rhetorical context" (p. 375). As writing teachers, we know that "writing technologies play a significant role in meaning-making—especially in terms of production (process) and distribution (delivery)" (Grabill & Hicks, 2005, p. 304). In an online discourse community where learning and production (the completion of projects) is the goal, "digital writers rely on rhetorically sophisticated combination of words, motion, interactivity, and visuals to make meaning" (WIDE, 2005, n.p.). Using CMS as a way to deliver content through an interface created both by and for students links technology and digital writing and supports Selber's (2004) notion of redefining rhetoric "at the nexus of literacy and technology" (p.145). The WIDE Collective also addresses the complexity of what we are teaching when we use ICTs or have students write within or use these environments. They write, "our instruction teaches composing with technologies as an integrated process and as a liberal art—that is, we see our task as helping students acquire the intellectual and critical capacities they need to critique and choose among available options and to acquire new knowledge for themselves as tools develop and evolve" (WIDE, 2005, n.p.). Maybe CMS can help us create these types of interfaces for our students to learn in.

REFERENCES

Bernhardt, S. A. (1993). The shape of text to come: The texture of print on screens. *College Composition and Communication, 44,* 151-175.

Blakelock, J., & Smith, T. E. (Eds.). (2006). Distance learning: Evolving perspectives [Special Issue]. *Computers and Composition 23*(1), 1-166.

Bolter, J. D. (1993). Hypertext and the rhetorical canons. In J. F. Reynolds (Ed.), *Rhetorical memory and delivery: Classical concepts for contemporary composition and communication* (pp. 97-111). Hillsdale, NJ: Erlbaum.

Bolter, J. D. (2001). *Writing space: Computers, hypertext, and the remediation of print* (2nd ed.). Mahwah, NJ: Erlbaum.

Bruffee, K. (1986). Social construction, language, and the authority of knowledge: A bibliographical essay. *College English, 48*(8), 773-790.

Cargile Cook, K., & Grant-Davie, K. (Eds.). (2005). *Online education: Global questions, local answers.* Amityville, NY: Baywood.

Digirhet.org. (2006). Teaching digital rhetoric: Community, critical engagement, and application. *Pedagogy: Critical Approaches to Teaching Literature, Language, Composition, and Culture, 6*(2), 231-259.

About Drupal. Drupal.org | Community Plumbing Website. Retrieved April 15, 2006 http://drupal.org/about

Faber, B., & Johnson-Eilola, J. (2005). Knowledge politics: Open sourcing education. In K. Cargile Cook & K. Grant Davie (Eds.), *Online education: Global questions, local answers*. Amityville, NY: Baywood.

Grabill, J. T. (2003). On divides and interfaces: Access, class, and computers. *Computers and Composition, 20*, 455-472.

Grabill, J. T., & Hicks, T. (2005). *Multiliteracies meet methods: The case for digital writing in English education, 37*(4), 301-311.

Gu, B., & Pullman, G. (2005). *CFP: Special TCQ Issue on CMSs*. Techrhet Listserve. Retrieved July 25, 2005.

Gurak, L., & Duin, A. H. (2004). The impact of the Internet and digital technologies on teaching and research in technical communication. *Technical Communication Quarterly, 13*(2), 187-198.

Hawisher, G., & Selfe, C. L. (Eds.). (1999). *Passions, pedagogies and 21st century technologies*. Logan: Utah State University Press.

Hewett, B., & Ehmann, C. (2004). *Preparing educators for online writing instruction: Principles and processes*. Urbana, IL: NCTE.

Horner, W. B. (1993). Introduction. In J. F. Reynolds (Eds.), *Rhetorical memory and delivery: Classical concepts for contemporary composition and communication* (pp. ix-xii). Hillsdale, NJ: Erlbaum.

Howard, T. W. (1997). *The rhetoric of electronic communities*. Norwood, NJ: Ablex.

Johnson, R. (1998). *User-centered technology: A rhetorical theory for computers and other mundane artifacts*. Albany: State University of New York Press.

Johnson-Eilola, J. (1997). *Nostalgic angels: Rearticulating hypertext writing*. Westport, CT: Ablex.

Lowe, C., & Barton, M. (2006). Databases and collaborative spaces for composition. *Computers and Composition Online*.
http://www.bgsu.edu/cconline/barton-lowe/barton-lowe.htm

Mehlenbacher, B., Miller, C. R., Covington, D., & Larsen, J. (2000). Active and inter-active learning online: A comparison of Web-based and conventional writing classes. *IEEE Transactions on Professional Communication, 43*(2), 166-184.

Miller, S. K. (2001). A review of research on distance education in Computers and Composition. *Computers and Composition, 18*, 423-430.

Open Source Initiative, The. (2006). Retrieved March 15, 2006 from http://opensource.org

OpenSourceCMS.com. Retrieved April 15, 2006 from http://opensourcecms.com

Ong, W. J. (1982). *Orality and literacy: The technologizing of the word*. London: Methuen.

Porter, J. E. (2003). Why technology matters to writing: A cyberwriter's tale. *Computers and Composition, 20*, 375-394.

Porter, J. E. (2005, April). *Repurposing delivery for digital rhetoric: Access, interaction, economics*. The Tag Lecture, Department of English, East Carolina University, Greenville, North Carolina.

Reynolds, J. F. (Ed.). (1993). *Rhetorical memory and delivery: Classical concepts for contemporary composition and communication*. Hillsdale, NJ: Erlbaum.

Selber, S. A. (Ed.). (1997). *Computers and technical communication: Pedagogical and programmatic perspectives*. Greenwich, CT: Ablex.

Selber, S. A. (2004). *Multiliteracies for a digital age*. Carbondale: Southern Illinois University Press.

Selfe, C. L., & Selfe, Jr., Richard J. (1994). The politics of the interface: Power and its exercise in electronic contact zones. *College Composition and Communication, 45*(4), 480-504.

Swales, J. (1990) *Genre analysis: English in academic and research settings.* Cambridge, MA: Cambridge University Press.

Welch, K. E. (1990). Electrifying classical rhetoric: Ancient media, modern technology, and contemporary composition. *Journal of Advanced Composition, 10*.1. Available at: http://jac.gsu.edu/jac/10/Articles/2.htm

Welch, K. E. (1991). *The contemporary reception of classical rhetoric: Appropriations of ancient discourse.* Hillsdale, NJ: Erlbaum.

Welch, K. E. (1993). Reconfiguring writing and delivery in secondary orality. In J. F. Reynolds (Ed.), *Rhetorical memory and delivery: Classical concepts for contemporary composition and communication* (pp. 17-30). Hillsdale, NJ: Erlbaum.

Welch, K. E. (1999). *Electric rhetoric: Classical rhetoric, oralism, and a new literacy.* Cambridge, MA: MIT Press.

WIDE Research Center Collective, The (WIDE) [DeVoss, Dànielle, Cushman, Ellen, Hart-Davidson, Bill, Grabill, Jeff, & Porter, James E.]. (2005). Why teach digital writing? *Kairos, 10*(1). Available at:
http://english.ttu.edu/kairos/10.1/binder2.html?coverweb/wide/index.html

All about XOOPS. XOOPS Website. Retrieved April 15, 2006
http://www.xoops.org/modules/wfchannel/

CHAPTER SIX

Topography of Educational Place(s): Technical Communication, Instructor Preparedness, and Hybrid Courses

Lisa Meloncon

> It was to satisfy man's curiosity concerning differences of the world from place to place that geography developed as a subject of popular interest.
> *Richard Hartshorne* (1939, p. 15)

In the broadest sense, Hartshorne's idea of satisfying man's curiosity about differences in place is the focus of this chapter. More specifically, my focus is the difference in the educational places that technical communication teachers are facing. Far more than writing about this place or that place, taking place as a key component of research means "thinking about the implications of the idea of place" (Cresswell, 2004, p. 122). In this chapter, the implications of the idea of place focus on the shifting dynamic of the classroom into places beyond four physical walls. What I mean by educational places are actual, material, or virtual spaces where technical communication instructors teach. I became curious about the difference of place for instructors if the class is in a traditional location—all meetings are held in a brick and mortar building where students and teacher(s) are face to face; hybrid—some (or all) meetings are held in a brick and mortar building where students and teacher(s) are face to face *and* the course is enhanced through technologies like e-mail, online collaboration, discussion boards, and online delivery of supplemental course content; or online—all meetings and interactions are held in an online environment where the students and teacher(s) are in different physical locations.

Changing educational places, like making the decision to use a content management system (CMS), raises specific questions regarding instructors and educational places: How do instructors know if they can be comfortable in these new places? How does the instructor's role change when she is in a different educational place? How do instructors prepare themselves for the difference of place? And how do we manage multiple, the physical and virtual in particular, educational places? The existing literature for technical communicators offers little in the way of help to answer spatial questions related to instructor preparedness in hybrid courses. I focus on the hybrid course because it seems most technical and professional writing programs offer courses that fit the definition of a hybrid course. In addition, most instructors will offer a hybrid course before a fully online course. The hybrid course would then be the first step in changing *educational places,* and this move is usually facilitated through a content management system (CMS), making explicit the connection between changing educational places and CMS technologies. "These tools [course management systems] were initially developed for use in distance education pedagogies, their use in on-campus classroom settings to complement traditional courses is now considered a viable and often preferred option" (Harrington, Gordon, & Schibik, 2004, para 2). If, as Kenneth Green (2003) believes, the true technology challenges facing higher education are not in specific technologies or products, but instead, about people, policy, and programs, then it is time to bring the people aspect to the foreground. Technical communication instructors, in particular, teach practical writing behaviors and skills that the students will use frequently in the workplace with clients and colleagues. Therefore, in a hybrid course, an instructor not only interacts with students, but also models behaviors and skills that the students will use with their future colleagues and clients—often in similarly hybrid settings. The proliferation of technologies and the pressures, like increased enrollments, competition from corporate universities, student demands for more flexibility, and industry practices that necessitate understanding multiple communication platforms, from inside and outside the academy to, at the very least, supplement courses online warrants an emphasis on preparation strategies for instructors.

Therefore, instead of focusing on more common topics—specific course design using technologies, tips and techniques, or reporting on successes or lessons learned—I focus on theoretical constructions of building new educational places for teaching technical communication and what that means for the technical communication instructor. By using "*place* as an analytical concept that involves the process of shaping meaning and practice in a material sense" (Cresswell, 2004, p. 81, emphasis added), I introduce a theory for understanding the role of place in educational settings. Topographies of educational place(s) merge constructions of place with Edward Relph's (1976) "outsideness and insideness" and his (1984) research method of "seeing, thinking, and describing" to enable technical communication instructors to make informed decisions about the impacts of expanding educational places.

This theory answers a practical need for ongoing discussions of educator preparation that Hewett and Ehmann (2004) illuminated with their principles for preparing educators to teach writing online and works in tandem with Selber's (2004) metadiscourse heuristics that help educators critically assess the use of technologies in their classrooms. Even though this theory is potentially useful for educators in any discipline, I target technical communication educators specifically throughout my discussion. First, I explain the importance of geography and place to technical communication, then I construct the theoretical topography of educational place. This theory considers how places are constructed and how instructors determine whether they are "inside" or "outside" the constructed place. The final section models this theory by examining a typical CMS, since they are the dominant way technical communication instructors implement and deliver hybrid courses. In addition, a CMS becomes the tool that allows technical communication instructors to change educational places. A CMS is unique in the sense that no other technological tool currently in widespread use alters the educational place like it or allows instructors the ability to control and manage the spatial configurations of their classrooms. Understanding the construction and influence of place and the impact technology has on these constructions is a critical step in developing powerful and useful instructional settings, because it helps instructors understand the pedagogical implications of using a CMS to alter the spatial configurations of their classrooms.

GEOGRAPHY, PLACE, AND
TECHNICAL COMMUNICATION

A CMS not only manages course content, it manages the spatial configurations of the course. So when an instructor asks, for example, students to respond to a discussion thread online, they are asking students to enter into an extended educational space separate from their physical classroom. How to understand if the instructor is ready for such a move is a distinctly geographic question. Geography derives from the Greek words meaning *earth* and *to describe* or *to write*. Geography, then, is the description of Earth's surface and the written expression about Earth. Historically, geography has three branches: (1) physical, which examines the physical aspects of the world around us; (2) human, which studies the impacts of people on the physical world; and (3) regional, which analyzes the political and economic issues associated with the other two branches. All three branches interrelate to provide a comprehensive picture of the world premised on concepts of space and place. Geography's emphasis on spatial relations of the physical environment and human interaction with that environment coincides and connects to teaching, especially teaching technical communication, in interesting ways. David Gillette (1999) reminded instructors that one "reason we move classes to a virtual environment is to escape the physical constraints of the classroom" (p. 21), which makes geography ideally suited to discussions of hybrid courses in technical communication. Since hybrid courses extend the boundaries of traditional classroom spaces, geography, specifically the concept of place, provides an exceptionally useful choice for analytic examination.

But why all this talk about place? How does place matter to technical communication? To begin, technical communication, as Tony Scott (2006) has reminded us, is unique in that it is an academic field and a profession in the nonacademic working world making it an "in here" and "out there" field. The *where* of technical communication is as important as the *how*. Material constructions of writing and communication are intimately and directly tied to the places that create them. For instructors of technical communication, notions of place matter a great deal as they teach students about the nuances that different work sites bring to bear on the writing experience. Documentation of two similar applications produced by two different companies will look remarkably different. For example, both company A and B use the same piece of specialized hospital equipment. Company A's documentation emphasizes how to use the equipment with patients because they offer direct care, while company B's documentation emphasizes the use of the equipment itself because they focus on training technicians. Technical communication, as a nonacademic field, has always been marked by the sites and locations—the places—where writing happens. Place offers technical communicators another way of understanding the world in which we work as well as understanding how we can contribute to knowledge making within different sites, regions, and locations.

What place means for the technical communication classroom is that fundamentally the classroom changes its *spatial* configuration when it is altered from a traditional course to a hybrid course. The technologies used to implement hybrid courses expand the classroom beyond the material, physical construction of a room. This change in spatial configuration means that teachers have to adapt to a new learning environment. In effect, they create a new place to learn. No longer is the classroom inhabited simultaneously by the students and instructors, nor is it a shared space like an online chat room. The education place is new in the sense that it has different characteristics than before—like anytime access, extended asynchronous discussion forums, and links to multiple sites. This emphasis on place allows teachers to understand and theorize about the material contexts of technical communication instruction and practice.

Geography's attention to place provides a way to systematically reflect on one's expectations and readiness to teach a hybrid course. Carl Sauer (1889-1975) was instrumental in changing the face of geography. In 1925, Sauer wrote *The Morphology of Landscape,* which initiated the discipline's movement toward including human interventions in transforming the surface of Earth and started cultural geography, which "is a sub-field of human geography that focuses on the impact of human culture, both material and non-material, upon the natural environment and the human organization of space" (Cosgrove, 1994, p. 111). After a decline in practical application, cultural geography experienced a renewed interest in the early 1990s. The new cultural geography movement began with different theoretical assumptions grounded in conflicts, differences, and inequality. How these cultural attributes are distributed spatially and how they relate to the spatial distribution of wealth, power, and justice ground the new cultural geography movement.

Cultural geography has provided valuable insights into better management and design of built environments, which are the man-made material constructions (like buildings, roads, and parks) that surround us. For example, the work of Doreen Massey (1994) has emphasized how space and place connect in profound and intricate ways to concepts of gender, while Don Mitchell (2003) highlighted the politics and power structures found in and produced by space. Mitchell claimed that all cultural clashes are territorial and "literally take place" (p. 5) on the streets during a protest rally, on editorial pages, and in the chambers of city hall as decisions about public spaces are discussed. As these two examples show, cultural geographers have a stake in built environments, in places, and technical communication instructors can use the same methodologies to understand differences in educational places and the impact on how it can change their attitudes about teaching and their approaches to teaching.

The critical emergence of place in the geographic tradition began in the late 1970s. Geographers who labeled themselves humanist geographers published a series of landmark works (Buttimer & Seamon, 1980; Ley & Samuels, 1978; Relph, 1976; Tuan, 1977) that brought the study of place to the forefront of academic exploration. "After decades of devaluation in orthodox social science—and within human geography itself—place has reemerged with an intellectual vigor that few would have predicted" (Adams, Hoelscher, & Till, 2001, p. xviii). This renewed interest in place enables critical discussion of hybrid courses in technical communication, because extending our classroom places into virtual realms means that teachers are literally redefining the educational places.

Scholarship in technical communication, rhetoric, and composition draws heavily on geographic metaphor for explanation. Scholars have built strong traditions in a variety of places—*contact zone, frontier, city, town,* and *borderland.* Additionally, these metaphoric places provide educators and students the opportunity to build *architecture* and *maps* and work in and from *margins, sites, paths,* and *locations.* The georhetorical tradition has continued from early work in composition (Shaughnessy, 1977) to an increasing scholarly interest in geography and space/place as it relates to writing (Bolter, 2001; Dobrin & Weisser, 2002; Ede, 2004; Johnson-Eilola, 2005; Mauk, 2003; McComiskey & Ryan, 2003; Nagelhout & Rutz, 2004; Payne 2005; WIDE, 2005). What has not been fully developed in this literature, however, is a sustained emphasis on material places and the effect of those places on writing.

Recently, scholars have begun to take up the issue of material spaces in a critical and useful fashion. In her *Geographies of Writing*, Nedra Reynolds (2004) uses postmodern geographic theories to introduce a robust interpretation of spatial metaphors and to connect cultural geography and composition as she argues for "geographic rhetorics," which study writing and "inquire into the relationships between writers, writing and all places, spaces, sites, and locations" (p. 4). Reynolds's walking tour with geography students from Leeds provides a good example of differences in place and the impact material places have on students. The best example of the consideration of material spaces, especially for technical communicators, is from Rebecca Rickly and Locke Carter (2005).

Rickly and Carter incorporated spatial concerns into their discussions of online instruction by cautioning online educators to identify and "mind the gaps." They noted that they became "mindful of space first and foremost" because it is the most obvious gap between traditional face-to-face classrooms and online learning (p. 124). Rickly and Carter's astute discussion of physical, virtual, and cognitive space shows the complexity of spaces incorporated into any—traditional, hybrid, or online—classroom environment. In a hybrid course, the spaces and places shift throughout the length of the course, which makes the need for instructors to be "mindful of space first and foremost" even more pressing. This emphasis on spatial dynamics and the acknowledgment of gaps as important educational tools helps in situating the rest of my discussion, since it implicitly acknowledges the importance of a material geography of place.

So what does place mean? Place is physical, intellectual, and emotional. Place is physical in the sense that one can identify and name places based on physical features of that place. Place is temporal because they can be conceived in the mind without physical attachment, and place is emotional because people give places their characteristics. Place is also an obvious, complicated, and contested term. Place is obvious in the sense that at any given moment people know *where* they are, where they come from, and in many ways where they are going; place is complicated because the physical area is embedded with cultures, identities, politics, and economics, which brings a variety of complex interactions into how to define the term; place is contested because of its physical locations and its complicated narrative woven together with identities, politics, cultures, economics, and power. Or as in *Space and Place*, Yi-Fu Tuan (1977) argued, "a place achieves a concrete reality when our *experience* of it is total" (p. 18, emphasis added). Tuan's totality of experience is particular to each person, but generally, for a place to be totally experienced, one must be immersed into the place and form some sort of affective bond with it. Total experience is a fluid construction. For example, most people can easily define home as place because they have experienced it totally. Home brings forth memories; home is a material location; home is a figurative ideal that marks a beginning or ending. Home is totally experienced because it can be lived and remembered. Historian Philip Deloria (2006) characterized place this way: "A place becomes a place only with the passage of time, and with human *experience*" (p. 26, emphasis added). Extending Tuan and Deloria's "definitions," Relph (1976) characterized places as "fusions of human and natural order and are the significant centers of our immediate *experiences* of the world" (p. 141, emphasis added). The common theme among these "definitions" is that places are constructed and given meaning and value by a person's experience within them, which causes a new set of problems for instructors as they create hybrid educational places.

In his discussion of creating communities in online settings, Terry Anderson (2004) argued that "it may be more challenging than we think to create and sustain these communities and the differences—linked to the lack of placedness and synchronicity . . .—may be more fundamental than the mere absence of body language and social presence" (p. 40). The spatial barrier Anderson describes illustrates the need for a set of principles, a theory, to understand place. To achieve this understanding I want to construct a theory of reflection that provides teachers of technical communication a framework to assess if and when to expand their classrooms into virtual places. As Stephen Daniels (1992) said, "it is the move from 'knowing about' places . . . to 'understanding places' . . . that remains the hallmark of humanist geography" (p. 311), and it is this move to understanding that teachers need to be able to facilitate the change of educational place. It is imperative that teachers of technical communication know the topographies of educational places so they can be better equipped to offer hybrid courses.

TOPOGRAPHY OF EDUCATIONAL PLACES

The topography of a place is a precise description of it or an analysis showing the relations among its components. The topography of educational places does both. It describes how places are made, and then it analyzes the components of educational places based on the concept of belonging inside or outside the place. Combining both definitions of topography gives technical communication teachers a more complex schema to apply to their own particular explorations into new educational places.

Current scholarship in technical communication, rhetoric, and composition overlooks questions about teacher willingness and preparation. The notable exception to this oversight is Beth Hewett and Christa Ehmann's (2004) book on teacher preparedness, but their emphasis is on one-on-one tutoring of writing. Most scholarship starts with the assumption that teachers have already made the decision to teach a hybrid course. While Kelli Cargile Cook and Keith Grant-Davie's (2005) edited volume is extremely useful because of the depth and breadth of exploring issues in online education from a technical communication perspective, no chapter deals explicitly with helping teachers answer these questions: Should I teach a hybrid course? Am I prepared to teach a hybrid course? Cook and Grant-Davie are not alone in assuming teachers who are investigating teaching a hybrid course have already decided to do so. Guest editors, Blakelock and Smith (2006), made clear that the special issue of *Computers and Composition* they edited was for teachers already teaching online because they wanted the issue to "address the shift in the interests of DL [distance learning] teachers from the basic principle of how to teach online to research regarding effective online pedagogies and methodologies" (p. 1). Directly addressing the lack of scholarship on teacher preparedness, Pamela Takayoshi and Brian Huot (2002) explained that current composition scholarship "does not address very well the needs of instructors new to a computer teaching environment" (p. 2). Further, as Catherine Schifter (2004) pointed out, "what is missing from this [distance education] literature is a significant discussion of the faculty, full- or part-time, who teach the courses and why some faculty members participate while others do not" (p. 23). One possible answer to the unwillingness of some faculty members to make a shift to hybrid courses is in the concept of place making.

Place Making

Since one's teaching practices are constituted by and constitutive of the places in which one teaches, teaching a hybrid course extends and complicates one's present practices, which makes it important to understand how places are created. Yi-Fu Tuan (1991) wrote, "A central task for geographers is to understand the making and maintenance of place" (p. 684), and one can also say that a central task for educators is to understand the making and maintenance of educational places. Place making is a complex process that has been the source of debate for many years in geography scholarship, but as the discussion above suggests, specific definitions of place—although elusive—share a common characteristic in *experience*. But how does one gain experience of a place? One way is through dwelling.

Martin Heidegger's (1971) essay, "Building, Dwelling, Thinking," proves helpful in understanding how one creates or builds a new educational place and how one experiences that place. One builds something new by noticing differences, and as Hartshorne pointed out in the opening epigraph, the curiosity about the differences can lead instructors to building courses in new educational places. Heidegger exemplifies the idea of place making in his essay. His question, "in what way does building belong to dwelling?" helps the instructor consider moving to hybrid courses because of its emphasis on creating or building new educational places and experiencing—dwelling—in those places. Heidegger limits his discussion to things constructed and uses the construction of a bridge as an example. Building the bridge allows the stream to maintain its course and allows people to cross from one side to the other. The building of the bridge allows the dwelling, but it was the initial desire for dwelling, for a specific location on the other side, that prompted the bridge being built; "Thus the bridge does not first come to a location to stand in it; rather, a location comes into existence only by virtue of the bridge" (1971, p. 150). The new location—the other side of the stream—came into existence because of the building of the bridge.

Heidegger insists that one cannot dwell until one has built a location. In this sense, location and place are interchangeable because both Heidegger's location and place are identifiable areas. What this means for the instructor is if they are willing to dwell in a new place then that place can be built. Heidegger, however, posts a caution against describing building as a means to an end, dwelling. This conception of dwelling and building is limiting. Instead, Heidegger wrote, "only if we are capable of dwelling, only then can we build" (p. 160). Teachers have already made the commitment to dwell in the most basic of Heideggerian ideals. Teachers already dwell in an educational place, the traditional classroom. Because they are capable of dwelling, they are able to build a new dwelling, a hybrid classroom. Teachers can examine traditional courses, an original dwelling, to learn *how* it came to be built. Those lessons can then be applied to new buildings and the subsequent dwelling in those new places. "Building and thinking are, each in its own way, inescapable for dwelling," and it is this process of reflection that gives us the ability to dwell and therefore build.

Building and dwelling enable teachers to gain valuable experience that in turn makes them more attached to their educational places. This increased or new attachment to place through experience is the foundation of place making. A CMS becomes particularly valuable in the process of place making because it facilitates the change in spatial configurations of the classroom. As the tool for expansion, a CMS helps to make educational places "placeless" in the sense that they allow the material constraints of the classroom to be eliminated while simultaneously providing a location for the instructor to dwell. Place making through dwelling is especially important for teachers because it can help alleviate misconceptions and expose new faculty members to hybrid (or online) educational places. In their limited survey, Blakelock and Smith (2006) found a reluctance and stagnation of teachers teaching online, which can be offset by understanding place making as the first step of a teacher's exploration into their willingness and preparedness. Understanding how teachers can help in constructing educational places equips faculty for the move to online courses, technologies of mobility, wireless communication, and whatever the next stage of educational technologies may bring.

Technical communication teachers need to pay particular attention to their identity in this new place. John Brinkerhoff "Brinck" Jackson (1909-1996) explained that place provides people with their identities (1984, p. 152). So if teachers are moving to a different educational place, they need to redefine themselves in light of the change in landscape. This notion of changing or shifting identities is a common refrain in scholarship about online writing instruction. Gillette (1999), Nancy Coppola (2005), and Susan Miller (2001) discussed the changes of the instructor's role and identity while Stuart Blythe (2001) and Wilhelmina C. Savenye, Zane Olina and Mary Niemczyk (2001) called for instructors who develop Web-based courses to "act like designers." Kristen Walker (2005) was surprised at the difference between teaching technical communication face-to-face and online (p. 207), and Patricia Peterson (2001) wants teachers' roles to be part of a larger conceptual map of issues faced in online learning. Although these authors specifically addressed the instructor's role or identity, they did not provide a way for an educator to understand why their old identity with the educational place is not sufficient for the hybrid educational place. Relph (1976) offered a way around this disconnect by asserting "the identity that a person or group has *with* that place, in particular whether they are experiencing it as an insider or as an outsider" (p. 45) is as important as the place itself.

Insideness and Outsideness

As the previous discussion has shown, places come into being through experience. Once a space is experienced, it becomes a built place, which means one can now dwell within it. Building for Heidegger is part of dwelling, so if instructors want to extend their classroom places, they are learning to dwell within them as they go through the decision-making process. This does not mean, however, that they can automatically dwell comfortably within the new educational place they have built. It simply means they are capable of dwelling once they gain more experience in/with the place. This is why Edward Relph's conceptions of insideness and outsideness are so helpful, because they provide a way for instructors to view the educational place they have built—even if only in their own thinking—in terms of their own pedagogies and beliefs.

Relph (1976) discussed attachments to places through what he calls modes of insideness and outsideness. He argued that outsideness and insideness constitute a primary aspect of human life and that through varying combinations and experiences of outsideness and insideness, different places take on different identities for different people. In the technical communication classroom, the instructors' feelings of insideness or outsideness depend on their interpretation, creation, and experience of the new educational places. Relph's modes, as they are adapted to the technical communication instructor's identity within academic places, enable instructors to locate their level of experience—how they identify— with hybrid classrooms. Table 1 is a summary of the Relph's modes of insideness and outsideness.

Although Relph classifies seven different modes of insideness and outsideness, his overall concept of place making is normally reduced to a binary, where one is either on the inside or on the outside; actually, the opposite is true. Dualism is not what Relph is trying to show. He is instead trying to relate a continuum of

Table 1. Modes of Insideness and Outsideness

Insideness	Outsideness
EXISTENTIAL A situation involving a feeling of attachment and belonging. Place is fully experienced, holds full significance, and is characterized by a deep and complete identity and affinity with the location.	**EXISTENTIAL** A situation involving complete uninvolvement and separation. Place is where the person feels separate from or alien and cannot be significant centers of existence.
EMPATHETIC A situation involving deliberate effort of perception in which a person willingly tries to be open to place and understand it more deeply. This kind of experience requires interest, empathy, and heartfelt concern.	**OBJECTIVE** A situation involving a deliberate dispassionate attitude of separation from place. Place is a thing to be studied and considered in terms of their locations and as a distinct object.
BEHAVIORAL A situation in which place is seen as a set of objects, views, or activities. Place is created by deliberate attention to the appearance of place. Place is clearest when it is restricted to a defined area.	**INCIDENTAL** A situation in which place is the background or setting for activities. Place is incidental to activities and is most common since what we are doing is usually overshadowed by where we are doing it.
VICARIOUS A situation of secondhand involvement with place usually through imagination.	

Source: Relph, 1976, pp. 51-55.

insideness/outsideness. Figure 1 represents Relph's modes adapted for use by technical communication teachers.

In Figure 1, Relph's modes have been adapted to a continuum that better represents the concept he was trying to make. In the adaptation of Relph's modes, vicarious insideness was omitted because it did not provide a useful category for the classroom experience, and objective outsideness and empathetic insideness were combined into one category. This combination of the outside and inside modes connects the two sides of the continuum. Relph's original explanations of objective outsideness and empathetic insideness were so close in meaning that to combine them clarifies the concept to one of a continuous

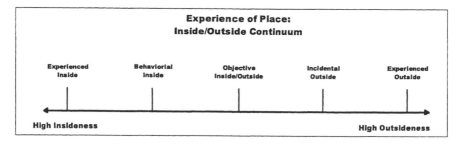

Figure 1. Instructor's experience of place.

exploration and a continuum of meaning rather than rigid binary categories. Teachers can use the continuum to determine their level of insideness or outsideness as it relates to the hybrid classroom. Each end of the scale represents the highest level of experience with the place.

Teachers (and students) can choose how inside or outside they would like to be in this new educational place. One can have a meaningful experience both inside and outside. For example, a new teacher may feel a sense of experienced outsideness on the first day of class but by the end of the semester may feel more like an objective inside/outside. A veteran teacher may feel a sense of incidental outsideness when she teaches a new course because she has not fully experienced the new educational place. As these examples show, inside/outside does not set up boundaries, but allows free movement, which illustrates the flexibility and application of Relph's conceptual structure.

A technical communication teacher can use the continuum as a way to gauge her experience or perceived experience or expectation with teaching a hybrid course. If a teacher has never attempted teaching a hybrid course, she can reflect on her own feelings of doing so by analyzing experience of place in relation to aspects of teaching a hybrid course. For example, a primary component of a hybrid technical communication course would be the use of online discussions. The teacher would need to assess her experience with discussion forums in general and any experiences that may be helpful or harmful to the implementation of online discussions. These experiences would be then categorized as feelings of insideness or outsideness. If she has had limited personal experience with discussion forums herself, she may feel a sense of incidental outsideness because she does not feel totally proficient in managing discussion forums. Or she may feel an objective inside/outside because she is aware of how they work, and she feels she can handle this task accordingly.

Most teachers of technical communication will be able to locate themselves, with regard to specific tasks, tools, assessments, or administrative functions, on the inside/outside continuum that Relph describes. The teacher needs to remember that if she locates herself on the outside of the continuum it may not be detrimental to classroom pedagogy. Sometimes an outside perspective can bring an additional richness to the classroom. In this case, instructors need to understand that they are entering a new place as an outsider who is willing to dwell. For example, travelers are initially incidental outsiders, but by the time they return home from their trip, they could be considered behavioral insiders. Relph's modes of insideness and outsideness provide a vocabulary for teachers to determine their own attitudes, biases, perceptions, and feelings toward hybrid educational places. This is an important first step in instructor preparedness, especially for hybrid teaching environments.

Doreen Massey and Pat Jess indicated that "our views of place are products of the society in which we live and to that extent the future of those views, even if constrained by circumstances, is in our hands" (1995, p. 50), allowing the instructor to move from the idea of experience of place—insideness and outsideness—to one of systematic methodology of place. To fully appreciate and determine one's level of experience with a place, one needs to see the place, think about the place, and then describe the place.

Seeing, Thinking, Describing

Relph's contribution to geographic methodology has often been overlooked because seeing, thinking, and describing seems so elementary and obvious. However, teachers often displace, deconstruct, and deflect their own feelings by giving in to pressures from administrators, students, or colleagues or by giving in to perceived needs of the workplace. "In this age of scientific explanation and technology, mere description based on personal efforts of seeing and thinking does strike people as laughably futile" (Relph, 1984, p. 222), but personal efforts of technical communication teachers drive courses and programs that directly affect the learning outcomes of students. Technical communication scholarship needs more emphasis on the personal efforts of teachers, especially as they decide whether to move their classrooms into different spaces; and one way of accomplishing this is by using Relph's methodology, whose seeing, thinking, and describing, are "analytic categories . . . distinguished by reflection" (Relph, 1984, p. 212). The reflective process is key for technical communication teachers. Most teachers take the time to reflect on their teaching practices. When teachers consider shifting or altering the classroom place, reflection takes on greater urgency.

Seeing is direct observation. It is meant to be self-centered and a reflection of what the teacher sees. In this sense, it can be joined with the experienced insider and behaviorial insider modes. In thinking, one must not impose fixed methods or strategies but should allow things to "manifest in their own being" (p. 217) while also considering inherent "biases, recollections, and intentions which condition our thinking" (p. 218). Thinking should be "held in tension" (p. 217) with seeing, so thinking is best aligned to the incidental outsider and the experienced outsider modes. Describing is the final step, where the information one gathered in the seeing and thinking phases are ordered into a tangible and accurate description of a place. In this sense, description contains characteristics of objectivity and is then aligned with the objective insider/outsider mode (see Figure 2).

The move to align seeing, thinking, and describing with stages on the continuum of experiences of place is an important and fundamental one. It forces teachers toward a methodological and analytical framework so they can experience all the parts of the inside/outside continuum. In doing so, teachers are able to understand how they dwell within new educational places.

This theory moves toward a robust analytical tool that helps to offset the rapid deployment of technologies into our pedagogies. Geography and place maintains its significance because as much as hybrid (and online) courses extol the virtues of anytime and anywhere, annihilating the mediating properties of time and space, technical communication classrooms, whether traditional, hybrid, or online, are still bound by place; they are still educational places. Relph (2001) tries to reconcile his methodologies and ideas in time of "confused geographies" where the "world continuously outruns theories and descriptions of it, and in the twentieth and twenty-first centuries, the pace of social and technological change has created a sort of theoretical vacuum that is now filling with simple concepts that are not always well connected with the everyday world" (p. 159). The theory of topography of educational places described here is an attempt to fill the vacuum and move away from simple concepts. It also moves toward Relph's idea of "critical description" which is a "revision and qualification" (p. 164) of his original seeing, thinking, and describing. His critical description calls for a grounding in everyday places, which is a crucial aspect of the theory introduced here. The technical communication classroom is an everyday place experienced by teachers. Teachers can approach decisions about what to teach, how to teach, and *where* to teach by using the topography of educational place to question what

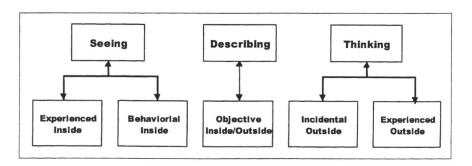

Figure 2. Relph's methodology aligned to the Instructor's experience of place.

they see, balance their thinking with student concerns as well as ethical and social concerns, and describe *critically* how they see *their* classroom in the age of technology. When teachers do this, they create powerful instructional settings and mimic what students should be doing when they enter the work*place*.

AN ASSIGNMENT FOR TEACHERS

In proposing the topography of educational place, I realize the abstractness of it, especially in light of weaving together different disciplinary strands. So to make the connection from theory to practice, I will model this theory by examining a typical course management system (CMS), since these systems dominate the delivery and implementation of technical communication hybrid courses. CMS as developed for higher education are designed to enable teachers, with little or no technology expertise, to design, create, deliver, and assess courses delivered totally or partially online.

Kate Kiefer (2006) pointed out that the "teacher can shape the emergent dynamic of a class by the choices about the ways a course is set up" (p. 135). Two important points are embedded in Kiefer's comment: the importance of instructor willingness and preparedness and the specific impact technological decisions have on the class. Technical communication classrooms are differentiated from other types of writing classrooms because of their aims. Technical communi-cation courses focus on bridging the theoretical/practical divide and providing students with a foundation of rhetorical skills they can bring to the workplace. When the CMS is added to the classroom, it expands the places and spaces of the classroom. Topography of educational places, as Graham (1998) suggested, helps to maintain conceptual links between new technologies and place. This linkage enables a fuller understanding of the interrelationships between them (p. 181). Therefore, the imperative facing instructors lies in making good decisions about the way hybrid courses are set up, including choosing which parts of a CMS to use.

CMS seem to be dual edged swords: offering teachers the hope of saving time and effectively "managing content" while restricting pedagogical approaches by being too normalizing and too uniform. Unlike decisions in the workplace, the major stakeholders, teachers, are usually not consulted when the CMS decision is made. The economic push and the technological pull found at many colleges and universities are encouraging teachers to increasingly consider using all or parts of course management systems. In their limited survey to assess the use of open-source tools, Reilly and Williams (2006) found teachers normally "make do" with the universitywide system because of ease of use, support, and student expectations (pp. 80-81). Harrington and colleagues (2004) and Blakelock and Smith (2006) also found a great reliance on commercial CMS software. What these studies show is that while CMS is an integral and visible part of higher education, it still falls to teachers to implement technologies into the larger pedagogical aims of their courses. It still falls to the teacher to determine whether using a physical blackboard or the commercial Blackboard will best facilitate the learner's construction of knowledge.

CMS as Place

An important reminder for those involved in teaching and learning is that "place serves as a multiple reality and many different kinds of projects might find their realization in a particular site" (Ley, 2001, p. 6). The projects of instructors, students, and administrators are all somewhat different in relation to CMS. Oddly, CMS has become somewhat synonymous with the phrase "course-in-a-box" software. A box, as a closed, fixed unit, removes any hint of the dynamic and fluid capabilities the Web has to offer. The CMS not only extends the classroom to a different place, it simultaneously creates a fixed location where students must enter. This dual role of expansion and contraction, mobile and fixed, highlights the important need of instructors to examine the CMS as a topography of educational place (see Figure 3).

Principle 1: Place Making

As I have outlined above, the first principle of the theory of experienced place is to understand how place is made and experienced. Before instructors can begin the specific tasks of determining the experience of place, they need to understand how their institutional place is created and why they are considering teaching a hybrid course. The following questions can act as a guide. These questions are by no means all the questions one can ask, and the questions are largely dependent on the teachers' experience and their location.

- Have you considered all the *places* affecting your educational place(s)? Personal, educational, technological?
- Do you know why you are considering teaching a hybrid course?
- How does the place operate?
- Are you ready to shift existing relationships among faculty/institution, faculty/student(s), faculty/pedagogy, and faculty/beliefs?
- Are there institutionwide (e.g., university, college, department, or corporation) initiatives for online learning?
- Can you agree with the institutional reasons for wanting to use CMS in hybrid courses?
- Is the traditional place functioning well?
- Are you willing to relinquish part of your classroom structure to the CMS's template-driven design controls?
- Has your institution offered you support and encouragement in the transition to hybrid instruction?
- Has your institution offered training and development?

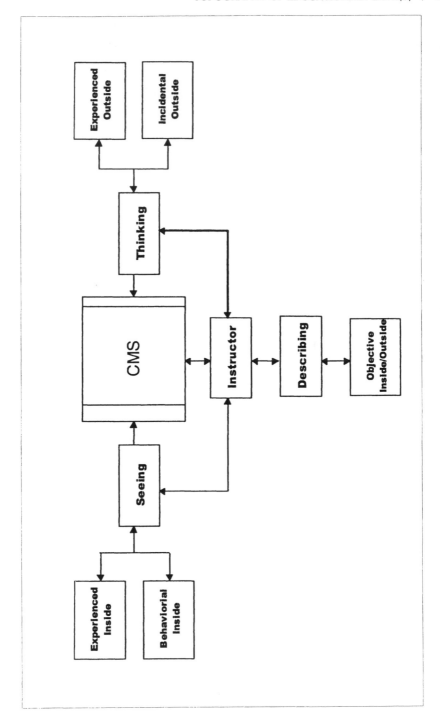

Figure 3. CMS as topography of educational place.

- Is hybrid teaching valued, expected, devalued?
- Are you ready to extend your teaching body, both in the physical and the knowledge-base sense, into another space?
- Are you ready to deal with the potential feeling of being disconnected from your students?

Principle 2: Assess Modes of Inside/Outside

- What are your present roles as teacher? Are your ready to change them?
- What tools are available to you?
- How can you change your content for this place?
- What is available to you for assessment?
- How can you manage administrative functions?
- What is important for you in a hybrid course?
- How can CMS help? How can CMS hurt?
- What do writing classrooms in particular have to gain from CMS?
- How do planning, implementation, and management issues change for instructors when using a Web-based course-management system?
- What are the time costs?
- How should the state of the landscape be described in context, space, and time?
- How does the place operate?
- What are the functional and structural relationships among its elements?
- How might the educational place be altered: by what actions, where, and when?
- What predictable differences might the changes cause?
- Should the place be changed? Can materials be adapted to a hybrid course?
- How should recent developments and innovations in online education cause us to reexamine our roles and responsibilities as educators in technical communication?

Table 2 provides a matrix for the instructor to see how they can use the experience continuum to assess their readiness to teach online. The matrix is useful in regards to specific tools as well as broader, more conceptual questions. The answers in the last area—ready and willing—are the starting point for the critical description. The teacher needs to explain why she has answered yes, no, or maybe to get a complete picture of her readiness.

Principle 3: Describe Your Educational Place(s)

Armed with your understanding of how your institutional place is made and your seeing and thinking assessment, your next step is to describe your educational place. The primary objective of this principle is to get a complete,

Table 2. Example of Instructor Preparation to Determine Willingness to Teach a Hybrid Course. Example Contains Course Tools Options Found in a Common CMS

Tools	Experience of place					Ready/Willing		
	Experience inside	Behavioral inside	Objective inside/outside	Incidental outside	Experience outside	Yes	No	Maybe
Announcements								
Send e-mail								
Discussion – add forum – decide settings – control – rules								
Collaboration – lecture hall – office hours – groups								
Digital dropbox								
Team site – use it? – edit/no – public – dates available								
Tasks								

critical description of the existing educational place *and* the hybrid educational place *and* the instructors' thoughts and feelings about both. This principle involves the greatest time and energy investment because, as Relph acknowledged (2001), "it is easy to propose a critical description. It is less easy to accomplish it" (p. 165). A word of caution at this point: one must be aware of histories and biases within the larger places of the university and department and within the instructor themselves. Following is a set of questions that may help guide the description process and work in tandem with the specific questions the instructor has already answered.

- How do technical communication teachers systematically determine whether we should be using a CMS in our classrooms?
- How do we as technical communication teachers understand and talk about the differences the CMS makes on our classrooms?
- In what ways do we see the CMS as empowering or disempowering our roles as teachers?
- How does the CMS help or hinder our abilities to be creative and innovative in our pedagogies?
- How does the use of the CMS situate teachers in relation to university, college, and departmental goals?
- How do these technologies situate our pedagogies against and in relation to what our students will need in the workplace?

Once the description is done, one may find that the feeling of outsideness is the most profound. In cases such as these, the instructor needs to remember that sometimes being a complete outsider provides the best views about what is going on inside. Even if an instructor feels total outsideness, it does not mean she should not teach a hybrid course; it simply means she should be self-aware of her concerns.

Principle 4: Build Your Educational Place

Deloria (2006) made clear that the forces of globalization redefine existing places as new spaces ready to be named, mapped, and claimed. The process of place making can be depicted as a practiced colonialization that is all about power and domination (p. 29), which is a sentiment echoed by Darin Payne (2005) in his discussions of Blackboard in the composition classroom. Content management systems with their rigid template structures can be seen as a way to dominate both teachers and students. Reilly and Williams (2006) found that "personal labor practices and institutional business decisions have a much greater influence over which tools are chosen than do ideology or pedagogy" (p. 68), which can be seen as disheartening. But Tony Scott (2006) encourages teachers to continue to be "dedicated both to helping students get along in the world as they find it *and* recognizing theoretical/analytical perspectives that are critical of the terms of work and the broad grim effects of late capitalism" (p. 239). A first step in this pedagogical process is for teachers to understand the topography of educational place and their feelings toward it; because even if instructors have to make capitalist-type decisions and implement the institutional CMS, the time saved should enable the teacher to create open educational places where critical discussions can emerge, even discussions about technologies that create the educational place.

FROM PLACE TO PLACE

Technical communicator instructors need to take educational place(s) very seriously, because technical communication as a practice is decidedly rooted to location. As Hartshorne suggested in the opening epigraph, geography helps to understand the differences from place to place. Using the topography of place the technical communication teacher can understand how the shifting of place affects the teachers' (and students') basic concept of classrooms and educational places. Teachers must first understand how places are created, how they experience those places through dwelling and being on the inside or outside, and finally how they can use the methodology of seeing, thinking, and describing to assess their readiness and willingness to teach a hybrid course. The CMS offers a practical model of the theory in use.

Instructors often devote so much time and energy to focusing on the students' "sense of place" within classrooms that they forget to attend to their own sense of place. When technologies change the classroom space, especially technologies like a CMS that control the spatial configurations of the classroom in such material ways, the students are not the only ones affected by that change. Technical communication instructors need to be aware that they too can feel displaced.

As institutions continue the push to educate more students with limited staff and resources, CMS and prepackaged course content will become permanent parts of universities and classrooms. Instructors need to be aware that even if the administration advocates use of a CMS, instructors can better prepare themselves for this change and teaching in this educational place by using the techniques outlined here. Even though she may not be completely comfortable in the hybrid or online space, the instructor has a better chance of negotiating and dwelling in this space when she understands how places are made and how she can feel on the inside or outside of those places. When change occurs, the topography of educational place becomes a tool for an instructor's critical and reflective assessment.

Place as a construct is constantly being reinvented, readjusted, and reinterpreted. Place as constructed in a hybrid technical communication course mimics the exigencies of the global business environment where "anytime, anywhere," and "24/7" are redefining place, but teachers do not need to be caught off guard. The assignment—or practical application of the topography of place—described here is a necessary part of the reflective process advocated by Cook and Grant-Davie (2005, p. 12). The emphasis on instructors to include their perceptions, thoughts, fears, and joys, fills a void in present scholarship and places the reflective gaze on those who drive courses, programs, and student learning. This type of critical self-reflection will also enable our students to approach decisions on the job with the same systematic awareness, which leads to better decisions. The act of critical descriptions matches Tony Scott's (2006) call to help our students "recognize, articulate, and change how they are situated as citizens/workers/writers by new technologies and coinciding labor trends" (p. 230), and the topography of place is the first step in answering the call of Reilly and Williams (2006, p. 89) to "interrogate the pedagogical efficacy" of distance learning applications.

As I have argued elsewhere (Meloncon, 2007), teacher willingness and preparedness is a key factor in any online education initiatives, and the topography of educational place can help teachers in their preparation. Teacher willingness is as necessary as technological and institutional realities, and this makes teachers' abilities to determine their own readiness and willingness to shift or extend educational places—to use a CMS and how much to use a CMS—especially important. The challenge for educators and administrators is whether or not and when "faculty attention can shift from preoccupation with adaptation of existing course structures and the mastery of difficult and newly evolving technology to a thoughtful experimentation with customizable pedagogies" (Katz, 2003, p. 58). Once technical communication teachers—both new and experienced—understand topographies of educational places, customizable pedagogies will follow that extend and modify the classroom beyond the physical, material construction of four walls.

What I hope I have done is to provide a reading of a particular place—the hybrid technical communication classroom—from a particular viewpoint, the instructor's. This particularized reading will generate an interpretation where the instructor becomes and is part of the interpretive circle. Most importantly, however, this reading is not totalizing, since place making is in a constant state of evolution, change—processes. Moreover, by seeing, thinking, and describing the classroom space through modes of insideness and outsideness, one senses the impact of extending learning places, particularly on the instructor's view of the classroom space. Technical communication teachers need to be proactive in understanding the ramifications of different educational places so they can help their students find their place too.

REFERENCES

Adams, P., Hoelscher, S., & Till, K. (2001). Place in context: Rethinking humanist geographies. In P. Adams, S. Hoelscher, & K. Till (Eds.), *Textures of place: Exploring humanist geographies* (pp. xiii-xxxiii). Minneapolis, MN: University of Minnesota Press.

Anderson, T. (2004). Teaching in an online context. In T. Anderson & F. Elloumi (Eds.), *Theory and practice of online learning* (pp. 271-295). Athabasca, Canada: Athabasca University Creative Commons Online Book.

Blakelock, J., & Smith, T. (2006). Distance learning: From multiple snapshots, a composite portrait. *Computers and Composition, 23,* 139-161.

Blythe, S. (2001). Designing online courses: user-centered practices. *Computers and Composition, 18,* 329-346.

Bolter, J. (2001). *Writing space: Computer, hypertext, and the remediation of print* (2nd ed.). Mahwah, NJ: Erlbaum.

Buttimer, A., & Seamon, D. (1980). *The human experience of space and place.* New York: St. Martin's Press.

Cook, K. C., & Grant-Davie, K. (Eds.). (2005). *Online education: Global questions, local answers.* Amityville, NY: Baywood.

Coppola, N. (2005). Changing roles for online teachers of technical communication. In K. C. Cook & K. Grant-Davie (Eds.), *Online education: Global questions, local answers* (pp. 89-100). Amityville, NY: Baywood.

Cosgrove, D. (1994). Cultural geography. In R. J. Johnston, D. Gregory, & D. M. Smith (Eds.), *The dictionary of human geography* (3rd. ed., p. 111). Oxford, UK: Basil Blackwell.

Cresswell, T. (2004). *Place a short introduction.* Malden, MA: Blackwell Publishing.

Daniels, S. (1992). Place and the geographical imagination. *Geography, 77,* 310-322.

Deloria, P. (2006). Places like houses, banks, and continents: An appreciative reply to the presidential address. *American Quarterly, 58,* 23-29.

Dobrin, S., & Weisser, C. (2002). *Natural discourse: Toward ecocomposition.* New York: SUNY.

Ede, L. (2004) *Situating composition: Composition studies and the politics of location.* Carbondale, IL: Southern Illinois University Press

Gillette, D. (1999). Pedagogy, architecture, and the virtual classroom. *Technical Communication Quarterly, 8,* 21-36.

Graham, S. (1998). The end of geography or the explosion of place? Conceptualizing space, place, and information technology. *Progress in Human Geography, 22*(2), 165-185.

Green, K. C. (2003). The new computing revisited. *EDUCAUSE Review,* January/February, 33-43. Retrieved March 15, 2006, from http://educause.edu/ir/library/pdf/ERM0312.pdf

Harrington, C. F., Gordon, S. A., & Schibik, T. J. (2004). Course management system utilization and implications for practice: A national survey of department chairpersons. *Online Journal of Distance Learning Administration, 7*(4). Retrieved March 15, 2006, from http://www.westga.edu/%7Edistance/ojdla/winter74/harrington74.htm

Hartshorne, R. (1939). *The nature of geography: A critical survey of current thought in light of the past.* Lancaster, PA: Association of American Geographers.

Heidegger, M. (1971). Building dwelling thinking. In M. Heidegger (Ed.), *Poetry, language, thought* (pp. 145-161). New York: Harper & Row.

Hewett, B. L., & Ehmann, C. (2004). *Preparing educators for online writing instruction principles and processes.* Urbana, IL: NCTE

Jackson, J. B. (1984). *Discovering the vernacular landscape.* New Haven, CT: Yale University Press.

Johnson-Eilola, J. (2005). *Datacloud: Toward a new theory of online work.* Cresskill, NJ: Hampton Press.

Katz, R. N. (2003). Balancing technology and tradition: The example of course management systems. *EDUCAUSE Review,* July/August, 48-59. Retrieved March 15, 2006, from http://educause.edu/ir/library/pdf/ERM0343.pdf

Kiefer, K. (2006). Complexity, class dynamics, and distance learning. *Computers and Composition, 23,* 125-138.

Ley, D. (2001). Introduction: Landscapes of dominance and affection. In P. Adams, S. Hoelscher, & K. Till (Eds.), *Textures of place: Exploring humanist geographies* (pp. 3-7). Minneapolis, MN: University of Minnesota Press.

Ley, D., & Samuels, M. (1978). *Humanistic geography: Prospects and problems.* Chicago, IL: Maaroufa Press.

Massey, D. (1994). *Space, place, and gender.* Minneapolis, MN: University of Minnesota Press.

Massey, D., & Jess, P. (1995) The conceptualisation of place. In D. Massey & P. Jess (Eds.), *A place in the world?: Places, cultures and globalization* (p. 50). Oxford, UK: Oxford University Press.

Mauk, J. (2003). Location, location, location: The "real" (e)states of being, writing, and thinking in composition. *College English, 65,* 369-388.

Meloncon, L. (2007). Exploring electronic landscapes: Technical communication, online learning, and instructor preparedness. *Technical Communication Quarterly, 16,* 31-53.

McComiskey, B., & Ryan, C. (Eds). (2003). *City comp: Identities, space, practices.* Albany: State University of New York Press

Miller, S. (2001). How near and yet how far: Theorizing and distance teaching. *Computers and Composition, 18,* 321-328.

Mitchell, D. (2003). *The right to the city: Social justice and the fight for public space.* New York: Guilford Press.

Nagelhout, E., & Rutz, C. (Eds). (2004). *Classroom spaces and writing instruction.* Cresskill, NJ: Hampton Press.

Payne, D. (2005). English studies in Levittown: Rhetorics of space and technology in course-management software. *College English, 67,* 483-507.

Peterson, P. (2001). The debate about online learning: Key issues for writing teachers. *Computers and Composition, 18,* 359-370.

Reilly, C. A., & Williams, J. J. (2006). The price of free software: Labor, ethics, and context in distance education. *Computers and Composition, 23,* 68-90.

Relph, E. C. (1976). *Place and placelessness.* London, UK: Pion Limited.

Relph, E. C. (1984). Seeing, thinking, and describing landscapes. In T. Saarinen, D. Seamon, & J. Sell (Eds.), *Environmental perception and behavior,* Research Paper 209 (209-23). Chicago, IL: Department of Geography, University of Chicago.

Relph, E. (2001). The critical description of confused geographies. In P. Adams, S. Hoelscher, & K. Till (Eds.), *Textures of place: Exploring humanist geographies* (pp. 150-166). Minneapolis, MN: University of Minnesota Press.

Reynolds, N. (2004). *Geographies of writing: Inhabiting places and encountering difference.* Carbondale, IL.: Southern Illinois University Press.

Rickly, R., & Carter, L. (2005). Mind the gap(s): Modeling space in online education. In K. C. Cook & K. Grant-Davie (Eds.), *Online education: Global questions, local answers* (pp. 123-129). Amityville, NY: Baywood.

Sauer, C. O. (1925). The morphology of landscape. *University of California Publications in Geography, 2*(2), 19-54.

Savenye, W. C., Olina, Z., & Niemczyk, M. (2001). So you are going to be an online writing instructor: Issues in designing, developing, and delivering on online course. *Computers and Composition, 18,* 371-385.

Scott, T. (2006). Writing work, technology and pedagogy in the era of capitalism. *Computers and Composition, 23,* 228-243.

Schifter, C. (2004). Faculty participation in distance education programs: Practices and plans. In D. Monolescu et al. (Eds.), *The distance education evolution: Issues and case studies* (pp. 22-39). Hershey, PA: Information Science Publishing.

Selber, S. (2004). Technological dramas: A metadiscourse heuristic for critical literacy. *Computers and Composition, 21,* 171-195.

Shaughnessy, M. (1977). *Errors and expectations.* New York: Oxford University Press.

Takayoshi, P., & Huot, B. (Eds.). (2002). *Teaching writing with computers: An introduction.* Boston, MA: Houghton Mifflin.

Tuan, Y. (1977). *Space and place: The perspective of experience.* Minneapolis, MN: Minnesota University Press.

Tuan, Y. (1991). Language and the making of place: A narrative-descriptive approach. *Annals of the Association of American Geographers, 81*(4), 684-696.

Walker, K. (2005). Activity theory and the online technical communication course: Assessing quality in undergraduate online instruction. In K. C. Cook & K. Grant-Davie (Eds.), *Online education: Global questions, local answers* (pp. 207-218). Amityville, NY: Baywood.

WIDE Research Center Collective. (2005). (Some) conclusions: Why we must teach digital writing. *Kairos: Rhetoric, Technology, Pedagogy, 10*(1). Retrieved March 15, 2006, from http://english.ttu.edu/kairos/10.1/index.html

PART III

CMS and the Profession
of Technical Communication

CHAPTER SEVEN

Content Management Systems and Technical Communication: Rolling with the Tide

Robin Evans

Technical communicators must be quick learners and rapidly adapt to changes in the markets in which we work. As those markets continue to change to accommodate global expansion, more technical communicators are using Content Management Systems (CMS) and writing using single sourcing to quickly reproduce and streamline documentation. This chapter will describe the relationship between using content management systems and single sourcing in technical communication, and reassure technical writers that the content management system is not a threat to their careers, but an enhancement, when writers and editors create content that is suitable to reuse in print and online formats. Single sourcing, which is writing content to reuse for different media, is quickly becoming the standard method of writing documentation. According to the Society for Technical Communication (STC), single sourcing is defined as "using a single document source to generate multiple outputs from a document or database (STC, 2003). The topic is so influential for technical writers that the editors of *Technical Communication* dedicated an entire issue to the topic. The wave of single sourcing is sweeping over organizations throughout the world as more companies are becoming global. The debate continues as to whether or not single sourcing will benefit an organization and its writers.

MOVE TO CONTENT MANAGEMENT SYSTEMS

Informed technical writers will need to adapt to the sweeping trend and greatly benefit from using Content Management Systems if writers use CMS as a tool to increase productivity and work more efficiently. Content Management Systems can ease the burden of reproducing the same content for different audiences in hard copy documentation, quick references, training manuals, Web resources, and online help. Documentation automation, also called single sourcing, is similar to mass production in a manufacturing environment. For example, Delphi Chassis manufactures suspension parts for several different automobile makers, such a Chevrolet, Daimler-Chrysler, and Ford. However, each shock, strut, or piston has to meet the same specifications, whether the production occurs in Dayton, Ohio, or in Singapore; the quality and expectations for the product are the same throughout the company.

In many large, international organizations, using a content management system has become inevitable due to global competition, niche marketing, smaller budgets, and pressure to produce technical products and documentation faster than ever. Ann Rockley (2001) provides a general overview of single sourcing in her article "The Impact of Single Sourcing and Technology," which discusses how increased importance placed on technological skills has decreased the emphasis on effective communication. According to Rockley, a paradigm shift is occurring in the field of technical communication because of e-commerce technologies, electronic publishing, and single sourcing. Rockley identifies four levels of single sourcing: identical content, multimedia, dynamic customized content, static customized content, and electronic performance support system. Changes in the roles of writers and editors brought about by single sourcing are also discussed, including the need for teamwork, information designers, and information technologists. In her article *Single-Sourcing—The Solution for Duplicated Efforts with Documentation,"* Wendy Yurick (2006) discusses how single sourcing eliminates or greatly reduces the time and money spent re-creating something that already exists she provides realistic scenarios to demonstrate the benefits of implementing single sourcing for a communications department that mass produces documentation. She argues that while the initial investment can be quite steep, the long-term benefits outweigh the start-up financial investment. In smaller documentation departments, however, the small production requirements will not justify the high initial investment for high-end content management systems.

Technical writers who are moving to a CMS environment should consider the CMS as a tool to enhance their rather than one of replacement. Instead of writing the same content repeatedly in documentation with every product release and format, writers using single sourcing become information and content developers; they learn to do more than just reorganize the content, they target the content for specific audiences and uses. In essence, both the organization and the writer benefit because of the increased opportunities to compete in a changing global market. For example, in an online help document, the reader will not need to go through the entire chapter in a help topic when he needs only the most pertinent information to perform a task. A writer using single sourcing will document the most basic elements of how to perform a specific task, include additional details for a set of instructions, add instructional notes for training manuals, or remove any information that does not directly relate to performing the task.

POINTS OF VIEW

From an employer's point of view, intense global competition places pressures on organizations to produce high-quality, adaptable documents rapidly. These organizations often have small groups of writers, or a single writer, which may make single sourcing overwhelming during implementation. According to Melissa Guthrie (2000), "several major companies that hire technical writers are also moving toward single sourcing, such as Nextel and Medtronic. Forces that push companies to move quickly to single sourcing are globalization and translation requirements in the documentation, niche marketing, which is marketing to several distinct markets simultaneously, the convergence of software and documentation of several versions, and shrinking cycle times and budgets." Single sourcing presents some incredible long-range benefits for larger organizations, such as faster, streamlined production of reused information and reduced duplication of effort. If the corporations that employ a large number of technical writers move to single sourcing, the writers must be willing and ready to move with the changes, be informed about single sourcing, and anticipate organizational changes.

From a writer's point of view, single sourcing appears to be a threat to job security. Technical writers may feel threatened by the change into a single source environment because they are currently unfulfilled in their work, and employers and organizations do not adequately prepare their employees for the drastic change from traditional documentation to single sourcing. Technical writers focus specifically on writing documentation for technical products; if the documentation is already written and reusable in future releases, then there is a perceived threat for the writers that they are no longer a valuable asset to the company. The company hired them to write, ostensibly, because they have special skills to produce documentation. When the content is reusable, then the writers fear they will no longer be needed because the documentation is written in such a way that the content can be repackaged and mass produced using technology and not writers. Instead of writing a separate document for print, online, and online help, which could take three writers, single sourcing repackages the same content for different purposes, which could be completed by one writer instead of three.

Locke Carter (2003) addresses the rational fear that technical writers often face when moving to a single source environment. Technical communicators share a rational fear of automation, similar to moving from craftsmanship to mass production in a manufacturing environment. Carter states that "When desktop publishing word processing became widely available, nearly every business employed typing pools to produce text. The typing pool disintegrated and its employees were either laid off or offered an opportunity to learn word processing" (Carter, 2003, p. 319). Writers are afraid that they will be replaced by the technology used to produce documents using single sourcing. In reality, this is not the case; they will be liberated from monotonous, mechanical reproduction of text to move to more challenging and interesting positions within the team or organization, which I will explain further in the next section.

TRADITIONAL DOCUMENTATION AND COLLABORATIVE AUTHORING

Instead of working as a part of a productive team, many technical writers of traditional documentation find themselves with very little autonomy or control over their writing and consider it unfulfilling, uninvolved, and mechanical. Melissa Guthrie refers to this type of mechanical writing as "drone syndrome," referring to the male drone bee, whose sole purpose is to reproduce more bees (Guthrie, 2000). These unfortunate documentation drones are often "forced to pour a quantity of words into a template to help an unknown audience perform poorly-defined tasks can feel like a career death sentence" (Guthrie). The "career death sentence" Guthrie refers to is a trap that technical writers may fall into if the organization has high production requirements or high demands of written content for several niche markets using traditional documentation methods. In both of these situations, the writers' role changes from writing to simple reproduction. In the manufacturing company, production workers who contribute to the generation of the finished part are not recognized for their contribution; the only name on the finished product is Delphi Automotive, and the company as a whole receives recognition for producing high-quality products. When writers use single sourcing, each section, paragraph, or sentence is an important part of the finished product and must be consistent with the style that the team agreed upon.

Technical organizations with large production requirements for documentation follow the same trend as in other major markets, such as manufacturing, to compete in global and niche markets and stay in business. In her article "Single Sourcing: It's About People, Not Just Technology," Ann Rockley (2003) discusses the need for structured and collaborative writing. She argues that many writers' creative content is focused on the document's format or other factors besides the actual writing. For the technical writer, single sourcing may present a broader scope of work, but a loss of creativity or sense of ownership in the writing. Although writers may feel they will lose creative control and sense of ownership, their focus moves away from the format and toward the content (Rockley, 2003, p. 352). When writers use a traditional writing method, particularly with a team of writers, they often lack creative outlets and autonomy in writing content using traditional documentation, according to both Guthrie and

Rockley. When using traditional documentation, the individual writer writes an entire manual, chapter, or section, but generally must adhere to a corporate style or documentation guide to present a unified document. Single sourcing maintains the same goal when working with several writers, to present a unified document; it simply makes the process faster and easier to present a unified document with one voice and one style.

Ann Rockley (2001) warns that organizational managers must plan to use a content management system and have a clear vision of the organization's goals and style requirements to avoid documentation disasters. An excellent source that clearly describes single sourcing methodology is *Managing Enterprise Content: A Unified Content Strategy*, by Ann Rockley, Pamela Kostur, and Steve Manning (2003). These authors identify a common problem in organizations in which authors are working "in isolation from other authors within the organization" (Rockley et al., 2003, p. 1), which may result in redundancies in work and result in wasted time and money. The "Unified Content Strategy" (UCS) is "a repeatable method of identifying all content requirements up front, creating consistently structured content for reuse, managing that content in a definitive source, and assembling content on demand to meet your customer's needs" (Rockley et al., 2003, p. 2). Increased collaborative work is one of the ways that members of single sourcing teams must adjust to make single sourcing work in their documentation.

Single sourcing will work only when all the elements are formatted and expressed in the same manner. Wendy Yurick provides a realistic example of a documentation product created by several writers who are located throughout several departments in her article "Single-Sourcing—The Solution for Duplicated Efforts with Documentation" (2006). The content is a "repair and replace" procedure that must be distributed across several formats for different audiences. The readers and purpose of the document will differ, but the core data is essentially the same, which makes this document a great candidate for single sourcing. Ideally, in an organization that uses single sourcing, all of the writers will have ready access to common information and likewise, they will remain aware of new developments, which can be especially useful for software products that can be utilized on more than one operating system.

Single sourcing methods will only be successful if the writers have clear, consistent, and standard guidelines. One way to involve writers in this process is to have them collaborate on a structured style guide for the content management system. If the guidelines for producing single sourced documents are not clear and consistent, the project will be doomed to fail, particularly since writers may write only a paragraph, a sentence, or just a step in a larger set of documents. Ann Rockley (2001) states that "Adding to their frustration, writers in these environments are often prohibited from experimenting with new layout and design techniques or software tools, because these decisions may be dictated by other groups or by technology choices that limit the organization's flexibility" (Rockley, 2001, p. 192).

ORGANIZATIONAL CHANGES FOR
TECHNICAL WRITERS

The change from traditional technical writing to single sourcing is illustrated by an example from Dr. Stephen Spencer's book *Who Moved My Cheese* (1998). The book describes four characters and their adventure through a maze. Hem and Haw are two small humanlike characters, and Sniff and Scurry are two mice. The four characters raced as two teams every day through a maze for the grand prize: a block of cheese that was always in the same location. Hem and Haw became complacent and assumed the cheese would always be in the same place, while Sniff and Scurry remained competitive and hunted for the cheese each morning. One morning the cheese disappeared from the location. Hem and Haw were not prepared for the change and thought it was not fair, while Sniff and Scurry quickly altered their course to search for new cheese and found a much larger supply (Spencer, 1998, pp. 28-33).

Change is inevitable in any organization; if writers refuse to change with the industry and blindly hope that the situation will return to a comfortable state, much like Hem and Haw, they are doomed to be left behind in an industry that relies on a constantly changing market of technology. Michael Albers considers the traditional technical communicator's role as a "jack-of-all-trades, but master of none" (Albers, 2003, p. 335). When single sourcing is used in documentation, the individual writer will not create alone, but in a collaborative effort to benefit the company as a whole. Content in single sourcing needs to fit multiple formats; it is important that the information be broken down into complete content units or chunks. When multiple authors write for the same source, as is often the case in single sourcing, having clear formatting and style guidelines becomes critical to readability.

In a traditional documentation environment, writers claim ownership for their assigned manuals or sections, so the manual they are writing becomes "their manual" and "their chapters," when in truth the documentation remains the organization's property. Even in a team environment where organizations use collaborative writing to accelerate and simplify documentation, each contributor becomes responsible for his own section. Just as Hem and Haw were bewildered when someone moved "their" cheese, technical writers are often unprepared for changes that occur within in their organizations. Hem and Haw quickly discovered that the cheese, did not belong to them, but was only a variable part of the maze. When technical communicators write documentation and content, they must realize that products they create, in print and online, do not belong to them; they are products of their position as an employee within the company. Technical communicators must change their drone mindset of thinking their sole purpose within an organization is to reproduce content, and they must look into the future of an organization and prepare content for reuse, not just reproduction using single sourcing. Locke Carter says that the "technique has broad implications for writers and writing that go far beyond software use, content management, or production initiatives involving quality speed, or efficiency. When production techniques are changed radically, workers often perceive this change as a threat to their jobs and their way of doing things" (Carter, 2003, p. 318). In many cases, the purpose of change is not to threaten the writers' jobs, but to improve them and keep the writers working; and the way they do things may be the catalyst for organizational changes. When single sourcing is effected within a technical organization, using clear implementation, it should provide ample opportunities for writers to escape the career death sentence and experiment with other roles within the writing group. For example, the writer with a sharp eye for detail will be able to specialize as the team's editor and focus on smoothly blending the pieces from the core content to create an intelligible document, or several documents, for mass production.

Writers need to change their attitude of "ownership" to one of teamwork to compete for promotions and performance-based rewards in an organization that uses single sourcing, or is moving to single sourcing. Robert Kramer (2003) advises technical writers to change their mindset to a "management-technologist" role to succeed in the future standard of technical communication. As a management-technologist, the "toolset controls the shape and design of the published documents, so again a shift must take place from what writers know about document design and text structure to accepting what the tools at hand produced within the already defined styles. One of the greatest challenges that writers face when moving to single sourcing is the lack of separation between writing and the roles of the editor, content developer, and technical expert" (Kramer, 2003, p. 328). In general, those who are willing to be flexible in their roles as technical writers will probably benefit from creating single sourced documents. Instead of "droning," or simply reproducing the same content with each new release, they can automatically perform updates for new content without changing static content, and move on to other projects. Ann Rockley (2001) defines some benefits to the writer in a single source environment, such as focusing on new content instead of updating entire documents that contain elements of outdated information (Rockley, 2001, p. 192). Rockley also illustrates clear career paths that emerged from single sourcing that provide clarity to the ambiguous title of "technical communicator" within many organizations.

The title "technical communicator" is defined by distinct positions on a team, which include writers who create reusable core content; information designers who build information models and facilitate the writing process; editors who evaluate the content and design of the product; and information technologists who manage all aspects of the output, which includes the tools and media for the product (Rockley, 2001, p. 194). Moving toward specialization for each member of the documentation team in a single sourcing environment may advance technical communication into being a profession, because, although each member of a technical communication team maintains the title of "technical communicator," the team does not focus on titles but on roles within the team.

AUTHORING TOOLS

Two of the metaphorical mountains that technical writers must climb to conquer single sourcing is adapting to new software and authoring tools. Mastering these tools can be overwhelming if you have no previous knowledge with the software, and selecting the right tool can be a bewildering task if you are uninformed of the tools available. Ann Rockley (2004) is one of the prominent subject matter experts in the field on single sourcing. Her conference paper, "Selecting the Right Single-Sourcing Tool," presented at the STC 50th Annual Conference, provides practical advice for evaluating and choosing the right tools for single sourcing. Her paper also provides a list of considerations for evaluating tools and discusses the various authoring tools available, such as traditional word processors and desktop publishing tools; authoring products, such as XML-aware tools and XML editors; as well as a brief discussion on content management and workflow systems.

XML is one of the more popular tools in single sourcing. In "Usability, Structured Content, and Single Sourcing with XML," Filippi Sapienza (2004) emphasizes that using XML language (Extensible Markup Language) allows technical writers to adapt content for multiple audiences simultaneously. Using XML or similar methods of structured writing specifies a standard process that writers must follow to view the text properly. According to Sapienza, adherence to standards when using XML will ensure "quality control and similarities in voice, logic, and tone" even on projects where there are many contributing writers (Sapienza, 2004, p. 400).

Another tool of single sourcing is discussed in "Single-Sourcing with FrameMaker," by Michelle Marques (2005). She examines how single sourcing can simplify a technical writer's publication process using Adobe FrameMaker. Marques provides simple, direct instructions on single sourcing multiple models of the same product line, creating different versions of a document for different audiences using FrameMaker as the primary tool in single sourcing when writers need to produce simple documents in multiple formats, such as online help and user documentation. Determining what tool will best suit your needs when moving to single sourcing is a decision not to be taken lightly. Managers and writers should collaborate to use the existing knowledge they have about the documentation and the audience to select the right tool.

PREPARING STUDENTS FOR THE "BRAVE NEW WORLD"

New graduates from current writing programs will have an advantage if their programs provide adequate and project-based training that uses single sourcing.

They will already be familiar with rhetoric and understand audience analysis before starting their career as a technical writer. Students will be familiar with writing chunks of information with the purpose of reusing the data on other projects or media (Guthrie, 2000).

Managers within technical organizations may perceive documentation as a "necessary evil," so technical writing departments within many corporations are often understaffed and may not experience initial success. Technical organizations have a consistent need for trained technical writers, which presents a unique challenge and opportunity to students trained and prepared to write content using single sourcing. Michael Albers (2003) focuses on teaching technical communicators to be effective in a single sourcing environment. New graduates, and undergraduate students who are seeking internships, have to be flexible and prepared to work in a single source environment. They must have experience with collaborative writing in order to be competitive and marketable as a technical communicator. Albers states that "when the company decides that the eight technical communicators (rather than one) will significantly improve corporate revenue; seven technical communicators will be added as fast as they can be hired" (Albers, 2003, p. 337). Adding value and justifying our profession is a constant issue in technical communications. Dave Clark and Rebecca Andersen (2005) suggest that technical communicators are undervalued by members of related fields, such as engineering, due to the faculty members' approach to teaching technical communication. Clark and Andersen argue that if technical communicators change the focus in training from tools to implementation and practice, or praxis, they will build better connections between academics and practitioners as well as create new connections with other fields (p. 291). To accomplish this praxis, the authors recommend training students and graduates to increase organizational credibility, training technical communicators to be business-minded mentors, and developing courses in technical communication and the fields in which technical communicators work (pp. 294-295). Universities that adapt and train their graduates to write using single sourcing will give them a competitive advantage when applying for technical writing positions. The students will already have experience with the tools and will also understand the rhetorical elements that affect the readers for which the documentation is being written. This competitive advantage will prepare graduates to work in the "real world" and apply the theory they learned to the practical application of technical writing, particularly when using single sourcing.

CONCLUSION

The move to single sourcing from traditional technical writing has become inevitable due to global competition, niche marketing, smaller budgets, and pressure to produce high-quality documents faster than before. The debate is not whether or not this change will be beneficial to the individual writer, but whether or not the informed technical writer will change with the sweeping trend and greatly benefit from it, or be left behind the new standard in technical communication and face bitterness and unemployment. It is true that writers have much less autonomy, control, and creativity in a single source environment, but that may provide opportunities for them to move into other positions on the technical writing team that are more desirable, such as manager, editor, graphic designer, and information architect. The world is full of traditional technical writers who are accustomed to writing and rewriting the same information from one release to another, as a drone, but learning to be an information architect or designer is more profitable and possibly more fulfilling than simply reproducing the same information year after year. The tide of documentation is quickly rolling toward single sourcing and automation; to stay competitive, and in many cases, employed, we will simply have to roll with that tide.

REFERENCES

Albers, M. J. (2003). Single sourcing and the technical communication career path. *Technical Communication, 50*(3), 335-344.

Carter, L. (2003). The implications of single sourcing for writers and writing. *Technical Communication, 50*(3), 317-320.

Clark, D., & Andersen, R. (2005). Renegotiating with technology: Training towards more sustainable technical communication. *Technical Communication, 52*(3), 289-302.

Guthrie, M. (2000). Avoiding the drone syndrome: How to keep your technical writing job interesting in an age of automated publishing. *Society for Technical Communication.* Retrieved February 6, 2006 from
http://www.stc.org/confproceed/2000/PDFs/00005.PDF

Kramer, R. (2003). IBM's SGML toolset and the writer as technologist, problem solver, and editor. *Technical Communication, 50*(3), 328-334.

Marques, M. (2005). Single-sourcing with FrameMaker [Electronic Version]. *Information in Focus*, 2006. Retrieved March 13, 2006 from
http://www.telchwr-1.com/techwhirl/magazine/technical/singlesourcing.html

Rockley, A. (2001). The impact of single sourcing and technology. *Technical Communication, 48*(2), 189-193.

Rockley, A. (2003). Single sourcing: It's about people, not just technology. *Technical Communication, 50*(3), 350-354.

Rockley, A., Kostur, P., & Manning, S. (2003). *Managing enterprise content: A unified content strategy.* Indianapolis, IN: New Riders.

Rockley, A. (2004). *Selecting the right single sourcing tool.* Society of Technical Communication Annual Conference, Baltimore, Maryland.

Sapienza, F. (2004). Usability, structured content, and single sourcing with XML. *Technical Communication, 51*(3), 399-408.

Spencer, S. (1998). *Who moved my cheese? An amazing way to deal with change in your work and in your life.* New York: Putnam Adult Books.

Society for Technical Communication (STC). (2003). *Useful links.*
http://www.stcsig.org/ss/index.htm

Yurick, W. (2006). *Single-sourcing—The solution for duplicated efforts with docu-mentation.* Retrieved February, 2006, from
http://www.marketingsource.com/articles/view/1411

CHAPTER EIGHT

Single Sourcing and the Return to Positivism: The Threat of Plain-Style, Arhetorical Technical Communication Practices

Jeffrey Bacha

Despite numerous attempts to overcome the stigmas of old, modern technical communicators may once again be running the risk of being marginalized to the status of organizational bottom feeders. Pressured to succeed during a hostile climate, companies are continually searching for cost-cutting programs to maintain financial stability, and in many instances this means eliminating bloated payrolls by dramatically reducing employee numbers and outsourcing projects to contractors who can handle the job more economically. In order to remain competitive, modern technical communicators have had to augment their roles in the corporate hierarchy, transforming themselves into technically proficient architects of knowledge warehousing.

The two main factors that have directly contributed to the shift in workplace practices of technical communicators is the corporate push for multiple-use documents, which can be reused time and time again, and the global distribution of collaborative work practices. To survive, modern technical communicators have been forced to become tool-specific specialists in order to remain competitive in the diversified global economic support system where electronic documentation and storage have replaced the traditional production of print-based technological artifacts. In other words, "single sourcing changes the traditional view of the writing process that considers audience, purpose and context as dependent on the single document or product being written" (Eble, 2003, p. 345). As a result, the role of the technical communicator in the modern-day corporate structure has been reduced to component production or implementation of content management strategies.

In the introduction to the August, 2005 special issue of *Technical Communication* "The Future of Technical Communication," Michael Albers concludes that "the future of the field will be technology laden. Technology permeates everything a practicing technical communicator does" (Albers, 2005, p. 271). How technical communicators respond to Albers' concluding remarks and the rise of component product writing strategies could potentially shape the field for years to come. If the trend to produce single source, multiuse documents succeeds in dominating the technical communication profession, it threatens to reduce technical writing to an arhetorical, or acontextual and audienceless, form of writing that challenges the modern-traditional values of rhetorical style in composition. In other words, technical communicators could unknowingly be perpetuating a return to what Robert Connors (2004) describes as "Engineering English" or the historical tradition of object centered documentation commonly associated with "positivism," which Carolyn Miller defines as "the conviction that sensory data are the only permissible basis of knowledge; consequently, the only meaningful statements are those which can be empirically verified" (2004, p. 49).

"POSITIVISM," RHETORIC, AND TECHNICAL COMMUNICATION

At its core, technical communication has always been embrocated with the practice of producing practical documentation that reflected the theoretical and rhetorical situation it evolved from. According to Kathy Pringle and Sean Williams' article "The Future Is the Past: Has Technical Communication Arrived as a Profession?" the field of technical communication "historically has been characterized by a tension between employing sophisticated rhetorical and analytical skill to create effective communications at the same time those skills relied on technology for their implementation and demonstration" (2005, p. 362). Does possessing more technological skill, however, make the technical communicator's products better, or will the material suffer as the technical communicator's writing becomes more content focused? And will the lack of audience and acontextual need presented by single sourcing only add additional tension to an already historically tumultuous profession? In order to gain a broader perspective of what the future may hold for the field of technical communication and the rhetorical situation technical communicators will be faced with, one first needs to be exposed to a brief history of how the technical rhetorical situation and the tensions that surround the field have evolved over time.

Robert Connors attributes the historical creation of the tension existing within technical communication to the developments leading to technical communication instruction becoming incorporated into the discipline of English composition. "Freshman composition requirements were almost universal, and the tacit assumption in engineering schools between 1880 and 1905 or so was that these first-year courses were all the introduction to writing that engineers needed" (Connors, 2004, p. 5). The technically oriented college program had some dramatically damaging repercussions; as Connors explains, "this period was, understandably, a rather dark time in the history of engineering education, a time when, by the schools' own later admissions, they turned out a large number of otherwise competent engineers who were near-illiterates" (p. 5). Connors labels this period as "Engineering English," where future engineers were shown how to reproduce preformatted letters and reports, a task most engineering students viewed as unessential byproducts of their work. What engineers were being exposed to in the first-year composition courses reflected the very utilitarian purpose of early composition studies. The foundational elements of "positivism" and "Engineering English" can be traced back to the rhetorical style guides and composition textbooks of the 1700s and 1800s and the call for effective documentation that communicated knowledge plainly and efficiently.

The concept of utility carried on throughout the 1800s and eventually became the backbone of early composition textbooks. By communicating thoughts in a plain, economical style, early composition theorists speculated that writers could limit their audience's misunderstandings, and by maintaining clarity through efficiency, less attention would be diverted from the main purpose of the composition. Under the dogmatic ideology of early composition theory, the writer's role in the composition process became that of a consummate observer who did not possess or create knowledge and was simply considered a demonstrator of accuracy. The historical need for efficiency, plainness of style, and clarity that developed inside the technical communication field prior to World War II reduced the role of the technical communicator to that of a simple transcriber of others' ideas or a mere record keeper for scientific facts. The role of the writer established by this dogmatic ideology is not unlike the potential shift in contemporary technical communication practice, because in response to increasing technological demands placed on technical communicators, technical communication could once again face the compartmentalization of text to plain style under the rubric of single sourcing and XML. The reductive tendencies of product-focused, or as James Kinneavy (2003) has labeled referential discourse where the dominant feature of the produced discourse is the subject matter being displayed (p. 134), is the first point of contention when discussing the potentially harmful effects of single sourcing practices and content management strategies, because in order for them to function properly, the technical document must remain subject driven and subject oriented. If contemporary technical communicators allow the field of technical communication to return to its legacy of reductionism, they will unknowingly be destroying everything the field has accomplished over the last 50 plus years; namely the shift to humanistic practices and the demand for more professional, humanistic documentation following World War II.

Compositions' dogmatism of utility, which developed out of "positivism," dramatically affected technical communication by placing the purpose of writing directly on a clear representation of a specific product. The technological need that swept through the nation following World War II, however, changed the field of technical communication because of the increasing demand for products to be accompanied by documentation. "World War II led to a huge increase in the number of military contracts. After the war, the government required that these contracts be accompanied by documentation" (Van Wicklen, 2001, p. 17). Engineers, however, still viewed the production of technical documents as subsidiary to the actual products they were creating. "As the amount of required documentation increased, engineers and scientists hired writers prepared for technical fields because they themselves didn't care for what they perceived as the mundane task of documenting their work" (Pringle & Williams, 2005, p. 363). Technical writing instruction mimicked this belief system passed down by engineers, as demonstrated by Morris Freedman's 1958 article "The Seven Sins of Technical Writing." In the article Freedman insists writers can produce functionally accurate technical documents if they avoid the following seven sins: indifference, fuzziness, emptiness, wordiness, bad habits, deadly passivity, and mechanical errors. "However, as technology became more and more readily available, consumers began demanding more professional and higher quality information products to accompany their purchases" (Pringle & Williams, 2005, p. 363).

The demand for products to be accompanied by more professional and higher quality publications forced technical communication specialists to reexamine the products they were creating in order to make them more accessible to the people purchasing the products. As Carolyn Miller explains in "A Humanistic Rationale for Technical Writing," technical communicators also began to see themselves linguistically crafting knowledge instead of demonstrating scientific and engineering discoveries. "The most uncomfortable aspect of this non-rhetorical view of science is that it is a form of intellectual coercion: it invites us to prostrate ourselves at the windowpane of language and accept what Science has demonstrated" (2004, p. 50). Throughout the 1970s and 1980s composition and technical communication theorists began questioning the "positivistic" and object-focused nature of the products that writers were producing, which were hard to read because they lacked an awareness of audience and did not take into account the social elements that continuously shaped their writing. What developed was a new form of technical communication, wherein writers became authors of information, translating socially constructed discourses between developers and purchasers, instead of record keepers of technical schematics. As Merrill Whitburn explains, "in the years since the 1970s and 1980s, academics in technical communication have made remarkable strides in broadening the scope of technical communication. They have responded to an increasingly global economy by exploring the extraordinary range of ways that international communication must be adapted to various cultures" (2000, p. 224).

During this period of change, technical communicators became document architects, crafting words into functional products that transformed technical knowledge into written tools. Technical communicators became collaborative members of the design process, ensuring technical artifacts clearly relayed production intent to the individuals who would be using the final product, and "whether they desire it or not, technical communicators are seen as variously adding, deleting, changing, and selecting meaning" (Slack, Miller, & Doak, 2004, p. 172). Technical communicators were required to produce material that a plethora of users could understand, navigate, and implement easily and effectively. The material also required a clear purpose because "purposes do not only guide the design team through the collaborative planning and drafting of a document, but may also serve as a standard for measuring success when it comes to reader-testing drafts of the document" (Lentz & Maat, 2004, p. 369). The shift in ideology from product centered to user focused documentation established a rhetorical need among technical communicators that emphasized a humanistic rationale for technical communication and put the technical writer in direct contact with an audience. "Any writer or speaker, 'technical' or not, works within a rhetorical situation. You need to say something to someone on some occasion. Rhetoric is the art of finding the right way to deliver the message that will produce the best results from everyone involved" (Killingsworth & Palmer, 1999, p. 4). Single sourcing and content management strategies, however, not only threaten to return technical communication to product centered communication practices, they may also be establishing the elimination of audience awareness from the creation of technical documentation, which is one of the critical aspects of any rhetorical situation.

By shifting the focus of technical communication away from the product toward the product's eventual audience, technical communicators became technical rhetoricians, carefully weaving knowledge into written products in order to produce textual meaning users could later use. "Briefly summarized, it holds that whatever we know of reality is created by individual action and by communal assent. Reality cannot be separated from our knowledge of it; knowledge cannot be separated from the knower; the knower cannot be separated from a community" (Miller, 2004, p. 51). The rhetorical situation that has developed for technical communicators incorporates four distinct portions of the communication process, which James Kinneavy labels as the encoder, the decoder, reality, and the signal (2003, p. 135). Specifically the technical communicator must consider the receiver of the information (the decoder), the information being passed (the signal), the documenter of the information (the encoder), and the context in which the information will be received (reality). Failure to satisfy any portion of the rhetorical situation will result in the production of unsuccessful products because "facts do not exist independently, waiting to be found and collected and systematized; facts are human constructions which presuppose theories. We bring to the world a set of innate and learned concepts which help us select, organize, and understand what we encounter" (Miller, 2004, p. 51). In other words, "as a technical writer or speaker, you face a special kind of rhetorical situation: Someone wants to solve a problem or satisfy a need and doesn't have the technical knowledge to do so" (Killingsworth & Palmer, 1999, p. 4). To satisfy the portion of a technically laden rhetorical situation that relates to the receivers of the information, technical rhetoricians must know their audience. As Robert Johnson (2004) points out, "the very nature of technical communication begs for conceptions of audience because technical writers are fundamentally charged with the responsibility of translating information from one context to another" (p. 92). In order to accomplish this, technical communicators must established a relationship with an audience, or what Johnson describes as an involved audience: "the involved audience is an actual participant in the writing process who creates knowledge and determines much of the content of the discourse" (p. 93). Dorothy Winsor (2004) further addresses this point, claiming "moreover, the textual construction of knowledge is social in nature because each document must convince other people of its validity in order to be accepted as knowledge" (p. 343), and "in effect, knowledge may be defined as that which most people in a discourse community are convinced of, and what a discourse community is convinced of is indicated by the texts it has accepted" (p. 343).

Once the technical communicator knows who will be using the products, she can then understand how and where the product will eventually be used or the context of the rhetorical situation. To satisfy the technical context of the rhetorical situation, the technical communicator must understand audience needs and the circumstances surrounding the product's eventual use, because a "document is effective only if it reaches its intended audience, for your document to reach its readers, you first need to learn about them" (Van Wicklen, 2001, p. 9). To accomplish this, a technical communicator must first understand the discourse community the user belongs to or works within and then must craft the written product to match the needs of the users discourse community because "to write, to engage in any communication, is to participate in a community; to write well is to understand the conditions of one's own participation—the concepts, values, traditions, and style which permit identification with that community and determine the success or failure of communication" (Miller, 2004, p. 52). Understanding the context surrounding the product's eventual implementation is critical because "communication is possible because we bring some innate psychological and some culturally learned or socially constructed knowledge that is shared with other discourse participants" (Campbell, 1995, p. 22). In other words, "a producer cannot hope to design an effective document unless he or she knows what information his or her recipients think is relevant, clear, adequate, and accurate" (p. 96).

Understanding and clearly satisfying the first two portions of the technical rhetorical situation will essentially help the technical communicator satisfy the final two portions of the communication process. By understanding the audience of the product, the audience's needs, and the context surrounding the implementation of a product, technical communicators can begin to create meaningful content and develop a format in which to present the content. "Thus, the design for addressing the user goals and information needs requires understanding both the overall requirements, how they vary within changing situations, and the different strategies that different people or user groups use to understand the information" (Albers, 2003, p. 266). Knowing how users will interact and use the information allows the technical communicator to create content that is easily understood and allows the technical communicator to anticipate problems with audience understanding. If the technical communicator anticipates problems, she can add specifications to the content as a way to circumvent later clarifications of the content and also ensure that the content provides enough information for the users to understand the product. According to Thomas Pearsall (2001), "when you write about what you have learned through your own education, you must consider how well your readers will understand the words, concepts, and techniques you write about. Accordingly, when you think your readers might need help with any of these aspects offer it" (p. 8). If the technical communicator fails to satisfy the first two portions of the rhetorical situation, the content she produces and the corresponding product could essentially become useless because the content and product's "existence defines a particular relationship with me and projects a particular power over my experience" (Dobrin, 2004, pp. 119-120). If the user has a negative experience with a product or the content of the product, the user may never use the product in the future, and the time spent creating the product will be wasted time. Single sourcing practices and content management strategies, however, could potentially increase the amount of users who have negative experiences with a product, because they remove the technical communicator from the discourse community and mandate the production of acontextual documents, because the information created must be able to function in multiple contexts and multiple platforms.

Modern technical communication, then, developed "as a discipline with a legacy of both scientific and humanistic stems; it is ultimately a recursive discipline that weds empiricism and rhetorical theory" (Kynell, 2000, p. 101). Technical communicators are now being asked to produce products users can understand by implementing rhetorical strategies of audience and socially constructed discourse communities. "Today's technical communicator, or content specialist, must not only assume responsibility for his/her role as a communicator with technical aptitude, but also understand the idiosyncrasies and sensitivities associated with communication in a multicultural, global world" (Whiteside, 2003, p. 304). Barbara Giammona's (2004) study of current global workplace practices further exemplifies the technical communicator's need to understand the rhetorical situation she works in, because modern technical communication practitioners are not only contributing members of production, they are also members of product-testing teams and usability experts. Giammona's study and

Aimee Whiteside's (2003) study of recently graduating technical communicators and managers both reveled the managerial perspective that all technical communicators must be able to write effectively in order to be successful. To write successfully, the technical communicator must understand and satisfy the rhetorical situation she has become a part of.

What technical communicators are required to write, however, has changed dramatically in recent years. The change in writing styles technical communicators are facing has the potential of eliminating the importance of understanding the technical rhetorical situation and returning technical communication back to the product-focused manacles of "positivism." The reason for this is an apparent need for acontextual documentation, loss of audience awareness, and the production of plain-style products associated with single sourcing practices.

THE INFLUENCE OF SINGLE SOURCING

Recently the biggest shift in the field of technical communication is the increased implementation of single sourcing practices, and as Locke Carter (2003) points out in "The Implications of Single Sourcing for Writers and Writing," single sourcing places "pressure on the seemingly stable constructs of the writer and the document in ways that many previous innovations have not" (p. 318). Single sourcing has forced modern technical communicators to not only change the way they write, it has also forced them into a new role of content producers and managers. Traditionally, technical communicators had the solitary purpose of producing a document or product designed to achieve a single goal for a specific audience. As a result of the technologies used to support single sourcing and content management strategies, however, the rhetorical situation has been eliminated from the production of technical documents, and the only portion of the communication process remaining is the narrow focus on the signal being communicated or the product itself. Single sourcing, then, forces the technical communicator to suppress the aspects of audience, context, and even the creator of the technical document. Contrary to the previously held belief that any communication must be "context-sensitive" in order to meet the rhetorical situation (Killingsworth & Palmer, 1999, p. 5), single sourcing requires and mandates the technical communicator to create products that can function in any situation.

The increasing popularity of single sourcing has also modified the traditional role of technical communicators to include content management and dynamic content delivery. "Dynamic, ever-changing publication of information resources at all levels by using internal and external electronically supported systems is a solution that many organizations are vigorously, and actively planning, developing, and implementing today. If they are not, they will soon find that they must or be mired in information wasteland" (Hackos, 2002, p. 8). Making information quickly and easily accessible is one of the biggest arguments used by single sourcing advocates. "Content management solutions hold an attractive premise—that all relevant content can be quickly, and easily available to those who need it to do their jobs, make decisions, acquire new knowledge, and satisfy their curiosity" (Hackos, 2002, p. 9). In order for information to be accessed easily, it must be retrievable; in order for it be retrievable, it must first be constructed in a contextless manner or deconstructed into various chunks of information and tagged with a unique identifier or numbered code. Knowledge, then, under single sourcing, must be reducible to a single descriptive phrase. "Single sourcing enables technical communicators to become knowledge, content, and information designers because knowing how to single source means knowing how to write, design, create, and (re)use content for various media" (Eble, 2003, p. 345). One example would be the creation of an online news service with an already-established print production. If a newspaper was converted by single sourcing practices, each article would be saved independently into a database before the product was paginated. Once saved the newspaper paginator and Web site designer could pull the same article from the database and place it within the various products they were creating.

As companies continue to produce material through the process of single sourcing, the amount of modular information will increase at a staggering rate and could potentially be stored at numerous locations in differing formats. In order for the content to be reusable, it needs to be accessible and searchable, which has forced technical communicators to look beyond their traditional role as document architects to become architects of knowledge warehouses. As Michelle Eble points out, "knowledge management specialist, content management specialist, information architect, and information technologist are just a few of the new roles that may be played by technical communicators" (2003, p. 349). One technological tool that modern technical communicators are utilizing in their roles as information managers is the coding system of Extensible Markup Language (XML). "The basics of XML starts with designing document type definitions (DTDs) that specify the elements that will be allowed in databases and the relationships among these elements" (Applen, 2002, p. 308). The DTDs or XML codes allow data to be retrieved from databases through multiple searches. By placing XML codes throughout modular content, information managers can create a DTD system where the same document can be found by searching for names, subject matter, dates, and even specific terminology. By making information searchable, technical communicators can make the information accessible to any member of the company, which makes the information reusable for future products.

With single sourcing, technical communicators may not know the context or audience they are producing material for. In *Single Sourcing: Building Modular Documentation*, Kurt Ament defines single sourcing as "a method for systematically re-using information. With this method, you develop modular content in one source document or database, then assemble the content into different document formats for different audiences and purposes" (Ament, 2003, p. 3). In other instances, "technical communicators use desktop publishing software to create a document, then reformat the document to create subsequent deliverables, with or without changes to the content" (Williams, 2003, p. 321). The biggest advantage associated with single sourcing is that material needs only to be edited once and can be used in multiple documents and multiple platforms with only slight modifications. An example would be using the same promotional material advertising a rate reduction special for a hotel's printed brochure and for the company's Web page, which makes the material in both products consistent. One problem associated with the above example would be attempting to use or reuse the same information in a different publication that does not focus inclusively on the company. In the example, the information does not require context to function because both products provide the situational elements for the information. Including the same information in a larger collection, like a directory of local hotels, would prove detrimental to the company, because the audience would need further explanation to understand the significance of the advertised reduction in rates. Another example would be the production of a company Web site by a team of technical communicators who are each assigned the task of producing different sections of the final product. "What the reader sees is not a document that an editor has carefully groomed, but rather a dynamic document which was compiled from a database and assembled just before the page is sent to the browser" (Albers, 2000, p. 191). In this example, each member of the production team must eliminate all occurrences of personal style from his writing in order to make the components read as if created by the same person and designed together to maintain consistency, essentially creating a situation where the technical communicators are required to produce stylistically neutral products. In single sourcing, the technical communicator who produces the content does not determine how the content will be built into the final product; instead how the content is presented in a final document will be determined by the production manager or technical editor. "The coherence and consistency of the information within and between each of the pieces of data (chunks) retrieved from a database are not a major concern of computer science, whereas in technical communication, coherence and consistency are of primary concern and determine how effectively the information communicates with the reader" (Albers, 2000, p. 192).

Single sourcing also requires the technical communicator to produce documentation that never requires additional information to function, which creates a problem for larger works of composition. As Bob Boiko points out in the *Content Management Bible,* "all in all, the structure of the repository in a composition system is an intertwined mass of highly interrelated components" (2005, p. 135). If all of the components are pulled together, they will function together, because the completed publication will contain information that explains other portions of the text and can draw clarifications from other sections of the work. If the same components are pulled separately, problems can arise because the individual components will be missing their interrelated counterparts. In other words, "many components risk losing much of their meaning and significance if torn out of the higher-level component within which they're embedded. For example, a biographer of Sigmund Freud could pull out chapters of her book to be delivered as a lecture series or publish them separately based on subject matter—Freud's time in Berlin, his relationship with associates, his major theories" (p. 135). Each paper, however, will need to be produced individually, and no paper will be able to draw information or clarifications from other sections of the biographical work, which could make the material hard to understand or make the information inaccessible for the user. This creates an additional problem because necessary explanations may not be added to the individual components.

Single sourcing has changed the traditional view of technical writing, because technical communicators are not producing completed documents from start to finish anymore; they are instead producing object-centered modular content that does not require context to function. "Technical communicators using single sourcing no longer write documents or products. Instead they need to learn and know how to write content that can be reused in various documents or products" (Eble, 2003, p. 345). Supporters of single sourcing claim its challenge to the traditional view of technical communication can lead to stronger products. "Although its primary goal is to save time and money, single sourcing improves the quality of your documentation. By requiring you to develop modular information that is usable in any format, single sourcing makes document usability an all-or-nothing issue" (Ament, 2003, p. 3). By eliminating the rhetorical situation from the process, however, the information technical communicators can produce must be stylistically natural and must not contain any information that would require additional explanation. But without negotiating all of the elements that constitute the technical rhetorical situation, how can technical communicators possibly know if the target audience for the information can disseminate the information or if what they are writing even fits the situational requirements the information will be used for?

THE THREAT OF "POSITIVISM" RESURFACING

How technical communicators eventually respond to the influence of single sourcing and the rising need for corporations to hire content managers could directly influence the field of technical communication for many years to come. "On one side of the issue is the possibility that single sourcing creates a new kind of writer, one who is more integrated than before. And by 'integrated' we mean that the writer is required to integrate more skills to retain the self-image (and the job description) of writer" (Carter, 2003, p. 319). By focusing on content instead of audience and context when producing technical communication artifacts, technical communicators run the risk of returning to what

Carolyn Miller describes as the traditional "positivist" view of writing, where writers simply record what they find. "Technical and scientific rhetoric becomes the skill of subduing language so that it most accurately and directly transmits reality. It aims at being an efficient way of coercing the mind to submit to reality" (Miller, 2004, p. 48). By doing so, technical communicators could unknowingly be contributing to the situation Pete Praetorius (2002) points out in "Technical Communication as Purveyors of Common Sense," where "a lot of technical writing is written as though it was created for and by machines rather than by one person for other people" (p. 346). Single sourcing also has the potential of removing the technical communicator from the discourse community she is producing content for, which could lead to the production of meaningless content or content the discourse community cannot understand.

Single sourcing then, has the potential "to place organizational needs ahead of user needs, limit the potential and negatively affect the perceptions of technical communicators, and contribute to less theorizing in the field of technical communication" (Williams, 2003, p. 325). In other words, single sourcing, because of its requirement of placing the object at the center of the writing process in order to reduce rhetorical influences that could limit its reusability for multiple uses, could return technical communicators to the historical role of simple knowledge transmitters, or worse still it has the potential of returning technical communication instruction and practice to the mechanical restraints of "Engineering English." Returning to the reductivistic practices of the past could essentially create a situation where "a technical writer should render his own act of writing invisible because technical writing is communication, not self-expression, and the information itself is far more important than the writer's attitude toward it" (Dobrin, 2004, p. 110).

As information continues to be developed into content chunks, project managers no longer require technical communicators to reproduce every portion of the final product and can instead search the company database for previously archived content. Once located, the previously archived content can be updated or modified to fit into the current project. If the single sourcing trend continues, the only time project managers will require the services of technical communicators is when new content is necessary to complete a project. From a managerial perspective, single sourcing has the ability to reduce company payroll, because there will be no need to employ full-time technical communicators when contract employees can be hired when their services are required. New technologies like XML are even allowing managers to shop around the globe for the cheapest contractor, because Extensible Markup Languages can be added to any document once it arrives at the office. "Most of us in management will be asked to consider the option or will face the reality of it in the near future—whether it means our entire function is sent offshore or whether certain work is sent outside the firm" (Giammona, 2004, p. 354). With single sourcing, project managers can now break a project down into fragments and ship each part to technical communication contractors anywhere in the world.

Single sourcing practices also tend to mimic the "positivistic" theory of efficiency first presented in the principle composition textbooks of the 1800s, specifically Adams Sherman Hills' *The Principles of Rhetoric* and Herbert Spencer's *The Philosophy of Style*. According to Hill, composition "is an art, not a science: for it neither observes, nor discovers, nor classifies; but it shows how to convey from one mind to another the results of observation, discovery, or classification; it uses knowledge, not as knowledge, but as power" (1895, p. v). Hill claims a work of composition should be viewed as a completely polished mechanism where every word, sentence, and paragraph contributes meaning to the work as a whole. To Hill, a completely polished mechanism was a work of composition structured logically through purity of grammar and style. Spencer took the theory of utilitarian discourse one step further by urging for a principle of economy within every piece of composition. In discussing a rationale and theory of composition, Spencer stresses "the importance of economizing the reader's or hearer's attention" (2001, p. 1155). Under Spencer's rubric of composition, language communicated in any form should be transmitted clearly, plainly, and as efficiently as possible in order to maintain the audience's attention and limit distractions that could hinder the associated thought being communicated. According to Spencer, composition should be viewed as "an apparatus of symbols for the conveyance of thought, we may say that as in a mechanical apparatus, the more simple and the better arranged its parts, the greater will be the effect produced" (p. 155).

The threat of "positivism's" return can be found in single sourcing's necessity for the creation of compact information that explains enough without the inclusion of too many detailed explanations; as Ament has pointed out, "to build usable and reusable text, shorten and simplify sentences. If a sentence contains serial items, format the items into an itemized list" (2003, p. 172). One example would be transforming the following sentence into an information list: When making a cake be sure to have a copy of the recipe, collect all necessary ingredients, and check to see if you have enough time to complete the task. The result would be:

Before making a cake:
• Locate recipe
• Gather ingredients
• Consider time constraints

In the example, single sourcing provides no room for the technical communicator to include explanations about why locating the recipe would be helpful, why gathering the ingredients first would be beneficial, or why time would be an issue when making a cake, because the explanations would be dependent on the type of cake being made and the context surrounding the production of the cake. The example also fails to take into account the context of the situation, specifically where the information will be used, because baking a cake at home could be very different than baking a cake in a commercial kitchen, where baking times may vary depending on oven capacity and cooking times.

In order to remain competitive, technical communicators may have to prepare for the worst and begin transforming themselves into technical specialists. Instead of possessing a broad range of desktop publishing, writing, and production skills, technical communicators may be required to specialize in specific portions of the single sourcing process by transforming into content writers or content editors. Writers will have to increase their ability to produce multiuse technical artifacts that do not require context to function and overcome the traditional craftsman approach to document production. "Writers who create structured content in a collaborative setting must accept this further degree of 'egolessness' or watch as their work is exported to countries where workers are more willing, as many software developers have had to do" (Williams, 2003, p. 325). Technical communicators will need to begin creating material that has to be written only once, because as Eble (2003) points out "writing content for single-sourced materials depends on the writer's ability to write 'medium-neutral' text without having to be rewritten" (p. 346). Technical editors will need to become more proficient with content management technologies and may need to become XML experts in order to create universal markup languages that make information easier to locate. Editors may also be required to distribute portions of the process to various departments within the same corporation, which could lead to multiple-source products without the direct collaboration or influence of usability testing that technical communicators are accustomed to.

Specialization in the field of technical communication can lead to a third problem attributed to single sourcing, which is the creation of a corporate hierarchical system that marginalizes the technical communicator to the bottom of the power structure. If technical communicators begin to specialize their skills, those who focus on writing content run the risk of eliminating themselves from the design process. By becoming excluded from the design process, technical communicators could reduce their role to what Dale Sullivan (2004) describes in the article "Political-Ethical Implications of Defining Technical Communication as a Practice" as a "good citizen" existing inside the corporate community. According to Sullivan, it is the community that "defines what the good is, and the individual is good when he or she performs well the functions required by society—that is, when the person is a good citizen" (p. 215). For the content specialist to produce "good" work and remain a viable asset to the corporation, she would be forced into the production of "medium-neutral" material, where the author remains invisible. In other words, "when people fill the role well, when they possess character traits that allow them to perform the functions of these roles with excellence, then their actions are considered virtuous" (p. 215). To be considered virtuous, the content specialist's work would need to be usable in multiple products without her being able to determine where the work should be located, which could return technical communication to what Sullivan calls "slave rhetoric" and has the potential of eliminating the humanistic and rhetorical aspects of writing that technical communicators have relied so heavily on. "Therefore, our present way of defining technical communication as the discourse appropriate for industry is equivalent to defining it as the rhetoric appropriate for slaves—those barred from making decisions about the ends, those whose decision-making authority is restricted to determining the most efficient means of obtaining predetermined ends" (p. 216).

Modern technical communicators are no longer viewed as traditional technical craftsmen, carefully weaving words together and are now seen as technologically proficient architects of socially constructed knowledge. By controlling the structure and completion of technical artifacts, technical communicators have ascended through the corporate power structure to become essential members of the production process. As Robert Johnson has pointed out, "if we are a part of the development continuum, then we might be perceived as a part of the development team, rather than just the scribes who 'write up' technical information" (2004, p. 96). As technological demand increases in the field of technical communication, specifically the shift to content management and single sourcing, practitioners need to further examine the impact these new technologies will have on their new positions of power or watch as their work becomes enslaved by the arhetorical mechanical nature of "positivism." If technical communicators are removed from any portion of the production process, they run the risk of being marginalized back to the traditional role of technical translators to remain virtuous members of corporations. By becoming content specialists, technical communicators risk further perpetuating the distribution of their jobs and establishing a situation wherein tomorrow's technical communicators may become obsolete members of industry. Current practitioners who specialize in portions of the single sourcing process without maintaining a broad set of skills also risk making themselves obsolete when new technologies replace single sourcing or XML. If technical communicators do not analyze the negative implications of single sourcing practices, they may unknowingly be returning technical communication to the arhetorical, mechanical, and unhumanistic past it has fought so hard to overcome.

REFERENCES

Albers, M. J. (2000). The technical editor and document databases: What the future may hold. *Technical Communication Quarterly, 9,* 191-206.

Albers, M. J. (2003). Multidimensional audience analysis for dynamic information. *Journal of Technical Writing and Communication, 33,* 263-279.

Albers, M. J. (2005). The future of technical communication. *Technical Communication, 52*, 267-272.

Ament, K. (2003). *Single sourcing: Building modular documentation.* Norwich, NY: William Andrew Publishing.

Applen, J. D. (2002). Technical communication, knowledge management, and XML. *Technical Communication, 49*, 301-313.

Boiko, B. (2005). *Content management bible.* Indianapolis, IN: Wiley & Sons.

Campbell, K. S. (1995). *Coherence, continuity, and cohesion: Theoretical foundations for document design.* Hillsdale, NJ: Lawrence Erlbaum Associates.

Carter, L. (2003). Introduction: The Implications of Single Sourcing for Technical Communicators. *Technical Communication, 50*, 317-320.

Connors, R. J. (2004). The rise of technical writing instruction in America. In J. Johnson-Eilola & S. A. Selber (Eds.), *Central works in technical communication* (pp. 3-19). Oxford, NY: Oxford University Press.

Dobrin, D. N. (2004). What's technical about technical writing?" In J. Johnson-Eilola & S. A. Selber (Eds.), *Central works in technical communication* (pp. 107-123). Oxford, NY: Oxford University Press..

Eble, M. F. (2003). Content vs. product: The effects of single sourcing on the teaching of technical communication. *Technical Communication, 50*, 344-349.

Freedman, M. (1958). The seven sins of technical writing. *College Composition and Communication, 9*, 10-16.

Giammona, B. (2004). The future of technical communication: How innovation, technology, information management, and other forces are shaping the future of the profession. *Technical Communication, 51*, 349-364.

Hackos, J. T. (2002). *Content management for dynamic Web delivery.* New York: John Wiley & Sons.

Hill, A. S. (1895). *The principles of rhetoric.* New York: American Book Company.

Johnson, R. R. (2004). Audience involved: Toward a participatory model of writing. In J. Johnson-Eilola & S. A. Selber (Eds.), *Central works in technical communication* (pp. 91-104). Oxford, NY: Oxford University Press.

Killingsworth, J. M., & Palmer, J. S. (1999). *Information in action: A guide to technical communication.* Boston, MA: Allyn and Bacon.

Kinneavy, J. L. (2003). The basic aims of discourse. In V. Villanueva (Ed.), *Cross-talk in comp theory* (pp. 129-140). Urbana, IL: NCTE.

Kynell, T. C. (2000). *Writing in a milieu of utility: The move to technical communication in American engineering programs, 1850-1950.* Stamford, CT: Ablex.

Lentz, L., & Maat, H. P. (2004). Functional analysis for document design. *Technical Communication, 51*, 387-398.

Miller, C. R. (2004). A humanistic rationale for technical writing. In J. Johnson-Eilola & S. A. Selber (Eds.), *Central works in technical communication* (pp. 47-54). Oxford, NY: Oxford University Press.

Pearsall, T. E. (2001). *The elements of technical writing.* Boston, MA: Allyn and Bacon.

Praetorius, P. (2002). Technical communication as purveyors of common sense. *Journal of Technical Writing and Communication, 32*, 337-351.

Pringle, K., & Williams, S. (2005). The future is the past: Has technical communication arrived as a profession? *Technical Communication, 52*, 361-370.

Slack, J. D., Miller, D. J. & Doak, J. (2004). The technical communicator as author: Meaning, power, authority. In J. Johnson-Eilola & S. A. Selber (Eds.), *Central works in technical communication* (pp. 160-174). Oxford, NY: Oxford University Press.

Spencer, H. (2001). The philosophy of style. In P. Bizzell & B. Herzberg (Eds.), *The rhetorical tradition: Readings from classical times to the present* (pp. 1154-1167). Boston, MA: Bedford/St. Martin's.

Sullivan, D. L. (2004). Political-ethical implications of defining technical communication as a practice. In J. Johnson-Eilola & S. A. Selber (Eds.), *Central works in technical communication* (pp. 211-231). Oxford, NY: Oxford University Press.

Van Wicklen, J. (2001). *The technical writer's survival guide.* New York: Checkmark Books.

Whitburn, M. (2000). *Rhetorical scope and performance: The example of technical communication.* Stamford, CT: Ablex.

Whiteside, A. L. (2003). The skills that technical communicators need: An investigation of technical communication graduates, managers, and curricula. *Journal of Technical Writing and Communication, 33,* 303-318.

Williams, J. D. (2003). The implications of single sourcing for technical communicators. *Technical Communication, 50,* 321-327.

Winsor, D. A. (2004). Engineering writing/writing engineering. *Central works in technical communication* (pp. 341-350). In J. Johnson-Eilola & S. A. Selber (Eds.), Oxford, NY: Oxford University Press.

CHAPTER NINE

Content Management in an International Outsourcing Framework: A Perspective for Technical Communicators

Kirk St. Amant

International outsourcing has become one of the more divisive topics of the new millennium. At the heart of this controversy is a concern related to exporting; namely the exporting of work (and jobs) from industrialized nations to developing ones. This focus on jobs has drawn attention from an equally important situation—the export of information, or content, to nations with different legal systems. Such practices, however, leave content, particularly personal information, open for abuse. One way to address this problem is to reconsider outsourcing from a content management vs. a professional staffing perspective.

This chapter examines the content-related problems arising from international outsourcing situations. It begins with an overview of what international outsourcing is and then examines how outsourcing practices increasingly involve content management factors. This examination reveals that the new focus on content-based activities is changing the nature of outsourcing and is creating problems related to content management practices. The chapter then explores how communication practices can address such problems and presents content management strategies that organizations can use to address these problems. Through this format, readers can gain an understanding of how international outsourcing situations can provide technical communicators with the opportunity to take a more direct role in an organization's content management activities in relation to international business practices.

AN OVERVIEW OF INTERNATIONAL OUTSOURCING

Outsourcing is the process of transferring the responsibility for completing a task from one entity to another (Bendor-Samuel, 2004). In many cases, "client" businesses or client organizations outsource work to entities that can perform tasks more effectively than the client company can. Within this relationship, the *outsourcing client* or the *client organization* is the company or the agency that sends work outside of that organization for completion. The *outsourcing provider*, in turn, is the entity that performs such outsourced work for the client organization. Such outsourcing, moreover, can occur on a local, a regional, or a national level depending on where the outsourcing provider is located in relation to the client organization.

Traditionally, such outsourcing has been used for two main reasons:

1. Cost: The outsourcing provider can perform a particular activity more cheaply than the client organization can (Gates, 1999; Partridge & Pal, 2001; Sawhney & Zabin, 2001)
2. Efficiency: The outsourcing provider can perform a particular task better, more effectively, or more efficiently than the client organization can (Gates, 1999; Partridge & Pal, 2001; Sawhney & Zabin, 2001)

Of these two items, cost often drives the push to outsource work. And to keep outsourcing-related production costs low, an increasing number of client organizations have begun to form partnerships with outsourcing providers located in other nations.

This move toward the international outsourcing of work is known as *offshoring*, and it is not a new process. Rather, for decades, companies have relied on overseas factories to produce goods such as clothing or consumer electronics (ROI thinking, 2004). In these instances, differences in labor costs often prompted companies to offshore manufacturing work to outsourcing providers located in developing nations (ROI thinking, 2004). That is, the employees working for these international outsourcing providers could perform production tasks for a fraction of the wage associated with workers in industrialized nations.

More recently, however, offshoring practices have expanded beyond basic manufacturing tasks. Now, an increasing amount of knowledge work, such as accounting, medical transcription, legal document processing, and computer programming, is being performed by *outsourcing employees* (individuals who work for outsourcing providers) in developing nations like India, China, Russia, and Vietnam (Relocating the back office, 2003). This shift toward the processing of information vs. the production of physical goods means offshoring increasingly involves the distribution and the management of content.

CONTENT MANAGEMENT AND INTERNATIONAL OUTSOURCING

Much of the knowledge-based work offshored today involves basic business practices including accounting, human resources processing, and information technology (IT) management (Relocating the back office, 2003). As a result, such *business process outsourcing* (BPO) is driven by information. That is, client organizations transmit data, such as financial records, medical information, or legal specifications, to an outsourcing provider and that provider then processes data into a particular kind of information product. In some cases, financial data is processed into tax returns, medical data is transcribed into a patient history file, and legal details are converted into contracts (Let's offshore the lawyers, 2006; Relocating the back office, 2003).

In all of these instances, the client organization is sending information, or content, abroad for outsourcing workers to use in the completion of a particular knowledge-based task. Outsourcing providers receive this content and process, convert, or combine it into new informational materials such as tax returns or legal contracts (Let's offshore the lawyers, 2006; Relocating the back office, 2003). Thus, BPO is a content-driven process in which overseas organizations are continually receiving and processing content for a client organization. As a result, the oversight for offshoring activities, particularly BPO activities, has become a matter of content management. Within this framework, client organizations need to make sure they supply outsourcing providers with the content needed to produce certain informational products. Outsourcing providers, in turn, need to make sure they adhere to audience expectations when processing content into materials to be used by the recipients of such informational products (e.g., the auditor reading the tax return or the insurance claims agent reading the patient file). Thus, success in BPO systems means organizations must keep track of how content is distributed, processed, and repackaged for various audiences. For these reasons, today's outsourcing practices are as much about content management as they are about the oversight of production processes.

In fact, the failure to track and manage content effectively in such outsourcing activities could result in unusable informational products, including misformatted tax forms or incorrectly crafted contracts. Such inadequate materials could then cost a client organization greatly in terms of lost business or even lawsuits related to faulty informational products. For these reasons, the rise of BPO and related content management issues involves more than just cheaper processing costs. Rather, the move to BPO practices is often related to the content management advantages that reduced labor costs can create in offshoring situations.

INCENTIVES TO OFFSHORE CONTENT-BASED ACTIVITIES

Traditional offshoring situations involved the export of basic and unskilled production work (e.g., the manufacture of tennis shoes) that could be performed by most laborers in a given nation. The production of information products, particularly sensitive ones involving financial, medical, or legal information, however, requires a level of training and skill beyond basic manufacturing practices (Let's offshore the lawyers, 2006; Relocating the back office, 2003). Rather, the content of the resulting informational products must be accurate for those products to be of value to the client organization. Thus, reduced labor costs alone are not enough of an incentive to prompt organizations to offshore content-driven tasks. Instead, the increase in BPO practices is fueled by practices that use cost factors to manage content more effectively.

To understand how such practices operate, one must first realize the difference in the cost of skilled/trained technical workers in industrialized vs. developing nations. Some reports, for example, note that "professionals in developed economies make roughly eight to ten times what similar employees in developing economies earn" (Dunn, Fernandes, & Jog, 2004, para. 7). As a result, it is not uncommon for gaming developers in Russia to earn roughly $100 US a week, while many middle managers in mainland China average an annual salary of $9,000 (Nussbaum, 2004; Weir, 2004).

Companies, however, do not simply absorb such cost savings as overall profits. Rather, such "freed capital" is often put back into BPO situations in ways that contribute to content management practices. In many cases, companies use the wage-based savings resulting from offshoring for development activities such as training outsourcing employees in how to manage content- and data-driven processes more effectively (Sink or Schwinn, 2004). Additionally, reduced management salaries mean companies can increase the number of managers who both oversee outsourcing activities (manage content) and who can spend more time training outsourcing employees in effective content management practices (Hagel, 2004; Nussbaum, 2004). For example, as the ratio of subordinates to managers is markedly lower in offshoring situations (8 to 1 in mainland China vs. 20 to 1 in the United States), it is easier for managers to identify inefficiencies and to work with employees to improve performance and avoid problems (Hagel, 2004). Such situations also allow managers to provide subordinates with more one-on-one training, which can make a difference in employee performance (Hagel, 2004; Lewis, 2003). As a result, the average international outsourcing employee can be more effective and more efficient with regard to content management activities.

Additionally, differences in labor costs mean companies can more easily hire well-educated and well-trained employees to perform BPO work. For example, while the average call-center worker in the United States has a high school education, his or her counterpart in developing nations usually has a college degree (Hagel, 2004; Reuters, 2004a). Similarly, most Indian IT workers are trained to operate at a much higher proficiency level than many of their counterparts in the United States (Hagel, 2004). This higher level of education and training can mean BPO workers have a better understanding of and appreciation for the importance of good content in performing tasks. It can also mean that such employees are more accustomed and open to formal training related to effective content management practices.

Moreover, such BPO workers tend to stay in offshoring jobs for longer periods of time. That is, most knowledge-based outsourcing jobs, such as working in customer call centers, tend to have high rates of employee turnover in the United States as individuals there often leave to look for better jobs. In many developing nations, however, secure employment is often hard to find (Farrell & Zainulbhai, 2004; Reuters, 2004a). In such regions, BPO jobs are generally viewed as long-term employment opportunities. These jobs also tend to be among the better paying ones in many developing nations. For these reasons, outsourcing workers in developing nations tend to stay with employers for longer periods of time. Such retention often means it is worthwhile for both client companies and outsourcing providers to invest time and money in training outsourcing employees in effective content management practices. A group of well-trained and long-term outsourcing employees who feel invested in an organization can, in turn, provide better content management in relation to information-based products.

It is perhaps for these reasons that the quality of content-driven outsourcing products and activities have increased over time (Reuters, 2004a; Farrell, D., 2004; Hagel, 2004). It is perhaps also for these reasons that some information-based offshoring activities have reported a better quality of service than do "domestic" counterparts who perform the same jobs (Farrell, D., 2004; Hagel, 2004; Reuters, 2004a). Certain call centers in the Philippines, for example, take 25% less time to handle incoming calls and receive higher rates of satisfaction than do their U.S. counterparts (Hagel, 2004). This increased efficiency means increased savings or profits for the related company—money that can be put back into that company to focus on core activities. This perception, moreover, is shared by key decision makers in many industries.

A final content-related advantage involving international outsourcing is direct access to overseas markets. The key to marketplace success in many developing nations is knowing someone in that region, or having an "in" (Rosenthal, 2001). Similarly, in-country outsourcing providers can introduce their clients to contacts within a particular culture as well as provide clients with advice on how to develop content-based products for consumers in that "other" culture (Rosenthal, 2001). Additionally, international outsourcing employees can serve as test subjects for informational products designed for a particular market. If, for example, a company wishes to introduce a product into the Indian market, Indians working in outsourcing practices there could work with that product and provide feedback for modifying it to succeed with Indian consumers. In such cases, these workers are providing a new kind of content—information that client organizations can compile into business plans for developing and selling information products in certain overseas markets.

THE EXPANSION OF CONTENT-BASED OFFSHORING

The manifold benefits of offshoring have prompted many companies to adopt it as a part of their core business strategy. As a result, the international outsourcing industry is booming. It is currently worth some $10 billion US and employs approximately 500,000 individuals in India alone (Baily & Farrell, 2004; Rosenthal, 2004b). Moreover, international outsourcing is poised to grow markedly in the future. Some researchers believe offshoring will grow by 20% a year through 2008, and by 2015, some 3 million business processing jobs will be performed by outsourcing employees (Baily & Farrell, 2004; Rosenthal, 2004b). Some critics expect this number to be much higher, with outsourcing accounting for at least 5 million jobs in the next five to 10 years (Garten, 2004).

The benefits associated with offshoring have also resulted in the spread of BPO across a variety of industrialized and developing nations. The competitive advantage of cost, quality, and market access realized by the U.S. and British organizations has, for example, prompted companies in many European nations to adopt such practices. French companies have begun working with French-speaking nations such as Senegal and Morocco on a variety of service-based outsourcing projects. These partnerships, in turn, have met with good initial results (Reuters, 2004a). Similarly, German firms have begun exploring outsourcing relationships with Eastern European nations, and while these relationships have not been as cost effective as those involving the United States, the savings related to wage differences are still there (Baily & Farrell, 2004; Farrell, D., 2004; Sink or Schwinn, 2004). To cut costs, Dutch companies have begun using international call centers located in South Africa, where Dutch-based Afrikaans is spoken (Rosenthal, 2004c). Additionally, markets in Spain, combined with the growth in the U.S. Spanish-speaking population, have led to an increase in the amount of work outsourced to Mexico and to Latin America (Rosenthal, 2004a). Even India, the one-time center for international outsourcing, is now outsourcing work to China and to Sri Lanka, where it can be done for less money (Reuters, 2004b). The average Indian programmer, for example, earns roughly $22 US an hour, while the average Chinese programmer earns $15 an hour for the same work (Gaudin, 2003).

Offshoring, however, is not without its problems. While the greatest attention has been paid to job losses related to international outsourcing, an equally important problem has gone relatively unnoticed. That is, offshoring activities increasingly expose content—particularly personal data—to abuse by outsourcing employees. The nature of international outsourcing, moreover, can make it difficult to track or to curtail such abuses once they take place. And while the controversy over job losses may cool over time, the prospects for content abuse are on the verge of growing (Lazarus, 2004a, 2004b). For these reasons, organizations need to understand how offshoring can contribute to data abuses, and they need to devise mechanisms for curtailing such abuse by controlling the dissemination and the use of such content.

THE RISKS ASSOCIATED WITH CONTENT-BASED OFFSHORING

In his book *A Short History of Financial Euphoria* (1990), economist John Kenneth Galbraith warns that the prospect of economic gain related to new developments can prevent individuals from recognizing the pitfalls inherent in these situations. This "euphoria" permits unexpected yet avoidable disasters to strike in ways that could financially destroy those involved in these new developments (Galbraith, 1990). Perhaps the best recent example of such a euphoria-based collapse is the bursting of the dot.com bubble in the 1990s.

International outsourcing, unfortunately, is becoming one of Galbraith's euphoric situations. That is, private companies and public agencies are increasingly relying on overseas workers to perform a variety of information-processing activities. In so doing, these client organizations are relinquishing the control they have over the uses of certain kinds of content. Thus, not only is content being offshored, but the oversight, use, and essentially management of that content is being offshored as well. Yet, if organizations are not careful, their rush to maximize profits via offshoring could lead to major losses in terms of customer confidence and even profits. At the heart of this relatively unrecognized problem are the prospects for the use and abuse of content, particularly content in the form of personal information.

The prospects of content abuse are related to the value associated with certain personal information. Marketers, for example, use compilations of personal data to fine tune the delivery of advertising materials for specific populations or even particular individuals via a process known as target marketing (Ward, 2006). Similarly, companies can use compiled personal data to plan product development around the number of prospective customers to which a certain product— particularly medical or pharmaceutical products—would appeal (Teasley, 2004). In so doing, companies can maximize the profits they can make from a product. This ability to use personal data to focus on specific groups or even individual consumers facilitates other business practices including the sales of goods and services to specific consumers (Teasley, 2004; The revenge of geography, 2003). Corporations, in turn, often collect and archive as much personal data as possible, even if such data has seemingly no value related to current corporate activities. The idea is that such information might have marketing value at a later date (Davis & Meyer, 1998; Siebel & House, 1999; Whitaker, 1999). Additionally, such data provides organizations with a base of valuable information that others might be willing to purchase. As a result, the value of personal information has skyrocketed, and so has the business imperative to collect as much of this information as possible (Davis & Meyer, 1998; Siebel & House, 1999; Whitaker, 1999).

These trends in data collection, however, have also given rise to consumer/ citizen worries related to privacy rights and privacy violations. To address these concerns, many governments have enacted laws that protect consumer information. In the United States, for example, the Fair Credit Reporting Act and the Credit Reporting Reform Act restrict how an individual's financial (and to some extent, medical) data may be used (Cate, 1997). More recently, the Electronic Communication Privacy Act has established some privacy protections related to computing use (e.g., keystroke monitoring) and online communication (e.g., "rerouting electronic communications to provide contemporaneous acquisition") (Johnston, Handa, & Morgan, 1997, p. 81). For these reasons, companies often find themselves performing a complicated balancing act related to consumer privacy. On the one hand, they have a vested interest in compiling and using consumer data; on the other, legal guidelines restrict their abilities to perform both of these processes.

Within this framework of privacy vs. profits, international outsourcing creates an interesting legal situation. If work is performed in another nation, then employees in that nation are operating under a different set of laws than the outsourcing client that provided the work/content. Therefore, a process that might be illegal in the nation of the outsourcing client (a "black market" activity) might be perfectly legal and acceptable in the nation of the outsourcing provider or the outsourcing employees (a "white market" activity). In terms of privacy and data protection, the various national laws dealing with such topics can range from the very strict, as in the European Union's Data Protection Directive, to almost nonexistent such as in the People's Republic of China (Swire & Litan, 1998). The result is a gray area in international law—which laws should apply where and how (Rosenthal, 2005)? Within this gray area, a new field of data collection could begin to emerge: *gray market informatics*.

Gray market informatics is an umbrella term that describes processes in which differences in national privacy laws allow content to be used or processed in ways not intended by the outsourcing client. In some cases, overseas outsourcing employees might compile and sell the personal information (content) collected as a part of their BPO activities. In other cases, outsourcing employees might "hijack" such personal data and threaten to sell or to publicly disclose such information unless the client organization agrees to pay a "ransom" for the return of such content (Lazarus, 2004a, 2004b). In fact, at least two cases of such content hijacking by outsourcing employees have been reported in the popular press to date, and both instances involved medical information sent abroad for transcription purposes (Lazarus, 2004a, 2004b). Thus, outsourcing both content and the management/oversight of how such content is used creates a serious problem area for client organizations engaged in offshoring.

In both instances, the appeal of gray market informatics has to do with tracking and punishing individuals who misuse content. Once content is sent beyond the borders of a particular nation, that nation's regulatory agencies might not have the capabilities—either in terms of time or resources—to track where such data goes. Moreover, once such data is received by an overseas worker, that individual can redistribute it to various subcontractors either within the same nation or in other nations. Many outsourcing providers already engage in such widespread subcontracting practices and often don't make clients aware of this fact until something goes wrong. Such redistribution only increases the difficulty of tracking where content is going. If violations cannot be tracked, it can be difficult to prove content/information abuses occurred. Again, the problem involves a failure to track and thus manage how content is used.

The situation becomes equally complex in terms of penalizing misuses of content. To punish violators, enforcement agencies must catch them in the act of abusing information. Even when violators are identified, if these individuals are working in a nation where such activities are legal, little can be done to prevent them from continuing with these actions (Bhagowati, 2004; Bierce, 1999). Moreover, even if certain data processing laws are in place, for them to be effective, the law enforcement agencies of the related nation must have the authority to apprehend and to punish violators (Bhagowati, 2004; Farrell, Khanna, Sinha, & Woetzel, 2004). If, however, an overseas government lacks the will to enforce such laws, then it could be difficult to stop the related process (Doyle, 2004; Orr, 2004). Thus, international legal differences create problems related to content management in international contexts.

These content management failures have the potential to spark consumer backlashes across multiple industries. In certain cases, large numbers of consumers might become aware that a company—or one of its offshoring employees—is using their personal information in "unapproved" ways. This consumer base could then become so outraged with such activities that large groups of individuals would boycott the offending organizations and refuse to purchase its products (Eisner, 2002; Goolsby & Whitlow, 2003). When done on a large enough scale, such a backlash could have crippling effects on a company's ability to generate profits. In fact, such a backlash in relation to the misuse of medical records served as the driving force behind many of the current practices designed to protect patient data (Smith, 1994). Additionally, such a backlash can gain enough momentum to create new regulatory conditions and agencies that govern how organizations use personal data (Flaherty, 1989). Such regulatory conditions, however, might reduce the speed and ease with which organizations engage in core business processes (e.g., human resources data processing).

Interestingly, many companies believe that they can avoid such problematic situations and protect content through written contracts that stipulate what an international outsourcing provider can and cannot do (Atwood, 2004; Doyle, 2004; Goolsby & Whitlow, 2003; Peterson, 2002). Unfortunately, for such contracts to offer any protection, they need to be viewed as "valid" in the nation in which the outsourcing provider operates (Bierce, 1999; Men and Machines, 2004). Even if such contracts are recognized as legitimate, there is no guarantee that the judiciary system in a particular country will enforce a particular contract. Moreover, in cases where overseas courts do recognize and enforce contracts, that enforcement might not be in line with what the outsourcing client had intended. In the Czech Republic, for example, all international contracts are tried in the Czech Republic and according to Czech law—a factor that could surprise outsourcing clients who expected to try contract violations in their own nations (Doyle, 2004). Thus, many of the conventional approaches to addressing gray market informatics lack true enforcement power that would prevent abuses of personal information.

Further complicating this situation are international trends related to economic development. The financial success experienced by the offshoring hotspots of India and China has prompted businesses in a variety of nations, including Malaysia, the Philippines, Russia, Ukraine, and Vietnam, to move into BPO activities (Gaudin, 2004; Goolsby, 2001; Malik, 2004; Reuters, 2004b; Rosenthal, 2004c; Weir, 2004). Each new country, in turn, brings with it a different set of laws and customs that will affect how content might be treated. The addition of new offshoring locations also makes it more difficult for organization to track international data flows and to isolate where abuses take place. Such complexity might actually act as a deterrent to enforcement, for the more time and money it takes to track data flows, the less likely organizations might be to pursue violators. Thus, the spread of offshoring brings with it an increased need to manage content in such situations.

The convergence of these factors means that now is the time for organizations to develop methods for ensuring the safe treatment of sensitive content in offshoring situations. The fact that many financial-services providers and many healthcare providers are just beginning to examine such processes means there is still time to implement content management approaches that allow for effective international outsourcing. Likewise, the fact that more developing nations are only beginning their expansion into international outsourcing means there is still time to devise effective content management practices that can be adopted by these nations as they begin working in outsourcing situations, vs. trying to impose such practices after the fact. Finally, the current political and business climate is right for such content management approaches to be developed in an atmosphere of support and interest. Within the context of this new situation, technical communicators are uniquely positioned to play a central role in developing the content management practices that will allow offshoring to operate effectively (from a cost perspective) and safely (from a privacy perspective).

THE MOVE TO EFFECTIVE CONTENT MANAGEMENT IN OFFSHORING SITUATIONS

The presidential race of 2004 brought international outsourcing to the forefront of public discussion by making it a central topic of each candidate's economic platform. As a result, a topic that had received relatively little media attention quickly became a hot-button issue that could not be ignored. This increased scrutiny prompted many companies to review their outsourcing practices in order to quell public concerns. Out of this review process came two key findings:

1. Organizations need to take a more active and a more direct role in content management relating to offshoring situations. In particular, such content management needed to focus on the tracking of where content went and the oversight on how content was used (Atwood, 2004; Bendor-Samuel, 2004; Eisner, 2002).
2. Communication is essential to effective content management in off-shoring situations, and mechanisms for effective communication needed to be established both between client organizations and outsourcing providers and within client organizations themselves (e.g., across divisions and between management and workers) (Atwood, 2004; Goolsby, 2003).

Many of the content management practices called for in relation to these two central findings involve skills central to technical communication practices. Perhaps the most important of these skills is being able to communicate complex ideas to different audiences and across different kinds of media—something at which technical communicators are highly skilled (Atwood, 2004; Eisner, 2002; Goolsby, 2003). The idea is that the more informed employees are of critical situations involving the handling of certain kinds of content, the more likely they are to address those situations effectively. Moreover, effective content management in such contexts requires the development of a system for regularly distributing information across media and audiences (e.g., newsletters, intranet updates, etc.) (Atwood, 2004; Goolsby, 2003). Again, technical communicators tend to be trained in how to create and to manage such systems.

The question then becomes, what are some of the content management activities technical communicators can engage in to address problems related to information distribution in offshoring situations? The answer lies with the management of content/information within an organizational context.

CONTENT MANAGEMENT SOLUTIONS TO OFFSHORING PROBLEMS

The key to addressing problems of information abuses is to revise content management practices in a way that effectively addresses the tracking and accountability loopholes created by offshoring situations. By developing communication-based approaches to content management practices, technical communicators can effectively address these offshoring problems. In so doing, they can also reveal how they can contribute to management practices in international outsourcing situations. While addressing such a complex situation can be a daunting task, technical communicators can begin by focusing on a few foundational strategies that reveal how effective communication is essential to managing content in offshoring situations.

Strategy 1: Develop categories for classifying content.

The greatest problem related to outsourcing and security has to do with the misperception that all content has equal value and thus should be treated equally. As discussed in this chapter, such a situation is not the case. Rather, certain kinds of data, particularly personal data, have greater value. As a result, such content is a prime target for abuse in offshoring situations. Thus, the first thing organizations need to do is to create categories for identifying what content is safe for offshoring and what content should be classified as "sensitive" and remain within a company for protection. The processing of sensitive content would take place "in-house" where both organizational regulations and national laws could manage its uses and protect it from abuses.

As technical communicators regularly develop classification systems and definitions as part of their jobs, they are well positioned to create sensitive data classifications. Moreover, as the in-house processing of sensitive content will likely become the task of technical communicators—who generally work with such data (e.g., results of clinical trials)—it makes sense that technical communicators would be the individuals best suited to develop such a classification system, that is, they would already be familiar with what kinds of personal information merit special treatment.

Should technical communicators wish to look for legal models to help in defining sensitive content, they could use the definition of "personal data" given in Chapter I of the European Union's Data Protection Directive (Directive 95/46/EC). This statute defines what personal data needs to be treated with extreme care, and it has become a foundational definition for the concept of sensitive data in other nations, including the United States (Eisner, 2002; Swire & Litan, 1998).

Strategy 2: Create content-based writing and editing practices.

Dividing content into safe and sensitive categories is only a partial solution to offshoring problems. At some point, this separated content will need to be reassembled into a uniform product (e.g., a manual, a report, etc.). The individuals—in house and overseas—working on a project, however, could have different understandings of how the information they are working with should be turned into parts of a final documentation project. As a result, different employees could write in different styles, use different organizational principles, or create incompatible documentation if left to their own resources. For this reason, the division of content for outsourcing brings with it the need for a new kind of content-based publications management.

Within this new management system, the division, outsourcing, collection, and reassembly of information and documentation would need to be closely structured and supervised. Individuals working on different content-related tasks of an overall process would need to be informed of everything from how to draft documentation to how to organize material and how to address a range of layout and design issues (e.g., the structure of headings). Finally, once the different parts of an overall project were collected, they would still need to be reviewed/edited to make sure the sections of the final document were logically assembled and stylistically smooth.

This editing process would be more than a mere final copy edit. Rather, it would involve major revisions across different, smaller documents in order to create

- consistency of style and terminology within an overall document,
- integration of information across sections of a larger document, and
- coherence of ideas and information presentation throughout a large, final document.

In essence, the technical communicator would be revising a collection of multiple, smaller documents into a single seamless and effective informational product.

Such writing and editing practices are familiar tasks within the field of technical communication. Many technical communicators are familiar with the concept of developing and using style guides to generate documentation. Additionally, many technical communicators are accustomed to either writing documentation as part of a team or relying on single sourcing practices to create integrated documents from different chunks of text. Such experiences provide technical communicators with insights related to what aspects of distributed documentation creation are most susceptible to problems and what kinds of strategies can be used to address such problems effectively. As a result, the creation and management of such content-based writing and editing practices would provide technical communicators with a unique opportunity to move into management positions in relation to the international outsourcing of work.

Strategy 3: Develop a communication plan for letting in-house employees know of the importance of content categories and content management approaches related to outsourcing.

If employees are made aware of what data is considered sensitive and how that data can be abused, they are more likely to take steps to treat the processing and the distribution of such data with greater care (Goolsby, 2003; Peterson, 2002). Informed employees are therefore more effective employees. The key to this situation is to remind employees regularly of such situations as well as inform them of new developments that could affect the processing or the abuses of sensitive data. Such information dissemination could be done via an organizational intranet site that is readily available. To further assist employees, such a site could have "FAQ" or "self test" modules that can answer employee questions or allow employees to test their knowledge of international outsourcing, privacy concerns, and data processing/data sharing policies.

Strategy 4: Create an intranet site that instructs employees (and managers) in how to recognize and address different content abuses they might encounter when working in outsourcing relationships.

To help with this process, technical communicators might wish to include descriptions of how to spot certain kinds of content abuses. They might also want to provide employees and managers with a list of whom to contact in which corporate office or government agency with concerns about a particular kind of violation (Peterson, 2002). By increasing the number of individuals monitoring international outsourcing activities, one decreases the chances that violations will go unnoticed. Also, by helping employees feel like they are a part of such processes, one increases the chances that these employees will play a more active role in these activities (Goolsby, 2003; Peterson, 2002). Such a site should also be designed to provide new, outsourcing-related news on a daily basis (encourages daily use of site) and include self-test scenarios so employees can evaluate if they are correctly working with outsourcers. Technical communicators should also make sure that outsourcing providers are aware that the company has adopted such measures in order to provide incentive to avoid data abuses (see Strategy 3).

Strategy 5: Work with clients and suppliers to draft job tasks related to outsourcing (don't leave activities ambiguous).

In the past, organizations have paid little attention to how outsourcers perform tasks related to using content to develop new informational products (Atwood, 2004; Goolsby & Whitlow, 2003). As a result, outsourcing providers might either be lacking the direction needed to treat certain content effectively, especially if their own nation does not call for any special treatment of such data. Likewise, outsourcing providers might engage in standard processes that actually create the potential for content abuse (Bhagowati, 2004; Goolsby & Whitlow, 2003). By developing descriptions of how to perform specific job tasks, companies can reduce the risks of the standard processes performed in other countries creating privacy problems (Peterson, 2002). Included in such descriptions would be a discussion on what sensitive content is, how it should be treated, how to identify prospective abuses of that content, and what steps to take to report such abuses to both the client and to legal officials in that nation (Doyle, 2004; Peterson, 2002).

As such an approach involves the writing of instructions (i.e., how to perform certain tasks), technical communicators would be well suited for heading up such tasks. Additionally, as some of the employees working for such companies will likely speak a language other than that of the outsourcing client, translation will become an important component of this process. As technical communicators are often the individuals who work with translators, they are well suited to both creating such job-task descriptions and having them translated for outsourcing suppliers.

Each of the aforementioned strategies is crucial to maintaining content security in outsourcing situations. Each strategy also conforms to the governance models proposed by outsourcing researchers. As a result, the individuals who spearhead such activities would be providing a valued service to their related company. Moreover, the emphasis that organizations are now placing on the oversight of international outsourcing means that these services are likely to be recognized in very public ways.

The focus such activities place on communication, instruction, translation, and user-centered design means that technical communicators are ideally suited to lead such activities. In so doing, they can increase

- their visibility,
- their contributions to the management of an organization, and
- the value individuals within a company assign to technical communication activities.

By pursuing such activities, technical communicators can establish a foundation of inherent value that allows them to advance within an organization. Such perspectives could also protect them from the international outsourcing trends currently affecting so many other knowledge-based professions (Giammona, 2004).

CONCLUSION

While international outsourcing offers a range of benefits, it also creates certain problem areas, especially related to the abuses of personal data. Fortunately, these problems can be addressed through content management practices that focus on effective communication. As a result, technical communicators are well-positioned to use outsourcing-related concerns to reveal how the skills they possess contribute to their abilities to manage offshoring situations. For this reason, technical communicators need to pursue such activities now, while offshoring remains somewhat limited in scope. While the strategies presented in this chapter can provide technical communicators with the means for realizing such opportunities, these steps are by no means definitive. Rather, these strategies are simply models or foundations for the kinds of undertakings technical communicators can pursue to manage content effectively in offshoring contexts. For this reason, readers should feel free to modify the strategies presented here or to adopt new approaches to addressing these issues.

REFERENCES

Atwood, M. (2004). The art of governance. *Outsourcing Center*. Retrieved December 27, 2004, from
http://www.outsourcing-requests.com/center/jsp/requests/print/story.jsp?id=4616

Baily, M. N., & Farrell, D. (2004, July). Exploding the myths of offshoring. *The McKinsey Quarterly*. Retrieved November 11, 2004, from
http://www.mckinseyquarterly.com/article_print.aspx?L2=7&L3=10&ar=1453

Bendor-Samuel, P. (2004). Lou Dobbs: Here's why you're wrong! *Outsourcing Center*. Retrieved December 20, 2004, from
http://www.outsourcing-requests.com/center/jsp/requests/print/story.jsp?id=4565

Bhagowati, B. (2004). India responds to growing concerns over data security. *Outsourcing Center*. Retrieved December 27, 2004, from
http://www.outsourcing-requests.com/center/jsp/requests/print/story.jsp?id=4720

Bierce, B. (1999). International outsourcing: The legal view of what's different. *Outsourcing Center*. Retrieved December 12, 2004, from
http://www.outsourcing-requests.com/center/jsp/requests/print/story.jsp?id=1216

Cate, F. H. (1997). *Privacy in the information age*. Washington, DC: Brookings Institution Press.

Davis, S., & Meyer, C. (1998), *Blur: The speed of change in the connected economy*. Reading, MA: Addison-Wesley.

Doyle, J. F. (2004). Avoiding outsourcing pitfalls. *Outsourcing Center*. Retrieved December 12, 2004, from
http://www.outsourcing-requests.com/center/jsp/requests/print/story.jsp?id=4626

Dunn, S., Fernandes, J., & Jog, S. (2004). Harnessing the full power of offshore outsourcing: What range of cost savings should a company expect? *Outsourcing Center*. Retrieved February 25, 2008, from
http://www.outsourcing-journal.com/nov2004-offshore.html

Eisner, R. S. (2002). Smoothing over the privacy potholes in BPO outsourcing. *Outsourcing Center*. Retrieved December 12, 2004, from
http://www.outsourcing-requests.com/center/jsp/requests/print/story.jsp?id=2451

Farrell, C. (2004, November 22). Giving thanks for offshoring. *BusinessWeek Online*. Retrieved December 30, 2004, from http://www.businessweek.com/pring/bwdaily/dnflash/nov2004/nf20041122_7377_dbb013

Farrell, D. (2004). How Germany can win from offshoring. *The McKinsey Quarterly*. Retrieved December 30, 2004, from http://www.mckenseyquarterly.com/article_page.aspx?ar=1496&L2=7&L3=10

Farrell, D., Khanna, T., Sinha, J., & Woetzel, J. R. (2004). China and India: The race to growth. *The McKinsey Quarterly*. Retrieved October 6, 2004, from http://www.mckinseyquarterly.com/article_print.aspx?L2=19&L3=67ar=1487

Farrell, D., & Zainulbhai, A. S. (2004). A richer future for India. *The McKinsey Quarterly*. Retrieved August 16, 2004, from http://www.mckinseyquarterly.com/article_page.aspx?ar=1440&L2+7&L3=10&srid=6&g

Flaherty, D. H. (1989). *Protecting privacy in surveillance societies: The Federal Republic of Germany, Sweden, France, Canada, & the United States*. Chapel Hill, NC: University of North Carolina Press.

Galbraith, J. K. (1990). *A short history of financial euphoria*. New York: Penguin Books.

Garten, J. E. (2004, June 21). Offshoring: You ain't seen nothin' yet. *BusinessWeek Online*. Retrieved December 30, 2004, from http://businessweek.com/print/magazine/content/04_25/b3888024_mz007.htm

Gates, B. (1999). *Business @ the speed of thought: Using a digital nervous system*. New York: Warner Books, Inc.

Gaudin, S. (2003, November 19). Offshoring IT jobs expected to accelerate. *ClickZ*. Retrieved November 30, 2004, from http://www.clickz.com/stats/sectors/b2b/print.php/3111321

Giammona, B. (2004, August). The future of technical communication: How innovation, technology, information management, and other forces are shaping the future of the profession. *Technical Communication, 51*, 349-366.

Goolsby, K. (2001). Nobody does it better. *Outsourcing Center*. Retrieved December 12, 2004, from http://www.outsourcing-requests.com/center/jsp/requests/print/story.jsp?id=1816

Goolsby, K. (2003, May). Governing attitudes: 12 best practices in managing outsourcing relationships. Dallas, TX: *Outsourcing Center*.

Goolsby, K., & Whitlow, F. K. (2003, June). *Haste makes waste: How to avoid outsourcing problems*. Dallas, TX: Everest Group.

Hagel, J. III. (2004). Offshoring goes on the offensive. *The McKinsey Quarterly*. Retrieved November 1, 2004, from http://www.mckinseyquarterly.com/article_page.aspx?ar=1406&L2=1&L3=106&srid=11

Johnston, D., Handa, S., & Morgan, C. (1997). *Cyberlaw: What you need to know about doing business online*. Toronto: Stoddart Publishing.

Lazarus, D. (2004a, March 28). Looking offshore: Outsourced UCSF notes highlight privacy risk. *San Francisco Chronicle*. Retrieved March 1, 2005, from http://www.sfgate.com/cgi-bin/article.cgi?file=/chronicle/archive/2004/03/28/MNGFS3080R264.DTL

Lazarus, D. (2004b, April 2). Extortion threat to patients' records: Clients not informed of India staff's breach. *San Francisco Chronicle*. Retrieved March 1, 2005, from http://sfgate.com/cgi-bin/article.cgi?file=/c/a/2004/04/02/MNGI75VIEB1.DTL

Let's offshore the lawyers. (2006, September 18). *BusinessWeek*. Retrieved November 10, 2006, from
http://www.businessweek.com/magazine/content/06_38/b4001061.htm?chan=search

Lewis, W. W. (2003). Educating global workers. *The McKinsey Quarterly*. Retrieved November 10, 2004, from
http://www.mckenseyquarterly.com/article_page.aspx?ar=1357&L2=7&L3=10

Malik, R. (2004, July). The new land of opportunity. *Business, 2*(0), 72-79.

Men and Machines. (2004, November 11). *The Economist*. Retrieved December 6, 2004, from
http://www.econcomist.com/printedition/PrinterFriendly.cfm?Story_ID=3351402

Nussbaum, B. (2004, September 20). Is outsourcing becoming outmoded? *BusinessWeek Online*. Retrieved October 11, 2004, from
http://www.businessweek.com/print/bwdaaily/dnflash/sep2004/nf20040920_0654.htm?cha

Orr, G. R. (2004). What executives are asking about China. *The McKinsey Quarterly*. Retrieved October 6, 2004, from
http://www.mckinseyquarterly.com/article_pring.aspx?L2=7&L3=8&ar=1478

Partridge, D., & Pal, N. (2001). Rebalancing management in the emerging e-marketspace: From control to leadership. In N. Pal & J. M. Ray (Eds.), *Pushing the digital frontier: Insights into the changing landscape of e-business* (pp. 91-116). New York: American Management Association.

Peterson, B. L. (2002). Information security in outsourcing agreements. *Outsourcing Center*. Retrieved December 27, 2004, from
http://www.outsourcing-requests.com/center/jsp/requests/print/story.jsp?id=2355

Relocating the back office. (2003, December 11). *The Economist*. Retrieved December 20, 2003, from http://www.economist.com/displaystory.cfm?story_id=2282381

Reuters. (2004a, July 18). France outsources, Senegal calls. *Wired*. Retrieved September 20, 2004, from http://www.wired.com/news/print/0,1294,64262,00.html

Reuters. (2004b, September 2). Outsourcing's next big thing—Malaysia? *News.Com*. Retrieved September 7, 2004, from http://news.com.com/2100-1011-5344618.html

ROI thinking: A best practices for ROI assessments. (2004, September). *Gantry Group Newsletter*. Retrieved November 10, 2006, from
http://www.gantrygroup.com/images/Newsletter1/News26.htm

Rosenthal, B. E. (2001). Business risk. *Outsourcing Center*. Retrieved December 21, 2004, from
http://www.outsourcing-requests.com/center/jsp/requests/print/story.jsp?id=1685

Rosenthal, B. E. (2004a). How real estate choices affect offshoring decisions. *Outsourcing Center*. Retrieved December 12, 2004, from
http://www.outsourcing-requests.com/center/jsp/requests/print/story.jsp?id=4718

Rosenthal, B. E. (2004b). META predicts offshoring will continue to grow at 20 percent clips through 2008. *Outsourcing Center*. Retrieved December 27, 2004, from
http://www.outsourcing-requests.com/center/jsp/requests/print/story.jsp?id=4714

Rosenthal, B. E. (2004c). Why the US and UK are calling South African call centers. *Outsourcing Center*. Retrieved December 12, 2004, from
http://www.outsourcing-requests.com/center/jsp/requests/print/story.jsp?id=4717

Rosenthal, B. E. (2005). New outsourcing risks in 2005 and how to mitigate them. *Outsourcing Center*. Retrieved January 2, 2005, from http://www.outsourcing-requests.com/center/jsp/requests/print/story.jsp?id=4721

Sawhney, M., & Zabin, J. (2001). *The seven steps to Nirvana: Strategic insights into ebusiness transformation*. New York: McGraw-Hill.

Siebel, T. M., & House, P. (1999). *Cyber rules: Strategies for excelling at e-business*. New York: Doubleday Press.

Sink or Schwinn. (2004, November 11). *The economist*. Retrieved December 6, 2004, from http://www.economist.com/printedition/PrinterFriendly.cfm?Story_ID=3351542

Smith, H. J. (1994). *Managing privacy: Information technology and corporate America*. Chapel Hill, NC: University of North Carolina Press.

Swire, P. P., & Litan, R. E. (1998). *None of your business: World data flows, electronic commerce, and the European privacy directive*. Washington, DC: Brookings Institution Press.

Teasley, B. (2004, December 28). Involvement data. *ClickZ*. Retrieved December 30, 2004, from http://www.clickz.com/experts/cm/analyze_data/print.php/3450561

The Revenge of Geography. (2003, March 15). *The Economist Technology Quarterly*, pp. 19-22.

Ward, S. (2006). Target marketing. *About.com*. Retrieved November 12, 2006, from http://sbinfocanada.about.com/od/marketing/g/targetmarketing.htm

Weir, L. (2004, August 24). Boring game? Outsource it. *Wired*. Retrieved September 20, 2004, from http://www.wired.com/news/print/0,1294,64638,00.html

Whitaker, R. (1999). *The end of privacy: How total surveillance is becoming reality*. New York: New Press.

CHAPTER TEN

The Technical Editor as New Media Author: How CMSs Affect Editorial Authority

Nicole Amare

Content management systems (CMSs) are changing the way technical communicators create texts, particularly in electronic environments. In this chapter, CMS means a computer software system for collaboratively creating and storing content, although CMS is a broadly used term (i.e., a manila folder is technically a CMS because it is one means of storing and organizing content). Prior to CMSs, technical writers wrote text and graphic designers created visuals that were edited mostly by people and partly by software (e.g., MS Word's grammar checker and HTML editors like Robohelp). The introduction of CMSs has influenced the process of writing itself as "content creation" to be managed by technology; namely a CMS, although even the *creation* of the "original" content in document production can be controlled by CMSs. The purpose of the CMS is to "save money, time and resources" (Carter, 2005, p. 25), and it accomplishes these tasks by filing content as data that is easy to recycle. The goal is to create text that is easily retrievable and reusable, a task that is best achieved when the writing is composed "generically" and with "'basic' modules of text" (Carliner, 2002, n.p.). A CMS works best with short blocks of text: "The less information in the module, the more likely that it might be reused" (Carliner, 2002, n.p.); it works even better if the writer follows some kind of template or preferably writes the content using a *document type definition* (DTD). A DTD contains tags or attributes that limit what can be written for the sake of consistent document formatting. Therefore, technical writers either create documents as potential templates to be reconfigured by the CMS or, as is the case more frequently, compose documents not as original text to be later manipulated but composing as a process of inputting information or content that agrees with the DTD.

In terms of the traditional rhetorical triangle (author, text, and reader; Kinneavy, 1980), the new CMS author is instructed to think more about future uses of the same text (or graphics) in terms of production rather than focusing on audience; any textual adaptation is left to the CMS and to editors who may revise for different audiences, media, or software tools. The author is now one more step removed from the reader (author ↔ text ↔ edited text ↔ reader). Figure 1 by Rob Prideaux offers a pictorial representation of how a CMS functions in terms of authorship, text, publication, and audience. Clearly, this CMS-influenced approach to authoring has several ramifications for the field of technical communication, particularly for the role of editors who work with CMSs. The editor or editorial team may, for instance, create a DTD for any document written for the fda.gov (the U.S. Food and Drug Administration) Web site because the FDA must regulate how a new drug can be described for consistency's sake and because of legal liabilities. I will discuss in this chapter how this document regulation, along with usability issues, influences both authorial creativity and editorial authority.

Rockley (2005) notes that CMSs "chang[e] the way people think and work," and this change is particularly difficult for authors: "Collaborative authoring is required to ensure that content can be reused across many different products and across many different types of documentation." And because "authors may be protective of their content," companies will need to change their management approach to encourage "structured writing and collaborative writing" (Rockley, 2005, n.p.). Although authors "may experience feelings of loss of creativity, or what they believe are invalid restrictions on their writing style" (Rockley, 2005, n.p.), the goal is to create easily reusable "data" (words, texts, visuals). In this chapter, I argue how this changing role of technical authorship through CMSs is elevating the technical editor's role in document production, although I show that this shift in emphasis from the creation of content to its delivery has been developing for some time, especially through the proliferation of the Internet and software authoring tools. Using relevant theoretical and industry issues from the field of technical communication, I debunk the myth that technical editors should not be valued as much as authors and merely serve as what Rude (2006) refers to as "grammar janitors." Technology, particularly the Internet and CMSs, has had a profound effect on the editor's role in production. I then discuss the implications of this paradigm shift in authority for both authors and editors who work with CMSs.

BEFORE CMSs:
THE DEVALUING OF TECHNICAL EDITORS

Before I discuss the implications of CMSs for editorial authority, it is necessary to establish how this change in editorial authority occurred and why it is so significant for technical editors. In *Technical Editing*, 4th ed., Rude (2006) describes the duties of a technical editor:

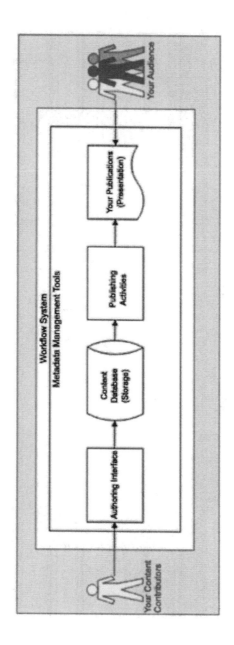

Figure 1. Pictorial representation of how a CMS functions. **Source**: Rob Prideaux's *What Does a Content Management System Do?* http://www.techsoup.org/learningcenter/webbuilding/page5062.cfm

> Editing does require high standards of language use, but you will find that cleanup is a small part of what technical editors do. Technical editing, *like writing*, requires information design—*creating* documents that work for the people who use them. Functional documents require more than correctness. Editors who help *to create* these documents must be able to *imagine* documents in use by particular readers, to use good judgment as well as grammar handbooks, to manage long-term projects, and to *collaborate* with others (p. xv, emphasis added).

The italicized words in the above definition emphasize the technical editor's role as author instead of "grammar janitor." Although many editors are also authors and vice versa, technical communicators continue to make a professional distinction between authors who write (create texts and visuals) and editors who edit (correct the texts and visuals). This definition, regardless of the semantic assumption that the word "correct" implies authority, confines the editor to a helpmeet role, one always second to the authority of the author. For example, Allen and Voss (1998) argue in "Ethics for Editors: An Analytical Decision-Making Process" that the editor's allegiances should be to the author, not necessarily to the reader or to the company they work for, let alone to themselves.

> When rewriting is necessary to improve clarity, editors should take care to preserve the author's style. Even when editors have a responsibility to maintain the house style, they must avoid doing so at the expense of the author's voice. Indeed, the document **belongs** to the writer; the editor should make only those changes that can be justified as assisting the reader while respecting the author's ownership of the work (p. 58; emphasis in original).

Allen and Voss's assertions about the roles of editors and authors and concerning the concept of document ownership represent the ideological author worship some of us still maintain as technical communicators. If there is any doubt that our profession still glorifies the author over editors and even writers (yes, there's a distinction), we just need to read the title to Benz's and Nichols's (1998) STC paper: "Be An *Author*, Not a Writer: Breaking Into Retail-Market Computer Book Publishing" (emphasis in original title) as if being an author were more prestigious than being a writer, both of which are still more valued than being an editor. Every technical communication conference I have attended in the last decade has had at least one session or workshop on *How to Publish a Book* or some variation of creative authoring, signaling that some of us may work as technical writers and editors but still harbor a belief that our life's goal is to write the great American novel. If anything, the pervasiveness and function of CMSs is forcing us to acknowledge finally the expertise of the editor in text production and the declining value of originality and therefore traditional concepts of authorship.

Perhaps because they are a decade old, Allen and Voss's (1998) assertions about editorial and authorial roles misrepresent (1) what most technical editors and authors do, (2) the legal relationship between copyright law and actually textual ownership, and (3) the ethical connection between editors and authors—especially those working with CMSs—and their readers/customers/end users. Most technical editors today are indeed authors (not just "also authors") in that they spend the majority of their time writing, creating, and imagining documents, although they are also often responsible for storing, sorting, harvesting, and publishing text(s). It is by the very nature of what they do that makes technical editors new media authors, and as such they should be granted more authority, power, recognition, and pay, particularly with the rising use of CMSs. Although CMSs may be sold as editing and archival tools, the fact remains that editors are needed now more than ever to author or "re-author" text. Jeffrey Veen (2004) contends that "content management is not a technology problem. If you're having trouble managing the content on your Web site, it's because you have an editorial process problem" (n.p.). Although Albers (2000) predicted that document databases *could* possibly reify the technical editor role as "nothing more than a copyeditor/proofreader" (p. 194), he concludes that "regardless of the production method, an editor must ensure the resulting document communicates to the reader" (p. 198). I agree with Albers that the use of CMSs only enhances technical editors' expertise because of editors' innate content management skills; that is, the ability to align the document's message with user needs. Kostur (2006) argues that "many organizations tend to focus on the system instead of on the content the system is intended to support" (p. 193). I believe that it is technical editors who are the ones who will guarantee that the attention be on content and not on the technological tool. Considering technical editors as new media authors in light of recent technology changes like CMSs and the Internet will not only allow us to value the technical editor's role in production more fully but will hopefully encourage better research about editing theories and practices with regard to document production changes like CMSs.

LITERATURE REVIEW: THEORY

To date, a handful of researchers have called for a reconsideration of the technical communicator's role based on a critique of authorship. In "The Technical Communicator as Author: Meaning, Power, Authority," Slack and colleagues analyze three levels or "models" of communication theory—transmission, translation, and articulation—to argue that technical communicators do indeed transmit or translate messages, but they do much more: like authors, they also *articulate* knowledge, language, and meaning. This process of articulation is what we as technical communicators recognize as related to power: "only by looking through the lens of articulation can we rearticulate the technical communicator and technical discourse as participating fully in the articulation of meaning and thereby fully empower the discourse as authorial" (Slack, Miller, & Doak, 1993, p. 15). It is hardly a stretch to see how technical editors also articulate when they delete, change, and add knowledge, language, and meaning to texts and visuals. This knowledge base goes well beyond writing skills, as technical editors are expected to be SMEs not only of language but of technology (Anderson, 2005; Dayton, 2006), company policies (Amare, Nowlin, & Weber, 2009), ethics and legal issues (Allen & Voss, 1998), production management (Eisenbaum, 2006; Weber, 2003), global contexts (Maylath, 2006), and usability (Tarutz, 1992; Weber, 2003), to name a few. With this knowledge base, technical editors today are able to "offer so much more: analysis, evaluation, imagination. and good judgment applied to information design and management" (Rude, 2006, p. xv).

In sum, technical editors are today's new media authors with regard to CMSs and other types of document databases for two reasons: First, as Albers (2000) observes, editors must ensure that the content matches user needs, which Kostur (2006) believes should be accomplished through a highly iterative usability process, where both the content and users are assessed. Second, through the creating of authoring templates and DTDs, technical editors not only determine what happens to a document after it has been authored, but actually establish guidelines, through tools like DTDs, which essentially shape how the document will be written. Take, for example, online instructions for any PDA. In order for the future online instructions to cohere with the print instructions, the technical editor would include in the DTD tags and attributes that would limit how the instructions would look. A technical editor's work with these instructions in a CMS goes way beyond formatting issues, however. If the company creating the PDA was subject to legal regulations, then the tags and attributes would encourage the author to create content that fell within these guidelines. If the author decides to override these tags and create whatever s/he wanted, the technical editor would have to step in and re-create the entire document to fit both user needs and company regulations, not to mention matching cost needs such as space issues and the preferences of the marketing department, who want certain buzzwords in all materials associated with the PDA. Another option to managing the content against all of these needs after the author takes creative license would be to completely restrict the author's text options for inputting from the start (although this might create hostility between the technical editors and the members of the document-composing team).

A CMS, however, is not our field's first introduction to the rise of editorial authority in lieu of the declining authorial role. In addition to communication theory, Slack and colleagues refer to critical theory, specifically Foucault's "What Is an Author?" in order to link the power of the author to the potential of considering technical communication as a field of "authored discourses" (Slack et al., 1993, p. 13). In his essay, Foucault challenges our herolike worship of certain authors and our disregard for others (e.g., Fitzgerald as author of a novel vs. author of a legal contract), remarking that "the author is not an indefinite source of significations which fill a work; the author does not precede the works" (Foucault, 1979, p. 159), implying that we should perceive of writing as not necessarily "birthed" by an author. Although Foucault speaks largely of literary authors and works in his essay, he does discuss "scientific" texts (including technical communication) as being largely anonymous, published without the same "author-function" (p. 149) as one ascribes to Shakespeare. Nevertheless, we still perceive of authorship—even of a text that is anonymous—as creation and origination.

A traditional (and misrepresentative) description of the process of creating a technical manual might read something like this: a software engineer creates software; a technical writer creates the help menu for the software; a technical editor edits the manual. This linear and restricted process is usually not the case, at least not for successful and effective products and specs. As I argue in the next section on Practice, technical editors are not limited to proofreading any more than engineers are the grand Author-gods of "new" software development, because technical editors must know both the product (software) and the process (writing), as well as everything else about the discursive context of said product and process, including the demographics of target consumers, laws and policies, and such. This is especially true with CMSs, where most of the authority for document work and rework lies in the hands of the editing team.

Building on Slack and colleague's discussion of authorship and communication theory, Henry (1994) posits in "Toward Technical Authorship" that the author in anonymous technical documents is always implied.

> Technical authorship, then, consists of using the diverse knowledge and skills of the communicator in a technical composition. This composition "represents" the culture from which it emanates, in its values and norms, and locates that culture in broader cultural contexts. The communicator— or writer, or composer—communicates far more than technical information. S/he communicates these values anew. Because the implied author conveys these values, the communicator is in a sense "writing culture" . . . (p. 455).

I would argue here that the implied author should most certainly include the technical editor, who articulates and mediates the "broader cultural contexts" relevant to target audience and uses "diverse knowledge and skills" to create a document that is usable and well received by the same target audience. Like Slack and colleagues (1994), Henry refers to critical theory to make his argument, using Foucault's essay and Roland Barthes' "The Death of the Author" (1977) to make the case that the author role and author function is text and context dependent. Again, I would argue that the shifting author role is not limited to a technical writer or engineer/SME and does signify technical editors as well, particularly editors involved in CMSs. Within the context of CMSs, the editor is the one who can control what Kostur (2006) refers to as "viral content" (p. 193). In order to create documentation that is desirable to users, the editor would measure user need against company goals, costs, and the like. When a company purchases a CMS, oftentimes all previous documentation is simply entered into the CMS without first assessing whether or not that content is still usable. The outcome is bad content that is being "managed" by the CMS—tagged, restructured, and reformatted—to create even more "bad content *everywhere* it is used" (Kostur, 2006, p. 193; emphasis in original). Viral content is one result for organizations that don't recognize the crucial shift from the authored content to the expertise of the editor: companies that blindly enter in the old content value the authored documents but not whether those documents still benefit users, which the technical editor can ensure through employing usability assessments throughout the entire document production processes.

French poststructuralism is merely a theoretical springboard for critiquing authorial roles; CMSs make real the death of the traditional author in terms of creative control over content and authority shift to the technical editor who now negotiates the CMS, the author, the organization, and the content in terms of usability (users' needs) and consistency (cost effectiveness). In addition, collaboration as a writing and revision process contributes to the shift in authority from traditional authors to technical editors. In "What Experienced Collaborators Say about Collaborative Writing," Allen, Atkinson, Morgan, Moore, and Snow (1987) interviewed several collaborative authors across academe and industry and discovered that certain writing tasks, like planning the document and revision, were performed by all group members, regardless if the member was classified as a supervisor, editor, staff member, professor, or such. In other words, each group member was engaged in the editing process of revision, a task of reimagining all or part of the text and visuals, or what most of us actually call writing or rewriting. Whatever remaining threads of traditional author construction—the writer in isolation, creating new and original text for user consumption—is deconstructed by the necessarily collaborative paradigm created when organizations implement a CMS. For example, the technical editor no longer just edits text that has already been created by someone else; the editor influences document production before text enters the CMS and even before the document is written by an author per se via collaboration with others regarding usability assessments, cost analysis, style and format guidelines, legal regulations, and DTD tags and attributes. Once the editing team deems text acceptable for CMS entry, even more authority is required: "The maintenance of the information within a document database as useful containers of information ready to be coherently combined, rather than a degenerated collection of individual pieces of data, rests squarely upon a technical editor's skill" (Albers, 2000, p. 204).

LITERATURE REVIEW: PRACTICE/INDUSTRY

Considering technical editors as new media authors in research and in practice will encourage organizations to recognize editors' authority and power on the job in creating effective texts and visuals with and sometimes against CMSs. Unfortunately, corporations have thus far focused too much on CMS's ability to manage a lot of content and not on the need for an editor to manage both the document production, of which the CMS is merely a tool: "it seems that in the rush to adopt what appears to be the latest technology, content management has become its own goal, with much focus on the technology rather than on the content the technology is intended to manage" (Kostur, 2006, pp. 193-194). According to Tarutz (1992), the technical editor's role should be that of championing users' needs (p. 42), which is why CMSs cannot be the only content managers in the document production process. I agree with Anderson (2005) that "we need to expand our notions of the editorial process and gain a more complex understanding of the roles editors may carry out in their organizations" because "there is much more to examine and understand in terms of the social contexts and tools influencing editorial processes" (pp. 484-485). In her pilot research, Anderson found that editors did not fulfill the stereotype of introverted fussbudgets who obsessed over grammar. Moreover, Anderson also discovered that even the description of editors as taught in textbooks and scholarly articles didn't always reflect how editors actually function in organizations (p. 493). CMSs have changed the editorial role even further from the original misconception of editors as glorified typists. CMSs, while diminishing the traditional authorial role because of the need for fragmented and reusable content, have accelerated the technical editor's authority. The editor now manages—or should manage—the *entire* document production, including whether or not content should be entered into a CMS or if, based on costs and users' goals, an organization even needs a CMS at all.

Anderson agrees with Tarutz's assessment that "while traditional publishing environments are driven by production, desktop publishing environments are driven by the writing" (in Anderson, 2005, p. 493). This means that technical editors are involved in every stage of document production, from the planning stage to the initial drafting to reiterative drafts to usability tests in the production cycle. The editor must manage the iterative cycle of rewriting. Similarly, most CMSs now have an authoring tool that allows content to be updated remotely, removing the author from the process or shifting that role to other members of the production team.

> It is this authoring tool that is the key to the success of the CMS. By providing a simple mechanism for maintaining the site, authoring can be *devolved out into the business itself.* For example, your marketing manager maintains the press release section, while your product manager keeps the catalogue up to date (Robertson, 2003, n.p.; emphasis added).

This excerpt gives new meaning to Barthes' "The Death of the Author" (1977) essay. To reinstate the authorial role but in a new way, technical editors are stepping in, creating text or visuals, revising or managing the content before and after it enters a CMS, and testing the document against end user comprehension and satisfaction. Mikelonis and Constantinides (2005) assert that "to improve writing and editing, we would all agree that we must move beyond the level of the sentence to larger units of discourse" (p. 151). I would further this call by asking us to expand our technical communication discourses to include more and better informed discussion of what technical editors really do and how valuable their role is in the overall process, especially in the context of Web production and CMSs.

Prior to CMSs, writing could be seen more as a moment, an event where originality and creative ideas are channeled into text. Each new document brought about a new writing event and a chance for new ideas and text. However, CMSs tend to ground content around the CMS itself, regardless of what is being written or rewritten: what structure does this document need to take? What keywords does the document need to contain (or not contain)? IBM's Darwin Information Typing Architecture (DITA) is one such structure for creating and publishing technical documents around modules of text. Now, instead of an idea prompting pen to paper (or keyboard to blank screen), writing is the formation of data modules that can be reused easily because the CMS needs to catalog them for later recovery. What happens if data modules are poorly written or cannot be easily recovered? A new document may need to be composed, creating potential inconsistency with existing documents and wasted time. The CMS cannot do its job if the technical editor does not control the formation of data modules and create the appropriate metadata, tags, or semantic labels that need to be over the DITA structure. The technical editor helps the CMS to work more efficiently, saving the organization time and money. However, the editor's job is also to control the CMS in that the content still needs to be created with the user in mind, not only the CMS. In other words, what good are similar structures across media for PDA instructions if content does not help users? A technical editor's creating an authoring template, managing the data, controlling the CMS, and editing the document at the end of the production cycle does not guarantee good content if the editor is not also there to create and define the content against changing user needs.

The idea of the technical editor championing the user in the document production cycle is not new to users of CMSs, but it is something that needs to be reinforced now that many organizations use CMSs. Traditionally, research in technical editing, though, is still engendered with the author/editor binary, with the editor in the helpmeet position. Quoting Mancuso's definition of the technical editor as "diplomat in addition to being a language craftsman [sic]" (1992, p. 32) and Speck's definition of editors as therapists who embrace "the role of an empathetic listener" (1991, p. 306), Mackiewicz and Riley agree that editors should be placed "in a cooperative, advisory role [rather] than an authoritative one. For both practical and humanistic reasons, the editor must convince through tact and reasoning (rather than dictate through force and belittlement) . . ." (2003, p. 84). This insistence on a lack of an authoritative role is very problematic for technical editors who work in organizations with CMSs, for their expertise is needed in every stage of document production, especially to ensure that content matches the *user*, not just the CMS's software needs.

Recognizing technical editors as having more authority now than before the use of CMSs, though, will not happen without opposition, and surprisingly this resistance comes not only from the SMEs or even authors themselves, but mostly from our own field's approach toward technical editing as a profession. In terms of author resistance in a practitioner setting, Rockley notes that CMSs mean that authors have to engage in "structured writing [,] a very different way of writing that is often difficult for authors to adopt" (2005, n.p.). This "different way of writing" may include collaboration or the encouragement of generic writing, such as creating chunks of data/text that are easy to reuse and index for archival purposes, and the author may not appreciate the loss of creative opportunities and the realization that the technical editing team will have more expertise with content management.

What seems more pragmatic is to conceive of technical editors not as helpmeets but as consultants, *experts* who collaborate with SMEs and manage the ultimate document manager—CMSs—to shape information to be effective for end users. Technical editors' authority with CMSs keeps the human element in the design process and eliminates the use of CMS as technology for technology's sake. Editors as user advocates is a helpful concept for the customers, but this role may alienate editors from some authors. Technical communicators who call for editors to be therapists or diplomats are envisioning better documents as a result of author-editor collaboration, but this union should not have to be a hierarchical one, with the editor in the helpmeet role. This collaboration is also what Allen and colleagues (1987) found when they conducted their interviews. Contrast the definition of editor as helper with Anderson's findings: "'Editors' may be writers, project managers, public relations specialists, production managers, or even communication consultants" (2005, p. 486). She also found that editors relied heavily on nonwriting tasks—what Anderson labels "soft skills" (p. 489)—such as effective oral communication and management skills to succeed. Editors in Anderson's pilot study were not perceived as helpers per se but as experts integral to every stage of the production cycle. This expert role is especially emphasized by editors who work as new media authors using CMSs to create cost-efficient and effective documents.

Let's return to the PDA example. Prior to the company's purchasing a CMS, the PDA was sold with a small booklet, containing data on how to operate the

PDA. The marketing department determined the size of the booklet for cost and packaging purposes, so the print instructions are actually shorter and structured differently from the online instructions, which are in a PDF attached to the company's homepage. A toll-free call center contains instructions to help users troubleshoot their PDAs, but these instructions are nothing like the booklet or the PDF. Similarly, an internal memo is sent to company employees regarding the necessary update of these instructions for new PDA models; the attached instructions to that e-memo are an abbreviated version of the booklet.

The company purchases a CMS to help streamline documents and save money. The CMS functions as a means to make the documents consistent. Without consulting the technical editing team first, the company may decide to enter in all of the existing documents, meaning the CMS simply contains old data content. The technical editing team will now have a lot of work to do with the CMS itself, ensuring that documents do not contain poor content (this will require great skill on the part of the technical editors if all of the old data is unusable!). Ideally, if the technical editing team is consulted from the get-go, it can determine which documents, if any—or which parts of documents—should be entered into the CMS based on regulation requirements and usability. The technical editors can also create structures and work with DTDs to make the most effective documents. Finally, they can ensure usability throughout the entire process. For example, the online instructions can remain in PDF form, but they definitely need to be searchable, for users are not going to read through an entire PDF to find answers to their troubleshooting questions.

Therefore, CMSs inherently increase the need for and authority of technical editors, although some have argued that the (unrealized) editorial authority has always been there. Speck (1991) supports editorial expertise "to override auctorial authority" (p. 300). He argues that while (some) technical editors may be perceived as low status, all editors can use the rhetorical strategies of "editorial dialogue, define the audience, cite authority, and teach" (p. 311). Using these strategies will help perceived low-status editors to gain authority and higher-status editors to maintain or reestablish the authority that is requisite with editors' expertise and role in the production cycle. Traditionally, collaboration is one way in which editors and authors can work together as *equals* toward the common goal of producing effective texts and visuals. Yet, as Speck points out, "the myth of auctorial authority subverts that goal by suggesting that authors are more powerful than editors, when, in fact, the opposite is true" (p. 305). Speck's assertions, however, are pre-CMS; editors no longer need to emphasize grammar expertise to "override auctorial authority" as CMSs are already reinforcing technical editors' skills in the production cycle as equal to if not more valuable than those of traditional authors', as demonstrated in the PDA example.

THEORETICAL IMPLICATIONS OF CMSs FOR
EDITORIAL AUTHORITY

I have already discussed how the implementation of CMSs in organizations affects editorial authority. Beyond this real-world shift, though, are historical and theoretical underpinnings for why editors have been so devalued compared with traditional authors prior to the introduction of CMSs. In this section, I provide some ideological background explanation as to why CMSs are having such a profound impact on editorial authority right now. Speck's editorial vs. auctorial authority has been a relevant issue in academic disciplines other than but also including technical communication. In "The Editor as Author: Re-Producing the Text," Fulton (1995) delineates between the traditional and valued theory of authorship and the skill of editing.

> For many years, the practice of editing texts was seen as just that: a practice, as distinct from a 'theory', by which manuscripts were presented in an accessible printed form for modern readers. More recently, however, contemporary critical and cultural theory has enabled us to view editing as a practice which is as theory-based as any other kind of linguistic or textual practice, and this new awareness has in turn led to a critical examination of established editorial methods (p. 67).

The editing theories Fulton refers to deal specifically with editing medieval texts, an important difference because the authors are dead and cannot be consulted. This theorizing of editing is relevant to modern-day work settings, however, because the CMSs—depending on the settings chosen by the technical editor—determine document attributes such as design, organization, and significance. Much in the same way, the editor of medieval texts controls these content elements as well.

Fulton's appeal for viewing editing as theory-based echoes such technical communication research as Dragga and Gong's *Editing: The Design of Rhetoric* (1989). Fulton refers to Michael Lapidge's definition of two editing methods that dominate the field of medieval studies; namely the conservative approach and the liberal approach. The conservative approach tried to keep the text true to itself by comparing it with other manuscripts, whereas the liberal approach focuses more on the author than the text, calling for the editor to revise the text so that it restores what the author would have written. Fulton notes that the liberal method dominated the twentieth century, with several attempts by editor-scholars to rewrite texts to represent the intentions of a now deceased author.

In medieval studies at least, the potential for editorial authority is great; because the author is dead, the editor is granted permission to speak for the author, making the editor "constructed as individually gifted as the actual author" (Fulton, 1995, p. 70). What is interesting is that the editor is allowed to assume an authorial role, yet still recognized as the editor who has created text with his or her own subjective intentions but based on some kind of subject expertise about the literary period, author, genre, and so on. As Fulton correctly notes, this type of authorship is crucial for editors yet dangerous for audiences who accept the revised text as authentic. To solve this double-bind, Fulton asks that we "liberate ourselves from the ideology of authorial intention" and remember that "editing must be linked to the function and audience of the edited text" (p. 77). Fulton's analysis, in a field historically linked to technical communication, shows us that editors cannot replace traditional authors per se. Nevertheless, her example demonstrates the need to reevaluate the role of authorship—of SMEs—and the relationship of power to the role of editing. What has happened instead is that the authorial role has evolved to where the usability of text and visuals—predominantly in Web authoring environments that may or may not depend on CMSs—has surpassed the creative muse who once spoke in the ear of the author, writing in isolation, with no authoring tools other than ink and paper.

The problem with the "ideology of authorial intention" and with the hero-author mythology that Foucault and Barthes criticize is our field's misconception not only with what editors do (activities that are authorlike) but mostly with our traditional valuing of the idea over the text. Authors and SMEs work with ideas, we tend to argue, and editors with grammar, and the creators of the big ideas—the Idea Gods—should get more credit for the work than the individuals who simply work with the language that represents those grand ideas. This assumption is faulty on three levels: (1) it fails to recognize editors as idea makers as well as linguistic creators, just as authors are also text fixers (as Anderson found in her workplace study); (2) it ascribes to the translation model of communication (from Slack, et al., discussed earlier in this chapter) when clearly editors deal with articulation; and (3) it places a value on ideas over words, a value that is displaced in that it is not recognized even by our own copyright laws.

In "Who 'Owns' Electronic Texts?" Howard correctly informs us that ideas have no legal value, no protection under the law: "According to the copyright statute in the U.S. Code, only the tangible expression of ideas belongs to the copyright holder. Ideas are not copy protected" (Howard, 1996, p. 403). Moreover,

> In terms of actual practice, current copyright law does not grant authors the right to demand remuneration for their intellectual labors, and it does this by protecting the ways authors express ideas. However, it does not allow them to claim ownership of the ideas they express; authors cannot expect to have and maintain a monopoly on truth (p. 403).

Nevertheless, we as a society and as a profession cling to the Romantic notion that authors own their original ideas. Plagiarism scholars (c.f., Angélil-Carter,

2000; Howard, 1999; Woodmansee, 1994) trace the idea of our valuing novel thought to the treatment of invention by Romantic authors like Wordsworth, Coleridge, and Shelley. However, the valuing of original thought can be traced back even further, to Aristotle, who asserted that the uncommon was valuable because it is rare, and this included not only tangible property but properties of the self: "Further, what is rare is a greater good than what is plentiful. Thus, gold is a better thing than iron, though less useful; it is harder to get, and therefore more worth getting" (1984, pp. 2170-2171). Because authorship is no longer a rare commodity, though, particularly in the electronic age, we should reassess our valuing of editors who have the power, authority, and expertise to effectively create, reuse, and improve documents for audiences.

Our traditional overvaluing of authors and our undervaluing of editors stem not only from our privileging invention but from our belief that authors own their texts. Again, this is a misconception; intellectual property rights are "a privilege we are granted by the government under certain specific circumstances" (Howard, 1996, p. 400), not rights based on natural property law. In fact, as Howard notes, English and American copyright law of the sixteenth century was not originally created to protect authorial texts at all but rather to protect the *public's* access to texts after the printing press book of the fifteenth century (p. 401). Today's copyright law, although protective of some author's texts (or some of an author's words), still largely functions as a means to make the public access to information fair while still granting remuneration to authors for their authorial labor.

The rub, of course, is that editors of academic journals or anthologies do not receive much remuneration, especially in terms of prestige. Creating ideas is still valued but not protected, whereas collecting texts and revising words is not. And, even when editors are renowned as authors, as in the case of an edited collection, prestige varies greatly, and recognition is still greater for those individuals who, say, authored a chapter in a collection as opposed to those who edited it. Tenure and promotion guidelines are changing, but the value is still based on the Romantic notion of creating original ideas, ideas that are reflected in the words on the page. Valuing editors as authors would be recognizing the value of the text over the idea behind the text, as if the two were somehow separable.

The introduction of CMSs in 1995 begat a culture that is focused on content consistency, recoverability, and reusability. These three areas are the technical editor's areas of expertise, which make the technical editor the natural fit for managing production, whether data is pre- or post-CMS. However, no matter how consistent the internal memo, the online help, the booklet, and the call center documents are for a company's PDA product, the content is worthless unless it meets regulations (e.g., ISO guidelines) and, most important, users' needs.

PRACTICAL IMPLICATIONS OF CMSs FOR
TECHNICAL EDITORS

Although academics seem to espouse most of the changing theory, it is the practitioners who have ultimately influenced the meaning of editor from grammar janitor to new media author. The proliferation of CMSs across organizations, while redefining creatively authored technical documents, has served to augment the role of the technical editor. Because CMSs encourage structured text creation in data modules for enhanced recoverability and reusability via DTDs, traditional authorship has been placed in a precarious role. Consequently, CMSs have influenced the document production process so tremendously that skills innate to technical editors are further extended, making editors new media authors. This increase in prestige warrants higher salaries and more respect for technical editors' multifarious expertise.

Although advocating technical editors as new media authors has many benefits for the practice of editing and the development of editing theories within the field of technical communication, there are some potential drawbacks, although much more so within academics, where the traditional model of print production is still pervasive. The greatest area of power abuse would probably occur with nonnative speakers who are working with or through a native-speaking editor to print or publish their work. In "Cross-Cultural Collaboration: Whose Culture Is It, Anyway?" Bosley (1993) provides quotes from two Asian students—one Vietnamese, one Japanese—quotes that reveal that nonnative speakers of English, especially those from cultures with differing communication styles and dynamics from Western countries, do not challenge other group members because to do so would be a sign of disrespect. Combine this cultural politeness trepidation with the power dynamics of, for example, NNE speakers trying to publish in an English-speaking journal but being told their article will not be acceptable without the inclusion of a native-English speaking author.

However, CMSs create a world potentially more open to a global playing field with regard to the above example, although one that may not be soon adopted by universities, who tend to value traditional modes of authorship. If an academic journal editor were to use a CMS (such as Drupal) for an online journal, the editor could set up DTDs to assist nonnative speakers in their article creation. Although many may argue that the CMS here would stamp out all creativity, it would actually be up to the editor which tags and attributes to request in the authoring template. I have already used such authoring templates when writing articles for conference proceedings, where the editors wanted all texts in the same structure, but tags and attributes could also be created for content as well as document organization. These DTD features would greatly assist nonnative speakers trying to publish in a particular journal and would make the editor a user advocate.

Although Rockley (2005) correctly argues how authors feel that their content creation is restricted by CMSs, the power dynamics created by editing and authoring texts in non-CMS environments is equally problematic. For instance, I worry about the power dynamics of professors as editors of students' work and of academic journal editors who subsume authorship even though they have not contributed substantially to the overall or even a majority of the document production. For example, Mathews found in his study of publication trends in the *Journal of Applied Behavior Analysis* that *JABA* published a disproportionate number of articles that included one of the editors as co-author. Although Mathews states that his findings are descriptive, he does note that "Journal editors are gatekeepers; they review and shape the work of others and influence the journal's direction and quality. They also contribute to the body of knowledge within a field as authors" (1997, p. 717). It is not clear whether these editors submitted their own collaboratively authored work to the journal an inordinate number of times, or if the editors became co-authors late in the production cycle by offering to serve as second, or third, or more authors once an article had already been submitted by an independent author or group of authors. However, the implementation of a CMS for an academic journal like *JABA* might help these authors, much like the nonnative English speakers. If academic journal editors use CMSs for the purposes of getting authors published and not to further their own careers, they will also function as user advocates while still encouraging high quality control with their journals.

In the context of Web production and CMSs, the technical editor essentially is today's new media author in terms of expertise and authority. Consider these lines of advice from Jeffrey Veen (2004) to current companies: "All publications require editorial expertise." "Put editors in charge." "An editor manages all content on the site." CMSs may not have completely eradicated the need for traditional authors per se, but the concept of original text and creativity has been dramatically altered. In addition, CMSs have brought to the forefront the wide-ranging expertise of technical editors, especially with regard to improving usability and managing the *entire* document production cycle. Much in the way the film industry will often recognize directors as having more authority with filmmaking than screenwriters, CMSs have further amplified the role of the technical editor.

REFERENCES

Albers, M. J. (2000). The technical editor and document databases: What the future may hold. *Technical Communication Quarterly, 9*, 191-206.

Allen, L., & Voss, D. (1998). Ethics for editors: An analytical decision-making process. *IEEE Transactions on Professional Communication, 41*(1), 58-65.

Allen, N. J., Atkinson, D., Morgan, M., Moore, T., & Snow, C. (1987). What experienced collaborators say about collaborative writing. *Iowa State Journal of Business and Technical Communication, 1*(2), 70-90. Rptd. in J. Johnson-Eilola & S. Selber (Eds.). (2004). *Central works in technical communication* (pp. 351-364). New York and Oxford: Oxford University Press.

Amare, N., Nowlin, B., & Weber, J. (2009). *Technical editing: Products and processes.* Upper Saddle River, NJ: Prentice Hall.

Anderson, R. (2005, July). The context dependent editorial process: Toward a more complex understanding of the technical editor. *Proceedings of the International Professional Communication Conference* (pp. 484-497). Limerick, Ireland: IEEE.

Angélil-Carter, S. (2000). *Stolen language? Plagiarism in writing.* Harlow, UK: Longman.

Aristotle. (1984). *The complete works of Aristotle* (Vol. 2). J. Barnes (Ed.). Princeton, NJ: Princeton University Press.

Barthes, R. (1977). The death of the author. *Image, music, text.* New York: Hill & Wang.

Benz, C. J., & Nichols, M. C. (1998). Be an *author*, not a writer: Breaking into retail-market computer book publishing. *STC's 45th Annual Conference*, Anaheim, California.

Bosley, D. (1993). Whose culture is it, anyway? *Technical Communication Quarterly, 2,* 51-62.

Carliner, S. (2002). Information developer's toolkit: How to write information so you can use it again. In *Models, processes, and techniques of information design.* Retrieved November 7, 2005 from http://saulcarliner.home.att.net/id/reuse.htm

Carter, T. (2005, December). Content management for the masses. *Intercom, 52*(10), 24-27.

Foucault, M. (1979). What is an author? In J. Hararí (Ed.), *Textual strategies: Perspectives in post-structuralist criticism* (pp. 141-160). Ithaca, NY: Cornell University Press.

Fulton, H. (1995). The editor as author: Reproducing the text. *Bulletin, 19,* 67-78.

Dayton, D. (2006). Electronic editing. In C. Rude (Ed.), *Technical editing* (4th ed.). New York: Pearson Longman.

Dragga, S., & Gong, G. (1989). *Editing: The design of rhetoric.* Amityville, NY: Baywood.

Eisenbaum, H. (2006). Project management. In C. Rude (Ed.), *Technical editing* (4th ed., pp. 419-437). New York: Pearson Longman.

Henry, J. (1994). Toward technical authorship. *Journal of Technical Writing and Communication, 24,* 449-461.

Howard, R. (1999). *Standing in the shadow of giants: Plagiarists, authors, collaborators.* Stamford, CT: Ablex.

Howard, T. (1996). Who "owns" electronic texts? In P. Sullivan & J. Dautermann (Eds.), *Electronic literacies in the workplace: Technologies of writing* (pp. 177-198). Urbana, IL: NCTE. Rptd. in J. Johnson-Eilola & S. Selber (Eds.). (2004). *Central works in technical communication* (pp. 397-408). New York and Oxford: Oxford University Press.

Kinneavy, J. L. (1980). *A theory of discourse: The aims of discourse.* New York: Norton.

Kostur, P. (2006). Incorporating usability into content management. *Proceedings of the International Professional Communication Conference* (pp. 193-196). Saratoga Springs, NY: IEEE.

Mackiewicz, J., & Riley, K. (2003). The technical editor as diplomat: Linguistic strategies for balancing clarity and politeness. *Technical Communication, 50,* 83-94.

Mancuso, J. (1992). *Technical editing.* Englewood Cliffs, NJ: Prentice Hall.

Mathews, R. (1997). Editors as authors: Publication trends of articles authored by *JABA* editors. *Journal of Applied Behavior Analysis, 30,* 717-721.

Maylath, B. (2006). Editing for global contexts. In C. Rude (Ed.), *Technical editing* (4th ed., pp. 347-366). New York: Pearson Longman.

Mikelonis, V., & Constantinides, H. (2005, July). Editorial smarts: Contextual and single sentence editing tools. *Proceedings of the International Professional Communication Conference* (pp. 151-160). Limerick, Ireland: IEEE.

Prideaux, R. (2005, May 17). *What does a content management system do?* Tech Soup: The Technology Place for Nonprofits. Retrieved November 7, 2005 from http://www.techsoup.org/learningcenter/webbuilding/page5062.cfm

Robertson, J. (2003, June 3). So, what is a content management system? In *KM Column*. Retrieved November 7, 2005 from http://steptwo.com.au/papers/kmc_what/index.html

Rockley, A. (2005). Change management for content management projects. In *STC: Indiana Chapter*. Retrieved November 7, 2005 from http://www.stc-indiana.com/articles-library.php?id=82_0_2_2_C

Rude, C. (2006). *Technical editing* (4th ed.). New York: Pearson Longman.

Slack, J., Miller, D., & Doak, J. (1993). The technical communicator as author: Meaning, power, authority. *Journal of Business and Technical Communication, 7,* 12-36.

Speck, B. (1991). Editorial authority in the author-editor relationship. *Technical Communication, 38,* 300-315.

Tarutz, J. (1992). *Technical editing: The practical guide for editors and writers.* Cambridge, MA: Perseus Books.

Veen, J. (2004, April). Why content management fails. In *Adaptive Path* April 1, 2004. Retrieved November 7, 2005 from http://www.adaptivepath.com/publications/essays/archives/000315.php

Weber, J. (2003). Working with a technical editor. In *Technical Editors' Eyrie.* Retrieved April 1, 2006 from http://www.jeanweber.com/about/workwith.htm

Woodmansee, M. (1994). *The author, art, and the market: Rereading the history of aesthetics.* New York: Columbia University Press.

CHAPTER ELEVEN

Applying Cohesion and Contrastive Rhetoric Research to Content Management Practices

Lyn F. Gattis

The literature of content management currently focuses almost entirely on practicalities: how content management technology functions, how to implement it, why organizations should or should not invest in it (Boiko, 2002; Hackos, 2002; Houser, 2003; Johnsen, 2001; Rockley, 2001, 2003a, 2003b). Proponents of content management systems (CMS) have asserted that the methodology helps organizations to deliver information in greater volume, to more readers, and in more forms than ever before. Moreover, proponents contend, CMS improve the consistency and timeliness of information across document suites and help organizations to coordinate content and physical design—all of which are features said to benefit readers (Boiko, 2002; Hackos, 2002; Rockley, 2003a).

However, current literature seldom distinguishes between *content* as discrete blocks of information and *text* as coherent, conceptually unified passages. CMS assemble documents from independent, stand-alone content units, thereby minimizing the need for transitions, contextual framing, cohesive ties between units, and other metalanguage. By reusing standardized content units, CMS improve consistency within document suites. However, such content is often (by definition) nonsequential and nonreferential, and whether end users find such content easy to understand is a question rarely addressed, for the CMS literature seldom discusses the linguistic, psychological, and cultural principles underlying reading comprehension. Further, aside from general localization issues, the literature says little about adjusting managed content for non-Western readers, a growing audience for technical material.

This chapter therefore takes the end user's point of view, examining scholarship in technical communication, linguistics, educational psychology, and reading that bears on the comprehensibility of managed content. Two research areas are especially relevant. One area involves studies of coherence and cohesion, rhetorical principles that help readers to create meaning at a text's global and local levels, respectively. Conventional writing practices employ many grammatical, lexical, and other devices to signal relationships among units of text so that readers can construct meaning more easily. By contrast, CMS require that writers avoid developing text that is too closely constrained by a specific logic or rhetorical structure. On one level, CMS are practical tools for retrieving and recombining units of text efficiently in particular situations. On another level, however, CMS radically limit the use of more traditional tools such as cohesive ties, which are themselves practical composing devices used for specific rhetorical purposes. Without textual guides to deeper understanding, which Brown and Duguid (2000) describe as "all the fuzzy stuff that lies around the edges" of information (p. 2), readers may lose perspective, resulting in narrow, superficial interpretations of information. Research on coherence and cohesion can therefore help to inform the new composing strategies emerging from content management methodologies.

The other research area of interest is cross-cultural communication, particularly the findings of contrastive rhetoric research, a linguistic specialization that examines textual patterns across cultures and genres. Contrastive rhetoric is based on empirical findings that "there are situationally, generically, or stylistically preferred compositional forms and that these are not the same from language to language or from culturally defined situation to culturally defined situation" (Scollon, 1997, p. 353). Considerable research suggests that, while cultures are more fluid and heterogeneous than was once believed, culture-based differences among end users do exist (Chung, 2000; Connor, 2002; Eggington, 1987; Fukuoka & Spyridakis, 2000; Goldman & Murray, 1992; Hinds, 1990; Kaplan, 1988; Scollon & Scollon, 2001; Ulijn & Salager-Meyer, 1998; Warren, 2002). Therefore, an important first step to improving managed content for those readers is to define their reading needs thoughtfully and accurately, heeding Carliner's warning about simplistic and "formulaic approaches . . . [such as] 'the five issues to avoid when writing for international audiences'" (2000, p. 569). For many CMS, content localization "is a complex issue, often barely recognized" by current software (Boiko, 2002, p. 337). Although software can organize localization tasks, humans still must analyze and perform the localization itself (Boiko, 2002). Hence genuine cross-cultural document development is no less challenging for writers in a CMS environment than for writers using traditional composing practices. As in conventional writing, cross-cultural content management must be grounded in research, drawing from the knowledge base for cross-cultural text reception to strengthen comprehension for a variety of end users.

This chapter begins by summarizing theoretical and empirical studies of textual cohesiveness, including writing practices and problematic rhetorical issues where applicable. The chapter then reviews selected reception studies in different cultural contexts. Although not all of the studies are recent, few (if any) of their findings have been applied to content management practices. The studies do not offer easy prescriptions, for responses of readers and writers can be difficult to measure, and studies sometimes yield contradictory results. However, by surveying existing studies, we can better frame questions for future work.

SCHOLARSHIP IN TEXTUAL COHESIVENESS

Although textual cohesion is not the only rhetorical issue associated with CMS, it does represent one conspicuous difference between conventional composing, which uses cohesive devices to link blocks of text, and CMS composing, which minimizes such links between blocks. Scholars do not understand completely how cohesive devices operate in text (Grabe & Kaplan, 1996), but many agree that cohesion is related to "the structure of the text itself" (p. 61) and that cohesion contributes to overall textual coherence, though in a subordinate way (Campbell, 1995; Halliday & Hasan, 1989). Whereas coherence "involves connections between the discourse and the context in which it occurs" (Campbell, 1995, p. 5), including the reader's world view, prior knowledge, and expectations of the text (Campbell, 1995; Grabe & Kaplan, 1996; Thompson, 1986; Ulijn & Salager-Meyer, 1998), cohesion is associated with specific linguistic cues at the surface of the discourse. In expository, nonfiction, and instructional texts, cohesion may relate more closely to usability than to coherence, to the extent that it helps users complete tasks more efficiently (Campbell, 1995). Thompson (1986) theorizes that cohesion also contributes to a text's predictability.

Little or no published experimental work in any discipline focuses specifically on textual cohesiveness in CMS. However, studies in several areas do address three broad linguistic theories of cohesion—semantic links, perceptual phenomena, and surface textual features—in ways that are relevant to managed content. By becoming more aware of these theories, writers in CMS environments may be able to develop managed content that end users can comprehend more easily.

Cohesion as Semantic Link

Early theoretical studies of cohesion (which continue to dominate the field) focus almost exclusively on semantic links among textual elements. In their seminal work, Halliday and Hasan (1976) define cohesion as a "semantic relation" that occurs whenever "the interpretation of any item in the discourse requires making reference to some other item in the discourse" (p. 11); that is, the second item assumes the discursive existence of the first. Together, the items sharing this semantic link form a cohesive tie, of which Halliday and Hasan identify several (sometimes overlapping) types. Ties of *reference* send the reader to related information elsewhere in the text, usually preceding. In English, these ties include comparatives, demonstratives, and personal pronouns. Ties of *substitution* are lexicogrammatical links that replace one word or phrase with another upon second occurrence; *ellipses* omit the second word or phrase entirely, leaving the reader to infer the meaning of the absent item. *Conjunctive* ties express relationships between two items, usually sentences. For example, one sentence may elaborate on the meaning of the other (*additive* tie); one may reverse the meaning of the other (*adversative* tie); one may have produced the other (*causal* tie); or one may relate sequentially to the other (*temporal* tie). Finally, *lexical* ties create cohesion through word choice, because the writer either repeats a word or uses a second word "systematically related" (p. 284) to the first, such as synonyms. Hoey (1983, 1991) has hypothesized that the cohesiveness of a given passage is largely the result of lexical networks formed by exact or near-exact repetition within that passage.

The effect of all these ties is to form from otherwise unrelated sentences a text, "a unit of situational-semantic organization . . . constructed around the semantic relation of cohesion" (Halliday & Hasan, 1976, p. 25). In short, cohesive ties help readers to connect the meaning of a given point with other information that precedes or follows that point. When composing by conventional methods, writers have regular opportunities to insert cohesive devices as needed, thereby making explicit the semantic relationships between blocks of text. By contrast, writers for CMS have fewer opportunities to insert cohesive devices, because content units must remain independent (both semantically and structurally) so they can be separated and reassembled as directed by document type definitions (DTDs).

Scholars disagree on the precise role semantic cohesiveness plays in reading comprehension, an issue particularly relevant to writers managing content for international audiences. One view holds that cohesion represents "the set of linguistic resources that *every language* has . . . for linking one part of a text to another" (Halliday & Hasan, 1989, p. 48; emphasis added); consequently, readers' sensitivity to cohesiveness may depend mainly on their overall linguistic competence. Some research has found only weak links between cohesive ties and reading comprehension (Freebody & Anderson, 1983). However, other research (Horiba, 1996; MacLean & Chapman, 1989) has found that readers do use cohesive ties to achieve coherence. Poor readers appear to process information below the sentence level and have more difficulty integrating small pieces of information into the larger context, while good readers are more successful in working with larger pieces of information and "maintaining the global unity of the text" (MacLean & Chapman, 1989, p. 26). Readers' ability to perceive cohesion in a given language may therefore be a function of verbal and cognitive maturation.

An opposing view is that some discursive traditions downplay textual coherence or achieve it without explicit cohesiveness (Hinds, 1987). For example, Reid (1992) found that native Arabic, Chinese, Spanish, and English speakers and writers use organizational and cohesive devices differently at the sentence level, although the language groups consistently favor some devices over others for specific types of discourse. Other scholarship has confirmed that conjunctive devices are "particularly problematical for Asian readers and writers of English" (Scollon & Scollon, 2001, p. 64). In the People's Republic of China, English instructional programs have tended to emphasize sentence correctness rather than discourse organization (Mohan & Lo, 1985). As a result, because learners in the PRC are less likely to study English sentence linkages or texts as entities, writing expository prose (except for translations) is difficult even for advanced learners (Johns, 1984). Moreover, writers tend to use fewer lexical cohesives than native English writers, possibly because of the Chinese tendency to teach English vocabulary words in isolation "rather than as part of a semantically-related chain" (p. 70). In one study of Chinese middle-school readers of four English passages (Sharp, 2002), comprehension scores were significantly and unexpectedly higher for the single test passage constructed without explicit cohesive devices. Researchers therefore believe the readers' responses to the absence of cohesive devices may reflect differences between Chinese and Western rhetorical conventions.

Implications for CMS

Research to date suggests that semantic cohesiveness matters most for readers of English texts, particularly native speakers, and may be somewhat less important for nonnative speakers with limited English reading experience. Of the types of semantic ties identified by scholars, lexical repetition (exact or near-exact repetition of words) may be the most feasible means of creating cohesiveness within and across discrete managed content units.

Cohesion as Perception of Structure

Halliday and Hasan (1976) tend to downplay the role of structure in textual cohesiveness, describing cohesion generally as a catalyst operating semantically on "elements that are structurally unrelated" (p. 27). However, later theorists have concluded that perceived structure does play a significant role in textual cohesion. Campbell (1991, 1995) believes that a "purely semantic" explanation of cohesion is inadequate for some genres such as business and technical writing, arguing instead that cohesion in nonfiction texts is "better understood as a general perceptual phenomenon" in which structure is an important factor (1991, p. 222). According to Campbell (1991), a text is cohesive if it foregrounds distinctive semantic elements against a consistent background of repeated semantic and structural features. Because the repetition makes explicit the relationships among semantic components, thereby unifying the text, the reader perceives and interprets contrasting elements more easily. Structural devices that appear to strengthen textual cohesion in this way include "thematic progression" (p. 227), which involves repeating topics or comments in successive sentences, as in given-new construction; "syntactic parallelism" (p. 228), or repeating syntactic features across sentences, lists, or headings in order to link semantic elements; and "graphic repetition" (p. 230), or using typography, enumeration, charts, and other visual elements consistently to heighten contrasts in semantic units.

In a sense, these structural devices complement Halliday and Hasan's (1976) concept of "tight" and "loose" semantic texture (p. 296). In a passage characterized by tight textuality, cohesive ties are stronger and highly interdependent; in loose textuality, ties are less numerous and dense. Texture within or across paragraph boundaries may be of either type. It follows, then, that if structural (especially graphic) features are highly similar, the consistent background they provide helps to tighten textuality across boundaries; if the structural features are dissimilar, then the background is less consistent and textuality is looser. When texture is looser, contrasting semantic elements may be more difficult to perceive and thus less meaningful to the reader. The complementarity of semantic and structural elements is supported by a recent study of secondary school ESL readers at three English proficiency levels (Chung, 2000), which found that, for low-level readers, conjunctives (semantic element) appeared to aid local reading comprehension; paragraph headings (structural element) aided global comprehension; and elements in combination aided both types of comprehension most effectively of all.

Structural elements may contribute to comprehension by calling readers' attention to selected aspects of the underlying content domain (Goldman & Murray, 1992) or text base (Lorch, 1989), leading readers to consider information more carefully. Lorch (1989) describes composition as a three-stage process in which the writer draws information from a mental text base, transforms the information into a surface or written representation that communicates the "semantic content of the underlying text base," and then applies various cohesive devices to emphasize content and organization without adding new semantic content (p. 210). Without such devices to direct their attention, readers may fail to "make inferences about what information is important, [and] how specific propositions are related to other propositions" (Goldman & Murray, 1992, p. 504), particularly if the readers are unfamiliar with the text's main topics.

Implications for CMS

In managed content, repeating structural cohesive devices such as paragraph headings and graphical elements across content units may strengthen readers' sense of overall textual coherence.

Cohesion as Surface Structure

A third theory of cohesion, drawing from both the semantic and structural models, suggests that the surface features of a text—of which cohesion is one—contribute significantly to coherence, either directly or through the interaction of reader and text (Grabe & Kaplan, 1996; Ulijn & Strother, 1995; Williams, 1990, 2005). At the surface, cohesion operates through "explicitly stated connections" and "linkage words," enabling readers to make inferences that aid in comprehension (Ulijn & Strother, 1995, p. 139). Williams (1990, 2005) contends that the single most important factor in cohesive text is the physical location of key words and topics, which should appear near the beginning of a sentence if the information they contain is given, or familiar, to the reader, and near the end if it is new. Top-level features that vary with text type and audience, that are easy for readers to discern, and that reveal the text's "hierarchical structure" through its "cohesive harmony" also appear to be important for comprehension, especially in everyday texts (Grabe & Kaplan, 1996, p. 61). Grabe and Kaplan acknowledge that coherence is more than cohesive signaling and that surface features can never reflect a text's underlying logic exactly. However, they suggest that a writer can strengthen coherence by using cohesive devices purposefully and skillfully. The result is what Ulijn and Salager-Meyer (1998) refer to as "considerateness of text" (p. 85): the intentional production of cohesive audience-appropriate texts that reveal their structures and purposes, show relationships among ideas, and are generally more comprehensible to readers.

In a variety of ways, studies of text signaling investigate whether and how text signals help readers mentally organize a passage, on the assumption that readers are more likely to comprehend a text if it seems coherent. The underlying "network of related propositions" (Lorch, 1989, p. 210) to which signals relate has been described in terms of discursive forms and text types (Geiger & Millis, 2004; Kintsch & Yarbrough, 1982; Sanders & Noordman, 2000); mental text bases (Lorch, 1989); and domain knowledge (Goldman & Murray, 1992). Some experimental evidence indicates that readers may comprehend texts on the basis of overall discursive structure, even when explicit text signals are missing (Sanders & Noordman, 2000). However, in one study of familiar rhetorical forms, participants were significantly more accurate in answering topic and main-idea questions for texts containing explicit text signals and "canonical ordering" of points than for texts that were less well organized (Kintsch & Yarbrough, 1982, p. 833).

Implications for CMS

If cues in well-organized texts activate schemata for specific structures, enabling readers to use comprehension strategies successfully, then writers of managed content should be able to guide readers with familiar surface text signals such as strategic ordering of points (content units) and topic sentences.

SCHOLARSHIP IN CROSS-CULTURAL CONTEXTS

Whereas scholarship in cohesion provides insights into how managed content can be made more comprehensible at the local or unit level, cross-cultural studies suggest how readers in different contexts may receive managed content at the global or document level. In any setting, the communicative power of managed content depends on how well writers "read" a prospective audience and, in turn, how well that audience "reads" the products of the technology. Consequently, to make informed decisions about disseminating, translating, or localizing managed content, communicators must understand culturally based ways of conceptualizing technical topics and the rhetorical conventions most appropriate in the cultures of interest (Hofstede, 1991; Warren, 2002). In addition to linguistic questions, contrastive studies in the past two decades have addressed cultural approaches to different discourse types and differences in writer/reader roles.

Contrastive Studies of Discourse Type

Discourse studies ask whether types vary significantly across cultures and how variance may affect cross-cultural reading comprehension. One issue receiving considerable scholarly attention concerns methods of introducing and developing main ideas, an area relevant to DTDs in managed content intended for cross-cultural dissemination. Kaplan's original contrastive study (1966) hypothesizes an opposition between Western rhetorical directness and Asian indirection, sometimes described as the difference between deductive and inductive organization, respectively. One empirical approach to the deductive vs. inductive issue is to measure what participants recall after reading a text, on the assumption that "people will integrate information into memory more easily when that information is presented according to a native organizing schema rather than an alien organizing schema" (Hinds, 1984, p. 46). For example, cultural preferences are evident in a study testing the ability of native Japanese and native English speakers to recall newspaper articles composed in *ki-sho-ten-ketsu*, a common Japanese prose pattern (Hinds, 1984). The pattern incorporates four functions—introduction (*ki*), development of the introduction (*sho*), subtheme (*ten*), and conclusion (*ketsu*)—and readers must use unstated information to interpret the form coherently. When participants were tested immediately for recall of clauses, no differences in the two groups were apparent, but when the groups were retested one week later, the Japanese readers recalled more of the texts, particularly the *ten* section, a rhetorical pattern not found in English. By contrast, English readers tended to emphasize and therefore recall the conclusions, a function more familiar to them.

The influence of cultural norms on text organization and document structure is apparent in other studies as well, a factor writers should be aware of when localizing managed content for specific audiences. Significant differences emerged for Asian readers in a study of comparison, causation, problem solving, and collection types of English expository text (Carrell, 1984), which could indicate preferences for native rhetorical patterns. In general, for the Spanish, Arabic, Korean/Chinese, and other participants in this study, recall tended to be greater for the more highly organized discourse types to the extent that readers recalled top-level organization of text. In a similar study (Kobayashi, 2002), English-proficient Japanese students wrote better summaries (a measure of overall comprehension) when they read clearly structured English texts than when they read unstructured texts. The level of structure tended to make little difference to less proficient students. In two other studies, perceptions of authorial purpose appeared to affect Japanese preferences for organization in Japanese expository texts (Fukuoka & Spyridakis, 1999, 2000). When readers believed authors to be presenting views as theses or conclusions, rather than reporting facts, comprehension as measured by recall was higher for inductively organized text. Following tests of Korean adult learners of English in the United States, Eggington (1987) concluded that over time, "information is retained far better when it is presented in a manner compatible with the reader's expectations" (p. 166). In this case, one Korean group read an English academic text written in English linear style, while the other group read an English passage in traditional Korean style, which resembles classical Chinese with a beginning theme, development, change to subtheme, and conclusion. An immediate recall test showed no difference between the groups, but a retest one week later showed a significant difference between the traditional and English-influenced texts.

In attending to cultural preferences, however, communicators must continually reevaluate existing binaries to develop authentic, rather than stereotypical, perspectives on how texts function dynamically in cultures (Connor, 2002) and how readers in a given culture respond to different writing strategies. With the growth of online communication, global publishing, and opportunities for education abroad, readers in many cultures have greater exposure now to nonnative rhetorical patterns and may adjust their responses accordingly. For example, Kobayashi (1984) found that Japanese students composing in English in the United States tended to favor rhetorical patterns and topic statement types different from those of Japanese students writing in English in Japan. Although the results indicate some cultural preferences for first-language rhetorical patterns and statement types, the second-culture context may have produced some hybrid writing practices. Similarly, culture-specific patterns were insignificant factors in recall results for a study involving an English expository text (Connor & McCagg, 1983, 1987). When native English, Japanese, and Spanish students at an American university were asked to paraphrase the text of an English newspaper article and answer comprehension questions on main ideas, the nonnative writers were more likely than the native English writers to reproduce the original structure of the propositions. These results suggest that the English rhetorical structure may have constrained the writers or functioned as a counterbalance to their first-language patterns.

Implications for CMS

When writers of managed content in English have information about a cross-cultural audience's exposure to Western writing conventions, they will be better equipped to determine whether the document structure should incorporate organizing patterns from the readers' first languages for greater comprehensibility.

Contrastive Studies of Writer/Reader Roles

Beyond textual and experimental studies, contrastive researchers have examined ways in which social and cultural factors may shape rhetorical practices and normative roles for readers and writers. For example, Matalene (1985) links Chinese rhetorical patterns to cultural attitudes toward tradition, the need to memorize thousands of written characters, and an expectation "consistent with the nature of the language" that readers will "infer meanings rather than . . . have them spelled out" (p. 801). Other researchers contend that contrasts in Chinese and English expository prose have been exaggerated (Mohan & Lo, 1985). Evidence from comparative studies in British Columbia and Hong Kong suggest that apparent differences in rhetorical preferences may have more to do with instructional practices and developmental issues than with "a preference for 'indirectness' in the language and culture of Chinese" (p. 522). That is, positive response to linear rhetorical patterns may be a function of exposure to English composition above the sentence level.

In a widely cited study (1987), Hinds proposes a new "language typology" to distinguish between such "reader-responsible" and "writer-responsible" cultures, respectively (p. 141). In contrast to the Japanese perspective that it is up to readers to "determine the relationship between any one part of any essay and the essay as a whole" (p. 151; see also Connor, 2002; Kaplan, 1988), English expository writing acknowledges that "readers expect, and require, landmarks along the way" (p. 146). Writers in English therefore include linguistic markers such as obvious transitional devices that would be more subtle or missing altogether in Japanese writing. A subsequent analysis (Kubota, 1997) challenges Hinds' hypothesis, arguing that the reader-/writer-responsible dichotomy over-generalizes with regard to Japanese and fails to account for changes in Japanese punctuation, linguistic features, and rhetorical patterns resulting from the flow of Western materials into the country since the mid-1800s. However, Carson (1992) supports Hinds on this point, agreeing that Japanese speakers do expect listeners and readers to understand and interpret messages correctly, though Chinese speakers tend to assume (as do English speakers) that "the responsibility for clear communication [rests] on the speaker/writer" (p. 54). According to Carson, the source of varying discourse patterns lies not in the Chinese or Japanese languages themselves but in differing cultural expectations.

Relating the issue of rhetorical indirection to communicative roles, Hinds (1990) has used organizational patterns in expository texts from Japanese,

Korean, Chinese, and Thai to argue that texts that delay introducing main ideas are not necessarily inductive. Rather, they are intended for readers with a common set of cultural norms, and "the author *does* expect that the minds of readers work in a very similar way to his or her own" (p. 98). Hinds contends that readers in those cultures "expect that the purpose of an article is to introduce a set of observations related loosely to a general topic" and that their roles as readers is "to sort and evaluate these observations" and come to their own conclusions, an approach Hinds characterizes as "quasi-inductive" (p. 99). Noting that inductive and deductive organizing patterns have long been common in both Asian and Western discourse of different types, Scollon and Scollon (2001) hold that apparent cultural preferences for these patterns have more to do with cultural roles than with rhetorical conventions per se. That is, specific usages relate to different expectations for "the cultural structuring of situations and participant roles" (p. 95) rather than to linguistic factors alone.

Implications for CMS

For writers seeking a research-based strategy of managing English content for cross-cultural readers, current theories suggest that audience expectations may determine the organizing pattern most appropriate. Audiences with exposure to Western educational methods and texts are more likely to have communicative practices that combine first- and second-language conventions, and they will likely comprehend texts that are linearly organized. Audiences with more limited cross-cultural exposure will likely be more receptive to document structures that incorporate familiar, first-language organizing patterns.

STRATEGIES AND QUESTIONS FOR DEVELOPERS OF MANAGED CONTENT

Linguists, educational psychologists, and reading specialists have investigated the effects of cohesion and cross-cultural factors on comprehension for more than two decades, but applied few of their findings to specific software issues. Conversely, technical communicators have focused on describing and implementing content management technology without analyzing its cognitive implications for readers. Thus technical communication scholarship has only begun to theorize managed content in terms of cohesion or cross-cultural issues. Sapienza (2002, 2004) frames the problem as a series of constraints on the writer, who is limited formally by the "predominantly restrictive rules of logic" of computer programming (2002, p. 163), a science not generally concerned with consistent communication or textual coherence (Albers, 2000). Rhetorically, the need for decontextualization in a CMS environment forces writers to avoid devices such as obvious transitions or use of the given-new principle between modules at a specified level of granularity, because "the writer either does not know where the module will be displayed, does not know in what relation to other content it will be arranged, or must contrive multiple givens" (Sapienza, 2004, p. 403). Within these constraints, some structural devices such as thematic progression and repeated syntactic features across text blocks (Campbell, 1991) are difficult to incorporate as well, given that the writer must not restrict content units to a unique context or arrangement.

One solution to systemic limitations on cohesion has been to focus on developing tight textuality within, rather than across, the boundaries of information units. Here, Horton's (1994) advice to writers of online documentation anticipates CMS methodology. To maintain coherence within a decontextualized block of information, Horton recommends that writers answer a single question in each unit, design each topic to be independent of other topics, and keep topics "rhetorically neutral" (p.105), suitable for a wide range of users and purposes. This strategy does produce local cohesion within units, although it fails to address top-level structure or cohesion across an entire document.

Another response to systemic constraints on cohesion is the intensive use of graphic (Campbell, 1991) or lexical (Hoey, 1983, 1991) repetition and visual patterning (Johnsen, 2001) throughout documents. Typefaces, bullets, numbered lists, horizontal rules, and generous white space between sections and paragraphs are structural devices likely to appear in documents of managed content, providing a measure of visual cohesion. Lexical cohesion, such as consistent wording in topic headings and exact or near-exact repetition within and across units, can improve overall coherence as well.

Findings from existing cohesion studies raise interesting questions for additional research in content management. One such question concerns the best practices for writing cohesive, self-contained modules (Albers, 2000). Another issue involves developing a rhetorical theory that would support those practices (Sapienza, 2004), perhaps building on an earlier question of how "texts of different kinds are constructed so as to form semantic wholes" (Halliday & Hasan, 1976, p. 24). Other pertinent research questions include the ways readers in different cultures create textual coherence, and how they use what they know about language to understand what they read (Koda, 1994).

To learn more about the significance of "connections between particular language patterns and mental life" (Lucy, 1996, p. 37), scholars must expand the volume and quality of experimental research in cohesion and cross-cultural issues. The profession needs additional empirical work on these topics to complement descriptive and theoretical studies. For contexts in which the use of English is a given, the profession needs "much more information on how readers from different cultures and language backgrounds interact with texts, and how specific features of English technical writing facilitate or interfere with comprehension" (Thrush, 2001, p. 292). Well-designed empirical research will also focus on a central linguistic concept, rather than a limited group of vocabulary items, and examine authentic behavior in real-world, multilingual settings (Lucy, 1996).

Although communicators are learning that traditional "handcrafted" writing strategies are inappropriate for the information chunking and standardization inherent in content management systems, a writing method that compromises reader understanding for the sake of consistency may ultimately be counter-productive. Communicators thus have a responsibility to balance system effectiveness against audience needs. A review of existing research suggests new questions for study and possible writing strategies that will help us manage content efficiently in ways that are still rhetorically and culturally responsive to our readers.

REFERENCES

Albers, M. J. (2000). The technical editor and document databases: What the future may hold. *Technical Communication Quarterly, 9,* 191-206.

Boiko, B. (2002). *The content management bible.* New York: Hungry Minds.

Brown, J. S., & Duguid, P. (2000). *The social life of information.* Boston, MA: Harvard Business School Press.

Campbell, K. S. (1991). Structural cohesion in technical texts. *Journal of Technical Writing and Communication, 21,* 221-237.

Campbell, K. S. (1995). *Coherence, continuity, and cohesion: Theoretical foundations for document design.* Hillsdale, NJ: Lawrence Erlbaum.

Carliner, S. (2000). A three-part framework for information design. *Technical communication, 47,* 561-576.

Carrell, P. L. (1984). The effects of rhetorical organization on ESL readers. *TESOL Quarterly, 18,* 441-469.

Carson, J. G. (1992). Becoming biliterate: First language influences. *Journal of Second Language Writing, 1,* 37-60.

Chung, J. S. L. (2000). Signals and reading comprehension—Theory and practice [Electronic version]. *System, 28,* 247-259.

Connor, U. (2002). New directions in contrastive rhetoric. *TESOL Quarterly, 36,* 493-510.

Connor, U., & McCagg, P. (1983). Cross-cultural differences and perceived quality in written paraphrases of English expository prose. *Applied Linguistics, 4,* 259-268.

Connor, U., & McCagg, P. (1987). A contrastive study of English expository prose paraphrases. In U. Connor & R. B. Kaplan (Eds.), *Writing across languages: Analysis of L2 text* (pp. 73-86). Reading, MA: Addison-Wesley.

Eggington, W. G. (1987). Written academic discourse in Korean: Implications for effective communication. In U. Connor & R. B. Kaplan (Eds.), *Writing across languages: Analysis of L2 text* (pp. 153-168). Reading, MA: Addison-Wesley.

Freebody, P., & Anderson, R. C. (1983). Effects of vocabulary difficulty, text cohesion, and schema availability on reading comprehension. *Reading Research Quarterly, 18,* 277-294.

Fukuoka, W., & Spyridakis, J. H. (1999). Japanese readers' comprehension of and preferences for inductively versus deductively organized text. *IEEE Transactions of Professional Communication, 32,* 355-367.

Fukuoka, W., & Spyridakis, J. H. (2000). The organization of Japanese expository passages. *IEEE Transactions of Professional Communication, 42,* 166-174.

Geiger, J. F., & Millis, K. K. (2004). Assessing the impact of reading goals and text structures on comprehension [Electronic version]. *Reading Psychology, 25,* 93-110.

Goldman, S. R., & Murray, J. D. (1992). Knowledge of connectors as cohesion devices in text: A comparative study of native-English and English-as-a-second language speakers. *Journal of Educational Psychology, 84,* 504-519.

Grabe, W., & Kaplan, R. B. (1996). *Theory and practice of writing.* New York: Addison Wesley Longman.

Hackos, J. (2002). *Content management for dynamic web delivery.* New York: John Wiley.

Halliday, M. A. K., & Hasan, R. (1976). *Cohesion in English.* London, UK: Longman.

Halliday, M. A. K., & Hasan, R. (1989). *Language, context, and text: Aspects of language in a social-semiotic perspective* (2nd ed.). Oxford, UK: University Press.

Hinds, J. (1984). Retention of information using a Japanese style of presentation. *Studies in Language, 8,* 45-69.

Hinds, J. (1987). Reader versus writer responsibility: A new typology. In U. Connor & R. B. Kaplan (Eds.), *Writing across languages: Analysis of L2 text* (pp. 141-152). Reading, MA: Addison-Wesley.

Hinds, J. (1990). Inductive, deductive, quasi-inductive: Expository writing in Japanese, Korean, Chinese, and Thai. In U. Connor & A. M. Johns (Eds.), *Coherence in writing: Research and pedagogical perspectives* (pp. 87-110). Alexandria, VA: TESOL.

Hoey, M. (1983). *On the surface of discourse.* London, UK: George Allen & Unwin.

Hoey, M. (1991). *Patterns of lexis in text.* Oxford, UK: Oxford University Press.

Hofstede, G. H. (1991). *Cultures and organizations: Software of the mind.* London, UK: McGraw-Hill.

Horiba, Y. (1996). Comprehension processes in L2 reading: Language competence, textual coherence, and inferences. *Studies in Second Language Acquisition, 18,* 433-473.

Horton, W. (1994). *Designing and writing online documentation* (2nd ed.). New York: John Wiley.

Houser, A. R. (2003). Managing and delivering your content as data. *Intercom, 50,* 13-16.

Johns, A. M. (1984). Textual cohesion and the Chinese speaker of English. *Language Learning and Communication, 3,* 69-73.

Johnsen, L. (2001). Document (re)presentation: Object-orientation, visual language, and XML. *Technical Communication, 48,* 59-65.

Kaplan, R. (1966). Cultural thought patterns in inter-cultural education. *Language Learning, 16,* 1-20.

Kaplan, R. (1988). Cultural thought patterns revisited. In A. C. Purves (Ed.), *Writing across languages and cultures: Issues in contrastive rhetoric* (pp. 275-304). Newbury Park, CA: Sage.

Kintsch, W., & Yarbrough, J. C. (1982). Role of rhetorical structure in text comprehension. *Educational Psychology, 74*(6), 828-834.

Kobayashi, H. (1984). Rhetorical patterns in English and Japanese. *TESOL Quarterly, 18,* 737-738.

Kobayashi, M. (2002). Method effects on reading comprehension test performance: Text organization and response format. *Language Testing, 19,* 193-220.

Koda, K. (1994). Second language reading research: Problems and possibilities. *Applied Psycholinguistics, 15,* 1-28.

Kubota, R. (1997). A reevaluation of the uniqueness of Japanese discourse: Implications for contrastive rhetoric. *Written Communication, 14,* 460-480.

Lorch, R. F. (1989). Text-signaling devices and their effects on reading and memory processes. *Educational Psychology Review, 1,* 209-234.

Lucy, J. (1996). The scope of linguistic relativity: An analysis and review of empirical research. In J. J. Gumperz & S. C. Levinson (Eds.), *Rethinking linguistic relativity* (pp. 37-69). Cambridge, MA: Cambridge University Press.

MacLean, M., & Chapman, L. J. (1989). The processing of cohesion in fiction and non-fiction by good and poor readers. *Journal of Research in Reading, 12,* 13-28.

Matalene, C. (1985). Contrastive rhetoric: An American writing teacher in China. *College English, 47,* 789-808.

Mohan, B. A., & Lo, W. A.-Y. (1985). Academic writing and Chinese students: Transfer and developmental factors. *TESOL Quarterly, 19,* 515-534.

Reid, J. (1992). A computer text analysis of four cohesion devices in English discourse by native and nonnative writers. *Journal of Second Language Writing, 1,* 79-107.

Rockley, A. (2001). Dynamic content management. *Intercom, 48,* 28-32, 42.

Rockley, A. (2003a). *Managing enterprise content: A unified content strategy.* Indianapolis, IN: New Riders.

Rockley, A. (2003b). Single sourcing: It's about people, not just technology. *Technical Communication, 50,* 350-354.

Sanders, T. J. M., & Noordman, L. G. M. (2000). The role of coherence relations and their linguistic markers in text processing. *Discourse Processes, 29,* 37-60.

Sapienza, F. (2002). Does being technical matter? XML, single source, and technical communication. *Journal of Technical Writing and Communication, 32,* 155-170.

Sapienza, F. (2004). Usability, structured content, and single sourcing with XML. *Technical Communication, 51,* 399-408.

Scollon, R. (1997). Contrastive rhetoric, contrastive poetics, or perhaps something else? *TESOL Quarterly, 31,* 352-358.

Scollon, R., & Scollon, S. W. (2001). *Intercultural communication.* Oxford, UK: Blackwell.

Sharp, A. (2002). Chinese L1 schoolchildren reading in English: The effect of rhetorical patterns. [Electronic version]. *Reading in a Foreign Language, 14,* 111-134.

Thompson, I. (1986). Readability beyond the sentence: Global coherence and ease of comprehension. *Journal of Technical Writing and Communication, 16,* 131-140.

Thrush, E. A. (2001). Plain English? A study of Plain English vocabulary and international audiences. *Technical Communication, 48,* 289-296.

Ulijn, J. M., & Salager-Meyer, F. (1998). The professional reader and the text: Insights from L2 research. *Journal of Research in Reading, 21,* 79-95.

Ulijn, J. M., & Strother, J. B. (1995). *Communicating in business and technology: From psycholinguistic theory to international practice.* Frankfurt, Germany: Peter Lang.

Warren, T. L. (2002). Cultural influences on technical manuals. [Electronic version]. *Journal of Technical Writing and Communication, 32,* 111-123.

Williams, J. M. (1990). *Style: Toward clarity and grace* (4th ed.). Chicago, IL: Chicago University Press.

Williams, J. M. (2005). *Style: Ten lessons in clarity and grace* (8th ed.). New York: Longman.

Contributors

NICOLE AMARE is an assistant professor of technical communication at the University of South Alabama, where she teaches composition, technical writing, editing, ethics, stylistics, and grammar. She has written *Real Life University*, a college success guide, and has edited *Global Student Entrepreneurs, Beyond the Lemonade Stand*, and *Giving Back*. Some of her research has appeared in *Business Communication Quarterly, IEEE Transactions on Professional Communication, Women & Language, Technical Communication*, and the *Journal of Technical Writing and Communication*. She can be reached at namare@usouthal.edu.

JEFFREY BACHA received his Bachelor of Arts degree in English from the University of Michigan-Flint in 2000 and his Master of Arts degree in Rhetoric and Composition from Georgia State University. Currently he is a Ph.D. student in the Rhetoric and Digital Writing program at Michigan State University.

MICHELLE F. EBLE is an assistant professor of Professional and Technical Communication in the Department of English at East Carolina University, where she teaches undergraduate and graduate courses in professional writing, publications development, electronic writing, grant writing, medical/healthcare writing, ethical issues in professional communication, and editing. Her research on writing technologies, rhetoric, and the theory and practice of professional writing has appeared in *Computers and Composition, Technical Communication,* and *Technical Communication Quarterly.* She is currently investigating technologies used to deliver courses and content online and the implications for rhetorical theory informing this digital delivery. She is the coordinator of the ECU Outreach Network, a division of Regional Development Services, where she works with students and community organizations in Eastern North Carolina on funding opportunities/resources and grant writing. She also serves on her University and Medical Center Institutional Review Boards.

ROBIN EVANS is a doctoral student at Oklahoma State University in Technical Communication and Composition Rhetoric. She serves as the student president of the Society for Technical Communication at OSU and serves on curriculum and book review committees for the university. She has nearly 10 years of experience teaching writing at the college level. Her primary focuses are technical writing pedagogy, distance learning, and information design.

SUSAN FOWLER is a consultant at Keynote Systems, Inc., a principal of FAST Consulting and co-author of three software design books including *Web Application Design Handbook* (Morgan Kaufmann Publishing, 2004). She has done technical writing, training, application design, and usability testing for major Wall Street, pharmaceutical, reinsurance, and telecommunications firms. She was managing editor of *User Experience,* the magazine of the Usability Professionals Association, from 2004 to 2006. She taught technical communication and human-computer interaction at NJIT and at Fairleigh Dickinson University.

LYN GATTIS is assistant professor of Professional Writing in the Department of English at Missouri State University. Her research interests include intercultural technical communication, information design, and content management systems. She received her Ph.D. in Rhetoric and Professional Writing from Oklahoma State University.

CAROL SIRI JOHNSON teaches technical writing at New Jersey Institute of Technology. She has a B.A. from Mount Holyoke College and a Ph.D. from the Graduate Center of the City University of New York. She worked as a technical writer in the computer industry prior to her position at NJIT.

BECKY JO GESTELAND MCSHANE is an associate professor in the English Department at Weber State University, where she teaches classes in content management and professional and technical writing, editing, and theory. After completing a Ph.D. in American Studies at the University of Utah she worked for several years as a technical writer. Now Becky searches for ways to combine her interests in cultural studies and technical communication. Her latest project investigates the spiritual aspects of knitting and the conventions of knitting patterns. In her spare time Becky hikes and skis the Wasatch Mountains with her family: Sean, Jake, and Maggie.

RUDY McDANIEL is assistant professor of Digital Media for the School of Film and Digital Media at the University of Central Florida. His research interests include narrative theory, video game technologies, knowledge management frameworks, and XML. As a consultant, he has designed Web-based applications for clients such as the IEEE Society and the Library of Congress, and has written interactive video game scripts for the Federation of American Scientists. Rudy is currently director of the Partnership for Research on Synthetic Experience (PROSE) lab at UCF, and can be reached by email at rudy@mail.ucf.edu or through his Web site at http://www.dm.ucf.edu/~rmcdaniel.

LISA MELONCON is an assistant professor of English at the University of Cincinnati, where she teachers courses in technical and professional communication. Her research interests combine rhetoric, science, and technologies, as well as an emphasis in geography. She is currently working on a book about early modern medicine and rhetoric.

MICHAEL PENNELL is an assistant professor of Writing and Rhetoric at the University of Rhode Island. He teaches classes in research writing, business communications, and writing in electronic environments. He is currently working on a project exploring the literacy education of the American Industrial Revolution through early Rhode Island mill communities.

JULIE STAGGERS is an assistant professor of English at University of Las Vegas Nevada. She teaches classes in technical and professional writing. She is currently working on a project about secrecy culture, rhetoric, and risk on the Manhattan Project.

KIRK ST. AMANT is an associate professor of Professional and Technical Communication at East Carolina University. His research interests include international online interactions, international e-commerce, and international outsourcing, and he has previously taught courses in international business, business communication, and business ethics for the Consortium of Ukrainian Management Education (CEUME) and the Kyiv Mohyla Business School. He has also worked as an ESL tutor and tutor trainer, and has been the Director of Tutoring (and a specialist ESL tutor) for the Online Writing Center at the University of Minnesota.

MEREDITH W. ZOETEWEY is an assistant professor of Technical Communication at Rose-Hulman Institute of Technology. She teaches classes in technical communication, multimedia writing, and visual rhetoric. She is currently working on a project about public portraits of wireless technologies.

Index

Printed and bound by CPI Group (UK) Ltd, Croydon, CR0 4YY

22/10/2024

01777623-0009